Elliot

JOHN LAW

Books by

H. MONTGOMERY HYDE

The Rise of Castlereagh
The Empress Catherine and the Prince Dashkov
Londonderry House and its Pictures
Princess Lieven
Judge Jeffreys
Mexican Empire
A Victorian Historian: Letters of W. E. H. Lecky
Privacy and the Press
John Law
The Trials of Oscar Wilde
Mr and Mrs Beeton
Cases that Changed the Law
Carson
The Trial of Craig and Bentley
United in Crime
The Strange Death of Lord Castlereagh
Sir Patrick Hastings: His Life and Cases
The Trial of Sir Roger Casement
Simla and the Simla Hill States Under British Protection
Oscar Wilde: The Aftermath
The Quiet Canadian
A History of Pornography
Norman Birkett
Cynthia
The Story of Lamb House
Lord Reading
Henry James at Home
Strong for Service

With the Marchioness of Londonderry, D.B.E.
The Russian Journals of Martha and Catherine Wilmot
More Letters from Martha Wilmot: Impressions of Vienna

With G. R. Falkiner Nuttall
Air Defence and the Civil Population

With John Kisch
An International Case Book of Crime

John Law of Lauriston.

From the portrait by Alexis Simone Belle in the National Portrait Gallery

H. MONTGOMERY HYDE

JOHN LAW

The History of an Honest Adventurer

W. H. ALLEN LONDON 1969

First published 1948 by Home & Van Thal
New edition, revised and enlarged, 1969 by W. H. Allen
© 1948 and 1969 Harford Productions Ltd.

Printed and bound in Great Britain by Butler & Tanner Ltd., Frome and London
for the publishers
W. H. Allen & Co., Ltd.,
Essex Street, London WC2
491 00193 2

In memory of my mother

CONTENTS

ILLUSTRATIONS

PREFACE

This book was originally published more than twenty years ago in times of strict post-war paper rationing and other production difficulties which involved printing in Holland. Consequently its circulation was necessarily limited. I have now taken the opportunity afforded by this new edition of revising the work and adding some MS material from a French collection not previously available to me.

An additional justification for its republication is that no other work on John Law has appeared in English since I first wrote about him in 1948, and during that period only two biographical studies have appeared in foreign languages, one in French and the other in Italian, neither of which has been translated.

I wish to thank the following who have helped me in various ways – Dr. Marguerite Wood, Mr. John A. Fairley, Major J. G. Morrison, and the staffs of the British Museum, the Public Record Office, the National Library of Scotland, the London Library, and the Méjanes Library in Aix-en-Provence; also my wife, who visited the latter library with me.

I am grateful to the trustees respectively of the National Portrait Gallery and of the British Museum for permission to reproduce the portrait and the letter written by John Law which are in their custody.

Westwell House,
Tenterden, Kent.
June, 1969.

H. M. H.

CHAPTER I

THE BEAU

Anyone who chanced to read the first number of the *London Gazette* for the year 1695 would have found some curious and interesting advertisements in that issue. There was an announcement of horse racing near Epsom: 'on Banstead Downs will be two Plates run for yearly for three years successively.' Holders of winning numbers of a Government lottery known as 'The Million Adventure' were urged 'to make more haste to prove their claims', otherwise 'great inconvenience and Disappointment may ensue'. A reward was offered to the finder of 'a Blue Shag Spring Purse', the property of a nobleman. Copies of a sermon preached at the Temple Church 'on the Sad Occasion of Death of our Gracious Queen' were now on sale to the public. Likewise a 'Collection of New Ayres, composed for Two Flutes, with Sonatas, by some of the Ingenious Masters of this Age'. Further, for the sum of five shillings could be obtained a bottle of 'the famous Oyl for giving present Ease in the Gout and Rheumatism . . . as also in the Palsy and Weakness of any Part'; this concoction, the manufacturer added, was in particular 'fit for those that use the Bagnio'. Finally the reader's eye might have been caught by the following:

> Captain John Lawe, a Scotchman, lately a Prisoner in the King's-Bench for Murther, aged 26, a very tall black lean Man, well shaped, above Six foot high, large Pockholes in his Face, big high-Nosed, speaks broad and low, made his Escape from the said Prison. Whoever secures him so he may be delivered at the said Prison, shall have £50 paid immediately by the Marshal of the King's-Bench.

Here at last was a new topic of conversation for the customers of the St. James's coffee-houses, who were tired of the Queen's death and the frozen Thames and the ravages of the smallpox. This notice, which could hardly be described as flattering, had a particular interest for those who claimed acquaintance with its subject. The latter was remembered as 'Beau Law', the Laird of Lauriston, a handsome and softly spoken young man about town, very popular with the ladies, who had fought a duel with another 'Beau' named Wilson and had had the misfortune to kill his antagonist in this encounter. For this he had been arrested and charged with murder. Trial, conviction and reprieve had followed in quick succession. But he was not released from gaol. Instead, he had again been prosecuted by the dead 'Beau' 's brother. While the formalities attendant upon this second trial were in process, he had already made one attempt to escape, but he had been discovered after filing through several bars of the window in his cell. The next time he had tried he had evidently been more successful, and it now seemed that the authorities, whose confidence and assistance he must somehow have enlisted, had deliberately circulated an inaccurate description of the fugitive which was really designed to facilitate his flight.

That the tenor of the notice was misleading had become apparent about a fortnight afterwards when news was received in Whitehall that 'Captain Lawe' had been taken in Leicestershire while riding post-haste in the direction of the north. It looked as if he were heading for beyond the Tweed where he would be secure from the jurisdiction of the English courts since Scotland was then a separate kingdom. But on being brought before a magistrate the arrested traveller turned out to be quite a different person. As it happened the real escaped prisoner was by this time safe on the Continent.

Twenty-six years were to elapse before John Law was to return to London and plead the royal pardon before the judges of the Court of King's Bench. By 1720 he had become the most talked-of man in Europe – the great Mr. Law, the 'projector', the author of the celebrated 'system', a millionaire, virtual Prime Minister of France. Less than ten years later he was to die in a tawdry Venice lodging house, nearly destitute and largely forgotten.

For many months after his escape nothing was heard of Law[1]

---

[1] There are at least nine contemporary spellings of nomenclature – Law,

by his friends in England or Scotland. Then isolated pieces of news began to be received at varying and lengthy intervals. He was thought to be studying the principles of banking in Amsterdam. Next heard of in Paris he was reported to have persuaded a lady there to leave her husband and elope with him to Italy. Some time later he was said to be maintaining himself and his mistress by gambling and to be often seen at the green tables in Genoa and Venice. Then about 1705 he made a brief reappearance in Scotland where he advanced some novel proposals on the use of paper money and credit. He even published a short and cogent book setting out his views; at the same time he sent a copy of his draft scheme to Lord Godolphin, the head of the Queen's Treasury in Whitehall, who was stated to be greatly impressed by it. But he could not tarry to discuss his scheme with the English minister, since the approaching union of the two countries again exposed him to arrest; and so he had set out on his travels once more.

According to the next news received he was in Paris discussing financial projects with King Louis XIV's ministers, but whether it was because of the high play he indulged in at the same time, or because in the Grand Monarch's despotic eyes he was a Protestant and therefore a heretic, his second visit to that capital city was of short duration, and it was rumoured that he had received his passport from the chief of police with a broad hint to lose no time in quitting the Kingdom. Back in Italy he was said to be gambling so successfully that both the Genoese and the Venetian authorities likewise requested him to remove himself beyond their boundaries. In 1712 he was reported to be in Turin discussing with the Duke of Savoy a plan for opening a state bank in that ruler's principality. A year later news came from The Hague that Mijnheer Law had bought a fine house there and had opened a credit account with the Bank of Holland for £100,000. Then for a third time he was said to be in Paris and in fact to have settled down there with his family in expectation of an imminent change of government.

The chance for which he had waited so long had come in 1715.

Lawe, Laws, Lawes, Laus, Las, Lasse, Lass. The last is the form generally found in France and is so written by St. Simon, Voltaire and other French writers. The first form is found in the subject's baptismal record; it is that by which he is usually known in the country of his birth, and it is employed throughout this book. See further bibliography below.

Louis XIV died and the regent Duke of Orleans, who ruled in the name of the infant Louis XV, allowed Law to realize his dream and open a bank. It was a private bank with power to issue notes – a novelty never before seen in France; in a short time it had proved such a success that the Regent converted it into a state institution. But the banker had had another scheme in mind which also came to fruition at this time – the colonization of the vast tract of American territory drained by the river Mississippi and then known as Louisiana. Thus had been born the 'Mississippi scheme' or 'the system'. A company had been formed with Law at its head which after absorbing the other French trading companies had launched forth on a number of ambitious projects, including nothing less than the liquidation of the bulk of the country's national debt. Meanwhile the rise in prices of the company's shares had produced the greatest mania of speculation which France had experienced in her history. Writing half a century later Adam Smith, the so-called father of political economy, was to describe Law's system in *The Wealth of Nations* as 'the most extravagant project both of banking and stock-jobbing that perhaps the world ever saw'. The climax had been reached early in 1720 when Law, having been made a naturalized French citizen and embraced the Roman Catholic faith, was appointed Finance Minister, thus becoming after the Regent the most powerful and sought-after person in the Kingdom. Nor had his fortunes fared so badly on the other side of the English Channel. He had received the freedom of his native Edinburgh in a silver box. The British ambassador in Paris had been recalled because it was considered that he had given the great man offence, while King George I had sent over his royal pardon for the offence for which Mr. Law had been convicted in his youth. In short, as a contemporary account put it, 'after undergoing great variety of persecution from his enemies, he now appears a Minister far above all that the past Age has known, that the present can conceive, or that the future will believe'.

Then had come the inevitable crash, suddenly and violently. Confidence in the 'system' had been undermined, there was a mad rush to convert paper money to specie, the price of the Mississippi Company's shares tumbled, and thousands of investors were ruined. Law was dismissed from office and soon afterwards had been obliged to leave France – lucky to get away with his life, so the current gossip ran. It was rumoured that the Tsar had invited him to go to St. Petersburg to set the Russian finances in order, but the shadow of Siberia no doubt deterred him from making the experiment. At all events he had got no further than Copenhagen where he had found a vessel to take him to the Thames rather than the Neva.

Fear of his creditors seems to have kept Law in England for so long as three years. When in 1725 he ventured forth again on the Continent the French Regent was dead, and with his passing were doomed Law's hopes of returning to the scene of his former triumphs and reviving their glories. It is true that grandiose projects continued to revolve in his fertile brain, but unfortunately his restless wanderings in Europe failed to provide him with any opportunity of putting them into practice.

Lack of capital too – for he had left all his liquid assets behind him in France – prevented him from gambling on the same scale or with the same profits as formerly. He had finally settled in Venice, and when he died there in 1729, at the comparatively early age of fifty-eight, he seemed to be a needy and forgotten adventurer. Only in France did the event attract any notice when the Foreign Minister, hoping that he would now be able to discover the secret of 'the system' and Law's successes at the gaming-tables, instructed the French ambassador in Venice to get possession of the late financier's papers and despatch them to the Quai d'Orsay.

That John Law was at least an honest adventurer it took over a century to record. The church in which his remains had been deposited was pulled down during the Napoleonic Wars. Providence ordained that the Governor of Venice at this time should be his grandnephew Alexander Law, Comte de Lauriston and future Marshal of France. To him fell the duty of removing the financier's remains to their present resting-place in the Church of San Moisé not far from St. Mark's Square and the Grand Canal and by an appropriate coincidence just beside the old Ridotto – the famous seventeenth-century gaming-rooms which had witnessed so many of Law's spectacular winnings. On one of the stones in the floor just inside the west door of the church the Comte de Lauriston had an inscription cut in Latin which commemorated the fact that beneath it lay the bones of a native of Edinburgh who had become a 'most distinguished Controller-General of Finance in France'.

The passing of time and millions of feet across the threshold of the Church of San Moisé have obliterated most of the words of the inscription on his tomb, so that today no more than an occasional letter is visible to the scrutiny of the curious observer. The crowds in the big square outside, the loungers beneath the shaded porticos of Florian's café, the lovers in the gondolas on the canal are just as numerous and intent on their business as they were in the days of the great 'projector'. Yet few of them, who enter the little church, ever give a thought to him whose bones lie beneath their feet, nor are they aware that the fundamental idea underlying the money they have in their pockets they owe in great measure to this ingenious Scotsman.

2

For two centuries or more there had been Laws in Edinburgh engaged in following the craft of goldsmith and silversmith as well as the business of banking as it was understood in those days. But with the exception of his father and his uncle, most of the male members of John's family had been sons of the manse, certainly for as many generations back as anyone could remember.

In 1595, exactly a hundred years before his great-grandson made such a sensational escape from the King's Bench prison in London, the Reverend Andrew Law became the minister at Neilston, an unattractive village with an equally unattractive kirk lying midway between Glasgow and Kilmarnock in Renfrewshire. In these severe surroundings the minister was destined to spend the remainder of his life. In 1631, feeling the weight of advancing years and being in indifferent health, he requested the Archbishop of Glasgow to permit his son John to assist him. It was necessary to obtain his permission as John had not yet been ordained. According to some accounts, James Law, the archbishop, was a brother of Andrew's. He certainly seems to have been a relative, whose promotion in the hierarchy had been the more remarkable in that as a young man he had once been censured by his local synod for playing football on the Sabbath day. What matters, however, is that he gave his consent to the innovation, saying at the same time he felt sure that the presbytery and the parishioners would be 'well content'. As things turned out these elements proved amenable, and in due course the young minister succeeded his father in the charge of Neilston Kirk and its congregation.

The ecclesiastical policy of the Stuart monarchs in Scotland forms a melancholy chapter in the history of that country. While James I of England and VI of Scotland united the crowns of the two Kingdoms in his person, he alternated between support of the Episcopalian and the Presbyterian elements in the Scottish Church. His son Charles I, on the other hand, made clear his determination to assimilate the churches of England and Scotland on the Episcopalian principle, until the outbreak of civil war on both sides of the border forced him to come to an understanding with the Covenanters, as the Presbyterians had come to be known politically. This understanding or 'engagement' was condemned in the extreme Presbyterian pulpits, but the minister of Neilston was among those who supported it. Unfortunately for him the triumph of Oliver Cromwell and the execution of Charles I led to the supremacy of the extreme Presbyterian party and the passing of an Act through the Scottish Parliament which excluded all men who had favoured 'the engagement' from holding any office either civil or ecclesiastical. Thus the Reverend John Law suddenly found himself deprived of his living 'for inefficiency'.

The dispossessed minister made his way to the Scottish capital where he seems to have lived a very difficult and precarious existence for the next ten years or so. At the Restoration he was found applying for 'charitable supply' from the Edinburgh presbytery, and in 1661 he succeeded in obtaining a small money grant from Parliament. Meanwhile he had had to face the problem of bringing up his family. The church was out of the question as a career for his two sons, so when the opportunity offered he apprenticed them both to two goldsmiths. It seems that the younger brother William was bound to serve a master named George Cleghorne, for it was on the latter's introduction that he was subsequently admitted to membership of the goldsmiths' guild in the city. What is of greater significance is that William Law married Cleghorne's daughter Violet towards the end of the year 1661. A few months afterwards he set up for himself in business in a small wooden shop which ran along the south side of St. Giles Church in Parliament Close.

The Edinburgh goldsmith of those days was regarded as a person of some consequence. He appeared in public wearing a scarlet cloak and a cocked hat and he carried a cane. But in his shop he worked with his coat off and his shirt sleeves rolled up. Several of the products of William Law's workmanship have survived, mostly in the form of church plate, and they show him to have been a fine craftsman. Even the smallest article had to be bespoken, however, as no stock was carried. Perhaps the most frequently manufactured articles were the silver tea-spoons which every intending bridegroom purchased as a gift for his bride and which according to custom were received and paid for over a friendly dram or a ¦pint of ale in a neighbouring tavern. On these occasions the goldsmith was usually treated to a history of the courtship while in return he was expected to retail the latest gossip of the town for his customer's information. So far as the goldsmith's banking functions were concerned, these were limited to lending money on security at a fixed rate of interest.

Less than twelve months after her marriage Mrs. Violet Law died in giving birth to a son named George, and not long afterwards the infant followed his mother to rest in Greyfriars Churchyard. About 1663 the bereaved widower found consolation in the charms of a certain Janet Campbell whom he married as his second wife at this time. For Janet it has been claimed that she was connected by blood with the ducal family of Argyll. Actually she was the daughter of a prosperous Edinburgh merchant named James Campbell whose people had been small landowners in Ayrshire in the south-west of Scotland. Besides a strong constitution which enabled her to withstand the risks of repeated childbearing, the second Mrs. Law brought her husband a useful dowry which enabled him to expand his business as well as increase his family. In 1670 William took over one of the adjoining shops in Parliament Close. It was in these enlarged premises that their fifth child and eldest surviving son was born.

The latest addition to William and Janet Law's growing family was baptized in St. Giles on April 21, 1671. He was called John after his grandfather, the dispossessed minister of Neilston.

Very little is known of young John's early years in Scotland. But he must have been a fairly robust lad, since four of his twelve brothers and sisters died in infancy or childhood. The household nursery seems to have been a kind of cellar underneath the main shop, whose sole natural illumination was received through a grating in the pavement of the street above. The younger members of the other goldsmiths' families in the close lived in similar insalubrious conditions, and it is hardly surprising that the rate of mortality among them should have been so high.

His education was simple but thorough. As a day scholar he attended the Edinburgh High School where the master or dominie gave him a useful grounding in the elements of mathematics and polite literature. When he was about thirteen years old he was taken away and sent to a boarding school called Eaglesham in Renfrewshire, the son of whose headmaster, John Hamilton, had married his eldest sister Agnes. It has been surmised that the real reason for this migration was his parents' desire to remove him from the temptations of the capital. In this academy he was said to have shown remarkable aptitude for arithmetic and geometry and to have mastered the complexities of that most irritating of all schoolroom studies, algebra, at an unusually early age. There was no doubt about it. Master John had a head for figures.

For the natives of Edinburgh particularly it was a barbarous age. From the first moment of his glorious restoration King Charles II set himself to break the power of the Presbyterian preachers beyond the border. However he may have been in Whitehall, the merry monarch proved himself an unjust and cruel ruler in Holyrood. Bones were crushed as brutally as consciences, and no day passed without the enacting of some revolting scene of corporal punishment in the neighbourhood of the goldsmith's house. Young Law must have become hardened early to these frequent hangings and scourgings and nailing of ears to the pillory. He must have remembered too the erection of a monstrous equestrian statute of Charles in the Parliament Close shortly after the King's death in 1688. Though only made of lead, it had cost £1,000. 'The vulgar people, who had never seen the like before, were amazed at it,' wrote a contemporary chronicler. 'Some compared it to Nebuchadnezzar's image, which all fell down and worshipped, and others to the pale horse in the Revelations, and he that sat thereon was death.'

Fortunately lighter incidents would occur from time to time which young John would overhear laughingly discussed in the family circle of friends and which helped to distract his attention from the harsh realities of the times. There was, for instance, the

story of a local minister named M'Queen, who was alleged to
have fallen besottedly in love with a certain Mrs. Euphame Scott
who made no encouraging response to his attentions. The minister
contrived by a trick to obtain possession of one of her under-
garments, out of which he made a waistcoat and a pair of drawers,
being under the deluded impression that by wearing these articles
he could induce the lady to give him her affections. Bishop
Paterson suspended him for this foolery, but it subsequently
appeared that his Grace, who was known as 'Bishop Band-strings',
was little better than the poor minister he had hypocritically
punished. For the bishop was said to have been in the habit of
kissing his band-strings in the pulpit 'in the midst of an eloquent
discourse, which was the signal agreed upon betwixt him and a
lady to whom he was suitor, to show he could think upon her
charms even while engaged in the most solemn duties of his
profession'.

Meanwhile John's father had been growing in repute as well as
in riches. In 1674, when a Royal Commission was appointed by
Parliament to enquire into the working of the Scottish Mint, one
of the three goldsmiths called in to assist in this investigation was
William Law. At the same time the banking side of his business
increased with such profits that he was able to become a landed
gentleman or laird. On June 4, 1683, he bought the estates
of Lauriston and Randleston situated in the ancient Midlothian
parish of Cramond a few miles out of Edinburgh. The price paid
is not known, but the purchase was agreed by the King of whom
the lands were held at an annual fee of two pence Scots money for
Lauriston and one penny for Randleston to be paid according to
the deeds, 'at the feast of Pentecost if asked only'. Lauriston
boasted a century-old castle with a circular tower, two angle
turrets, extremely thick walls and a secret chamber so constructed
that everything going on in the room beneath could be overheard
there.

There was apparently already a tenant in possession at Lauriston
whom the new owner did not wish to turn out, preferring instead
to draw the rents. He now settled the property on his eldest son
John, reserving to himself a life interest in the estates. But
William Law was not destined to enjoy them for long. He had
recently contracted a large stone, a common complaint in those
days, which was giving him considerable pain. In the same year

he went over to Paris to consult a surgeon who had been recommended to him. The consequent operation to which he submitted was unfortunately not successful. It is probable that sepsis developed which proved fatal. At all events William Law died in Paris towards the end of the year 1683 and was buried in the Scots College there.

Although he was not much more than fifty years old at the time of his death, when William Law's will was opened and admitted to probate, it was seen that the family, and in particular the eldest son, were left comparatively well off. Apart from the goldsmith's business and the rents of the Lauriston and Randleston properties, as a banker William Law had debts outstanding of over £25,000, a large sum for those days, which the executors were directed to liquidate. The fact that the creditors included members and heads of such noble families as Mar, Hamilton, Seaforth, Douglas, Argyll, Burghly, Roxburghe, Balcarres and Dundonald shows how considerable were his banking connections. The bulk of the estate was left in trust for John until he should attain his majority, while the executors were also directed to educate him and the other children at schools and trades 'as they shall think most convenient'. John was to come into his inheritance on his twenty-first birthday.

The testator's wishes were carried out during the next few years. The goldsmith's business was wound up and the banking debts called in, a process which seems to have taken some time to complete. Meanwhile young John had left school and returned to Edinburgh, where he showed an uncommon interest in these arrangements. In particular the banking side of his father's business exercised a peculiar fascination for him, and while yet in his teens he began to study and ponder on the current theories of money and credit. At the same time absence of parental control and the love of an indulgent mother freed him from those restrictions to which most young men were subject. He became proficient in such manly sports as fencing and tennis – he used to play tennis in the old court at the Water Gate near Holyrood Palace – but he was also strongly attracted by the more sensuous sports of the boudoir. Cards and dice also made an irresistible appeal to him. A strikingly handsome and engaging appearance naturally endeared him to the ladies, by whom he came to be known as Beau Law or Jessamy John.

From visiting acquaintances he heard of the superior pleasures of the English capital, so he made up his mind he must see London. He was still a minor when he took the road south – young in years but old in experience. Among his Edinburgh friends of this period was George Lockhart of Carnwath, the future Jacobite politician and author. According to this authority, John Law, even before he left Scotland, was 'nicely expert in all manner of debaucheries'.

3

Arrived in London the young Laird of Lauriston took a handsome set of lodgings in St. Giles-in-the-Fields and installed himself and a mistress there in considerable style. By this date St. Giles had grown from a village into a small town of some three thousand houses, but it was still separated by broad fields from the Royal Borough of Westminster and the City of London. Besides the area of the parish church and the old lepers' hospital it included the districts of Bloomsbury, Holborn, Covent Garden and Seven Dials. Its inhabitants varied from leaders of rank and fashion, who mostly lived in the country houses of Great Queen Street, to poor Irish immigrants and French refugees, who frequented the dingy network of alleys near the churchyard on the site of the present New Oxford Street and then known as 'the Rookeries'.

Prominently associated with St. Giles-in-the-Fields, as indeed he was with the whole Court of King William III and Queen Mary, was a picturesque character, whose acquaintance John Law was to lose no time in making and whose multifarious activities he was to study closely. This was Thomas Neale, Master of the Mint and Groom-Porter to His Majesty, conspicuous among the numerous 'projectors', or as we should now call them, company promoters, with whom London abounded at that time. He was particularly assiduous in getting up lotteries in similar form to those for many years conducted in various Italian cities. Amongst other projects Neale was then engaged in developing the property round Seven Dials. The diarist Evelyn records at this time how he 'went to see the building near St. Giles, where seven streets made a star from a Doric pillar placed in the middle of a circular area said to be built by Mr. Neale introducer of the late lotteries in imitation of those at Venice'.[1] As Master of the Mint he was responsible for the issue of the coinage of the realm, while his duties as Groom-Porter included the provision of cards and dice at Court and the arbitration of disputes at the card-table and the bowling-green. As Groom-Porter he was also authorized by the King to license and suppress gaming-houses and to prosecute unlicensed keepers of 'rafflings, ordinaries and other public games'. His crest, which used to appear on the lottery tickets, represented a naked woman, presumably Fortune, on a globe which was encircled by the motto, in Latin, 'Not always the same' (*Non eadem semper*).

Every evening Law would sally forth from his lodgings to one of the fashionable clubs or gaming-houses in the town and try his luck at hazard, which was the popular gambling game of the period. He began to study the game scientifically and, according to a contemporary account, after a while he was able in every instance to work out the odds against the player throwing any given combination of figures with the dice, thus anticipating by more than half a century the calculations of the celebrated Edmund Hoyle.[2] But he bought his experience at a price, for in order to raise money he was obliged to sell his interest in the Scottish property which he had inherited from his father. Fortunately for him his mother came to the rescue. In 1692, shortly before he came of age, he conveyed the estates of Lauriston and Randleston to her for a cash consideration, which is not known but which seems to have been fairly substantial, since it enabled him to keep up his luxurious style of living for more than two years. Indeed, he might well have continued to live for consider-

[1] The column, on the summit of which were seven sundials with a dial facing each of the streets, was removed in 1773 on the supposition (which turned out to be incorrect) that a considerable sum of money was lodged at its base. It can still be seen on the green at Weybridge in Surrey where it was erected in 1822 by the inhabitants to commemorate the long residence of Frederica Duchess of York at Oatlands Park.

[2] Long out of vogue in England, hazard has persisted in America under the title of 'craps' or 'the crap game'. Law is said to have been the first to discover that, where 7 is the 'main' and 4 the 'chance', the odds against the placer are 2 to 1 and so on in proportion. These odds were worked out by Hoyle in his *Essay towards making the Doctrine of Chances easy to those who understand Vulgar Arithmetick only*, first published in 1754.

ably longer in this manner, had it not been for a certain unfortunate 'affair of gallantry' in which he became involved and which,
as will shortly be seen, had disastrous consequences for himself.

If he spent his nights amusing himself with dice and women,
he devoted the more profitable hours of the day to studying the
principles of finance, which had already come to exercise a fascinat-
ing and absorbing influence upon him. These principles were
strikingly exemplified in the current controversies of the day. The
expansion of trade and the increase of wealth, which had followed
the Restoration, made the banker's function necessary and important. As in Scotland banking, as it was then understood, was
carried on by the goldsmiths who became the custodians of the
merchants' money which would be locked away in the vaults in
Lombard Street where they would be safe from fire and robbery.
The old-fashioned merchants complained that the goldsmiths
were fast becoming the masters as well as the treasurers of the
City, but though they set their faces against the new business,
it soon became clear that it had come to stay. Furthermore, its
development raised the question of the establishment of a national
bank on similar lines to those institutions which had long been
working so successfully on the Continent, particularly in Genoa
and Amsterdam.

Various schemes were put forward at this time, many of which
were undoubtedly of the wildcat variety. Two in particular
interested Law and he was later to come into varying degrees of
contact with their authors. The first, which was projected by a
clever fellow Scot named William Paterson, was designed to
create a bank and at the same time to provide the King with the
capital he required to continue the war against France. The money
borrowed from the subscribers to the loan (£1,200,000 at 8 per
cent) was to become the bank stock and the subscribers were to be
incorporated into a company whose trading activities were to be
confined to bills of exchange and bullion. The second scheme,
which originated in the frenzied brain of an eccentric doctor
named Hugh Chamberlen, was a bank which would issue notes
on landed security.

Paterson's bank came into being in 1694 as the Bank of England.[1] Chamberlen's so-called Land Bank remained the chimera

[1] Writing some years later Law described the Bank of England as follows:
'England set up a Bank to have the conveniences of that at Amsterdam and

of his imagination and has long been forgotten, although it was nearly realized in a modified form under the sponsorship of the rising Tory politician Robert Harley. It is mentioned here because Law was greatly attracted by its fundamental idea which he was later to embody in one of his own schemes. Chamberlen, who was popularly known as 'the man-midwife', was in his way as colourful a character as Neale. He had a considerable practice as an accoucheur which he owed to his use of the obstetric forceps, discovered some time previously by a member of his family. His leisure moments, however, he devoted to his economic scheme, as he himself put it, 'to make England rich and happy', and during these years he explained and defended it in no less than forty-five pamphlets. Briefly the plan was to advance money on the security of landed property by issuing notes of the bank to the landowners. The fallacy lay in Chamberlen's contention that a lease of land for a term of years might be worth many times the fee simple. For example, if a piece of land brought in £1,000 a year, the bank would be prepared to advance the owner £100,000 if he pledged it as security for a hundred years, although Chamberlen should have known that the fee simple was not worth more than twenty years' purchase. In his folly he was supported by another 'projector' named John Briscoe[1] who claimed that the creation of a national land-bank would make England 'the paradise of the world'. What particularly impressed Law about the scheme when he came to examine it was that shorn of its patent absurdities and fallacies, it contained great possibilities for the creation of credit and stimulation of trade.

A less ingenious but more successful method of raising money for the government was now introduced by Thomas Neale. While Chamberlen and Briscoe were explaining their crank project to

---

by their constitution to increase money. This bank was made up of subscribers, who lent the King £1,200,000 at 8 per cent for 11 years on a parliament fund, and were privileged Bankers for that time. The sum due by the Government was a security to the people to make good any losses the bank might suffer. This bank was safer than the goldsmiths' notes in use before. It made a great addition to the money, having a much greater sum of notes out than money in bank. And the sum lent the King, which was the fund belonging to the subscribers, was negotiated at profit and had the same effect in trade as money.' John Law, *Money and Trade Considered* (1705).

[1] John Briscoe was probably related to Samuel Briscoe, the publisher, under whose imprint the first biography of John Law appeared in 1721.

an incredulous House of Commons towards the close of 1693, the Groom-Porter was busy publishing the details of a huge lottery by which it was hoped to raise a million pounds for the King's Treasury. The lottery, which was really a lottery and loan combined, anticipating the present-day Premium Bonds, was advertised as 'a profitable adventure to the fortunate, and can be unfortunate to none'. The security for the sums advanced was to be the receipts from new duties on salt and beer which had recently been authorized by Parliament. The loan was divided into 100,000 shares or 'tickets' of £10 each, the interest on each share being 10 per cent or £1 annually payable for sixteen years. In addition certain of the shares were to be prizes, and their holders, who were to be determined by lot, were not only to receive the £1 yearly interest on their shares but to divide among them the sum of £40,000 annually for sixteen years. A special office known as the Transfer Office was opened in Lombard Street for the transaction of the business of the lottery, while the principal goldsmiths and bankers of the city were authorized to sell 'tickets'.

The first drawing of the tickets was carried out with appropriate ceremonial and attracted considerable attention. However, applications kept pouring in to the Transfer Office, and among the visitors who passed through its doors was John Law who took careful note of all the proceedings there. A second drawing was announced to take place on April 10, 1694. But whatever plans Law may have made with his friends for being present on this occasion, he was unable to fulfil. The reason was that on the date in question he found himself a prisoner in Newgate Gaol on a charge of murder.

4

It seems that in Law's lodgings in St. Giles-in-the-Fields there was a lady who objected to the presence of Mrs. Lawrence, the mistress whom he maintained there. This lady was a sister of Edward Wilson, a well known 'beau' of the period who far outdid Law in extravagant living, although he was a younger son of impoverished parents. Wilson was prevailed upon to remove his sister from the lodgings, whereupon the landlady, imagining that her house would now get a bad name, not unnaturally complained to Law. Whether she actually instigated Law to pick a quarrel with Wilson, as the diarist John Evelyn has suggested, it is impossible to say. The fact remains that on the morning of April 9, 1694, Law called on Wilson. About an hour afterwards the two men met by appointment in the then comparatively deserted neighbourhood of Bloomsbury Square, and in the duel which followed Wilson was killed. Before he could get away Law was arrested and taken to Newgate Gaol, there to await his trial on a charge of murder at the next Old Bailey Sessions.

Beau Wilson's life had long been a mystery even to his closest friends, and its abrupt termination in Bloomsbury Square brought a solution no nearer. Edward Wilson belonged to an old but impoverished county family. His father's income amounted to no more than £200 a year, so that he could spare nothing for his numerous children, of whom Edward was the fifth son. Yet young Edward, to quote Evelyn again, 'lived in the garb and equipage of the richest nobleman for house, furniture, coaches, saddle horses and kept a table and all things accordingly, redeemed his father's estate and gave portions to his sisters. . . . The mystery is how this so young a gentleman, very sober and of good fame, could live in such an expensive manner; it could not be discovered by all possible industry and entreaty of his friends to make him reveal it.' He did not gamble and was never seen about with women, so that it did not appear that he owed his riches to either of these instruments. All he would ever say was that 'if he should ever live so long, he had wherewith to maintain himself in the same manner'. His annual expenditure was estimated at over £6,000 a year.

During his lifetime the secret of Beau Wilson's wealth had formed a favourite topic of conversation in the London clubs and coffee-houses. Some spiteful people said that he had robbed the Dutch mail of a quantity of jewellery, for which another had suffered death in his place; other equally ill-natured persons averred that he was in receipt of 'some foreign pension for the transmitting of intelligence' to the French King Louis XIV; while others even more fanciful put it about that he had discovered the 'philosopher's stone' for the manufacture of gold, a story which reached the ears of the Fellows of the Royal Society. The most likely solution was advanced some years later and implicated the name of John Law, but no positive proof of it is possible.

According to this source, Edward Wilson was discovered one hot summer evening lying on the grass in Kensington Gardens by a lady who was taking the air there with her maid. In spite of his dejected expression the lady was greatly struck by his appearance. Being at that moment ripe for an adventure she instructed the maid to strike up an acquaintance with the young man. The result of this chance meeting was an assignation for the following night at midnight in St. James's Park. The assignation was kept by both parties and according to the maid, who is the authority for the story, 'my Lady was so charmed with her lover that till two of the clock she did not think of retiring'. Furthermore the mask which her Ladyship took care to wear concealed the intelligent but far from beautiful features of Mistress Elizabeth Villiers, thirty-seven-year-old favourite of the reigning monarch William III and future Countess of Orkney. Next morning the maid appeared at Wilson's shabby lodgings with a present for him of 1,500 guineas from her mistress. "'Tis your Lady's pleasure that you should put yourself in a condition fitting the favourite of love and hers,' she said as she handed him the largest sum of money he had ever seen. There were further instructions. He was to take the handsomest lodgings that he could find and form his equipage according to the richest fancy. 'Be everything that's great and noble,' she went on. 'To those that have money all things may be performed with expedition.'

In return for these favours only two things were expected of Wilson. 'All you have to perform on your part,' his visitor assured him, 'is to reserve yourself entirely for her, and never by an indiscreet curiosity endeavour to discover her.' The penalty for such 'indiscreet curiosity' was terrible. 'If you enquire and succeed in that enquiry, you must not only lose her but your life also.'

The maid then proceeded to inform Wilson of the arrangements for their clandestine meetings. He was to meet her at midnight in Pall Mall and she would then conduct him to her lady's chamber.

'You will find my Lady in bed. There shall be but one light in the chamber, but do not by it endeavour to see her face. Be satisfied that she's young and by some thought the handsomest. Make use of your good fortune. I suppose sleep will not be your business. When the clock strikes two, rise and be gone! A chair will wait to carry you home. Thus may you be blessed both by riches and beauty. And for the continuation of both that entirely depends on yourself!'

At first Beau Wilson obeyed these instructions faithfully, setting himself up in a magnificent establishment and having no relations with any other woman. Nor did his mistress make excessive demands upon his company. However, the irregularity of their meetings merely increased his natural curiosity and heightened the mystery for him. At last he could resist no longer, and in a rash moment told his mistress that 'if it cost him whatever was dearest to him, he could not be easy till she had given him that last proof of her love'.

'Ah, my dear,' said the frail lady to the maid after her lover had gone. 'What things these men are! Whilst we yet have any reserve, we are importuned: 'tis a supply to conversation which without a theme languishes. Love, however omnipotent he be counted, abates much of his divinity when he comes to full enjoyment. I must either see this creature no more, or resolve to disclose myself. I cannot wisely do the latter, for Wilson seems to be too weak a vessel to trust my secret to! His good fortune has turned his brain. Is he not satisfied that I love him more than I ought, without I love him as much as I can?'

Elizabeth Villiers thereupon sent her maid to acquaint Wilson that his mistress could see him no more, although she would out of her bounty continue to keep him in the state to which he had become accustomed. While the maid was delivering this message, Wilson informed her that he was already aware of his mistress's identity. This discovery, it appears, was due to the fact that he had given her a ring and had seen it on Mistress Villiers' finger as she chanced to lean out of the window of her carriage whilst driving in Hyde Park at the very moment that Wilson happened to be passing in his own. It was this unfortunate admission which apparently sealed his fate, for on hearing this news Mistress Villiers is supposed to have got hold of John Law and suborned him to fight the duel which cost her lover his life. A convenient pretext for a quarrel presented itself in the departure of Wilson's sister from Law's lodgings and the pretended umbrage taken by his landlady.

It is unlikely after such a long lapse of time that the truth or falsity of this alleged episode and Law's part in it will ever be established. One thing however is certain. Nothing was found among Wilson's belongings after his death which threw any light on the mystery of his wealth. As the Beau lay dying on the ground in Bloomsbury Square, he handed his keys to a friend nearby and requested him to burn all his papers. The friend immediately made off to the Wilson mansion, but the ensuing search revealed absolutely nothing of the slightest consequence. The most material document, we are informed, was a recipe bequeathed to the dead man by his grandmother 'to cure old women of the tooth-ache, so that no persons troubled with that distemper need doubt of a remedy'.

5

Immediately after his arrest Law was committed for trial at the next Sessions due to be held at the Old Bailey Court House. Nor did he have long to wait for this ordeal. Less than a fortnight later he pleaded not guilty to the indictment which charged him with the murder of Edward Wilson. The case was tried by the seventy-five-year-old Recorder of London, Sir Salathiel Lovell, an incompetent dodderer who was 'distinguished principally for his want of memory', although he was in the habit of boasting that he had been more diligent in the discovery and conviction of criminals than any other judge in the Kingdom.

Counsel for the prosecution in his opening speech outlined the circumstances which led up to the duel. There seems no doubt that the ostensible if not the real cause of the quarrel concerned Mrs. Lawrence whom the accused was maintaining as his mistress. Counsel quoted from a number of threatening letters from the accused to the dead man, which letters were full of invective and cautions to Mr. Wilson to beware, for 'there was a design of evil against him'. Counsel then called the rest of his evidence. The first witness was Wilson's servant Smith, who swore that the accused came to his master's house a little before the fatal meeting and drank a pint of sack in the parlour, 'after which he heard his master say that he was much surprised with something that Mr. Law had told him'.

The next witness for the Crown was Captain Wightman, described as 'a person of good information'. He said he was a close friend of Wilson's and had been with him and the accused in the Fountain Tavern in the Strand. They remained there drinking for a while and then the accused left. Shortly afterwards Wilson accompanied by the witness took a coach and drove to Bloomsbury Square where the accused met them. As the accused approached them, Wilson drew his sword and stood upon his guard; upon which, according to Captain Wightman, the accused immediately drew his sword, 'and they both passed together, making but one pass by which Mr. Wilson received a mortal wound in the upper part of the stomach of the depth of two inches, of which he instantly died'. This account was confirmed by a number of other witnesses who saw the duel and were all agreed that the antagonists drew their swords and 'passed at each other and presently Mr. Wilson was killed'. Such in brief was the sum of the evidence for the Crown.

Criminal procedure at that time did not permit an accused, in a serious case where a 'felony' was charged, to give evidence under oath on his own behalf or to call witnesses under oath or indeed to be represented by counsel except for the argument of points of law. Law's defence therefore took the form of an unsworn statement. In this statement the prisoner declared that he had been in Wilson's company on a number of occasions prior to the duel and there never had been any quarrel between them until they met at the Fountain Tavern as a result of their written correspondence. He pleaded that the meeting in Bloomsbury Square was entirely accidental, 'Mr. Wilson drawing his sword first by which he was forced to stand in his own defence'. The consequent killing of his antagonist, therefore, only arose from the sudden heat of passion and not from any malice aforethought. Several 'persons of good quality' then spoke as to the accused's character, alleging that he was not given to quarrelling nor was he 'a person of ill behaviour'.

The judge's summing-up to the jury was strongly against the accused. It is true that the Recorder did explain for the jurors' benefit that 'if two men suddenly quarrel and one killed the other this would be but manslaughter', but in the next breath he virtually directed the jury to convict. 'This case seems to be otherwise,' he said, 'for there was a continual quarrel carried on betwixt them for some time before; therefore, must be accounted a malicious quarrel and a design of murder in the person that killed the other.' The jury retired for a short time and, as might be expected, found the prisoner guilty of murder. On April 22, 1694, John Law was brought up for sentence and informed by the Recorder that he must suffer death by hanging.

During the next few days, as Law sat in the condemned prisoner's cell in Newgate, powerful influences were at work on his behalf. It is possible that Mistress Villiers, fearing some sensational revelation on the scaffold which might compromise her irreparably, sought with success her royal lover's intervention. Alternatively, duelling being regarded at Court as a necessary mode of settling differences between gentlemen whose honour had been affronted, the King was frequently moved to exercise his prerogative of clemency when any such meeting terminated fatally for one of the parties. At all events a reprieve was forthcoming, obtained, according to Law's own statement, 'by the intercession of several noblemen of Scotland'.

But the prisoner was not set at liberty. Wilson's family were naturally incensed at the turn events had taken, and his brother Robert proceeded to lodge what was known as 'an appeal of murder' in the Court of King's Bench. This was a curious and antiquated civil action which was sometimes brought by the widow or male heir of a deceased person after his killer had been acquitted or received the royal pardon. The appeal was in the nature of a private action between the parties by which, if the case went against the defendant and the plaintiff insisted on it, the death of the deceased was to be compensated for by the death of the defendant. In such a case the Crown could not remit judgement and the law had to take its course in the shape of the defendant's execution. To plead in this fresh process, therefore, John Law was, by virtue of a writ of *habeas corpus* at the instance of Robert Wilson, removed from Newgate to the custody of the Marshal of the King's Bench Prison.[1]

The Court of King's Bench sat in Westminster Hall and consisted of four judges of whom the Chief Justice, Sir John Holt, was by contrast with the Recorder conspicuous as one of the

[1] It seems that it was the King's wish that the Wilson family should have recourse to this civil action. The following is an extract from the Secretary of State's Domestic Entry Book: 'April 22 (1694) Whitehall. Caveat that nothing pass relating to a pardon for John Laws [*sic*] sentenced to death for the murder of Mr. Edward Wilson till notice first be given to Mr. Robert Wilson brother of the deceased at his house in Stratton St. Berkely Square.' *Calendar of State Papers (Domestic)* 1694–95, at p. 108.

ablest lawyers and one of the fairest and most humane judges of
the time. The prison attached to the Court was situated in the
neighbourhood of Southwark south of the Thames and close by
London Bridge, and the journey between the two places was as a
rule made by river craft. The King's Bench Prison, the largest
gaol in London after Newgate, was a forbidding-looking building
surrounded by a thirty foot high wall in Southwark High Street
generally known as the Borough. Its inmates consisted of debtors
and other unfortunates prosecuted by civil process. Living conditions were tolerable for those who had the means to pay for
them – they could leave the prison during the day and even at
night could sleep outside its walls in the nearby district called the
'liberties' – but the poor prisoners, on the other hand, who had
no money with which to purchase these privileges, frequently
suffered the most hideous cruelties at the hands of the warders or
turnkeys. Law, being a person of some substance, seems to have
been treated comfortably. On account of the somewhat special
circumstances of his case he was confined in a cell, but he was
allowed to receive visitors freely. Among the latter were several
lawyers whom, since the forthcoming trial was technically a civil
one, he was permitted to instruct to defend him.

On June 22 – exactly a month later – Law was brought up to
Westminster Hall to answer to the so-called appeal. He was represented by two of the most eminent senior counsel of the day, Sir
William Thompson and Sir Creswell Levinz, Serjeants-at-Law,
and an able junior, Mr. Thomas Carthew. Serjeant Thompson had
appeared in many famous trials including that of the duellist Lord
Mohun before the House of Lords for his part in the killing of the
actor William Mountfort. Serjeant Levinz had been himself a
judge in the reign of James II but had been dismissed from his
lukewarm support of that monarch on the Bench and had returned
to the Bar where he had appeared in several well-known cases,
among them the celebrated trial of the Seven Bishops in 1688.
Before the plaintiff was able to open his case this imposing team
of advocates put forward a series of legal arguments which affords
a good illustration of how trials were frequently upset on the
ground of legal quibbles and small technicalities. It was alleged,
for instance, that the plaintiff's statement in the court that the duel
had taken place 'about the first hour of midday' was bad for
reason of uncertainty: the time ought to have been stated

precisely. Similarly the place of the wound was 'not certainly expressed' as being 'in the upper part of the belly'. Also the town as
well as the parish in which the act complained of took place
should have been indicated. Finally, an objection was taken to the
return of the writ as having been personally directed to the sheriff
to 'attach' Law, whereas in fact Law had been arrested by the
sheriff's bailiff. Wilson's counsel, heard in reply, was Sir Bartho-
lomew Shower, a former Recorder of London and a law reporter
who has left an authoritative account of this curious action.

Before proceeding further with the case Chief Justice Holt
announced that the Court would take time to consider the legal
arguments of counsel and that it would give a ruling on them
during the next week. But it was now nearly the end of the term,
so that the hearing was again put off until after the Long Vacation.
The defendant was thereupon taken back to the King's Bench
Prison where he spent the succeeding months in planning to
escape. By the middle of October, he had succeeded in filing down
four bars of his cell window, but unfortunately for him, before
he could make any further progress with this enterprising arrangement, he was discovered, his instruments removed, and himself
placed in irons. In this uncomfortable condition he was brought
up again to the King's Bench Court soon afterwards to hear from
the mouth of the Chief Justice that the Court had decided to
overrule the legal arguments so ingeniously advanced by his
counsel. A date was appointed for the hearing of the action, but on
further consideration, in view of the heavy calendar for that term,
the trial was postponed until early in the New Year in the
following term.

Back in his cell again the prisoner refused to be daunted and
rallied all his friends to his aid, possibly including the King's
mistress. More files were introduced together with a plentiful
supply of money and a powerful opiate for use on the guards.
The escape was now planned to take place as soon as possible
after New Year's Day, 1695. His friends agreed to have a coach
waiting outside the prison to carry him off to the country where
he might make his way to the Continent. The only trouble was the
thirty-foot drop which Law would have to make from the top
of the walls in order to reach safety. However, he decided that he
must risk this.

As we have seen, the plan was successfully carried out. Its

execution, which is reminiscent of the escape of Benvenuto Cellini from the Castle of St. Angelo in Rome a century and a half earlier, was attended by one mishap fortunately not fatal for the prisoner. Like the great Italian artist, who had to negotiate a similar drop from the castle walls, Law sprained his ankle in the descent which took place under cover of darkness. He was immediately helped into the waiting coach and driven off to Sussex, where he remained in hiding till a boat could be found to convey him out of the country. In a few days arrangements were made with the captain of a vessel bound for a Dutch port and he lost no time in taking passage.

Whether Mistress Elizabeth Villiers had any hand in these arrangements it is impossible to say with any degree of certainty. Her maid and confidante, whose acquaintance we have already made, asserted that she had. The central figure in this dramatic episode, however, always denied the truth of the maid's story and was wont to declare 'that never any Lady employed him in this affair and the manner and means of making his escape very different from what is there represented'.

CHAPTER II

THE TRAVELLER

Relatively few details are known of John Law's life during the next ten years. It is extremely difficult to trace his movements since none of his correspondence for these years has survived, the evidence of contemporaries is scanty and there are few references in his own later writings to his activities at this time. According to his first and contemporary anonymous biographer, he made his way to France immediately after his escape from the King's Bench Prison. But France and England were then at war, and in view of that fact it is difficult to believe that he was able to put in at any French port at this time. The Jacobite agents, who regularly passed between the ex-King James II's Court at St. Germains and the exiled monarch's supporters in Britain, travelled as a rule through the Low Countries, and it is practically certain that Law, in eventually making his way to Paris as he did, used this route. Furthermore, French authorities seem agreed that he did not visit France until after peace had been signed between the two countries over two years later. It is more than likely that Law utilized the interval to acquire the detailed knowledge of Dutch banking of which he was later to give proofs in his writings.

The United Provinces of the Netherlands, of which Holland was the chief, occupied a pivotal position in King William III's scheme of defences against French aggression and Louis XIV's attempt to dominate Europe. In 1686, three years before he was called to the English throne, William, then Prince of Orange and Stadholder of the Union, had formed the famous confederacy of European states – the League of Augsburg – which, strengthened by the adhesion of England after the Revolution, had been engaged in an extensive and exhausting struggle with French arms on land and sea. The Hague had in consequence become the diplomatic centre of Europe, particularly since the League's diplomatic representatives were at William's suggestion in frequent and often continuous conference there. The Union's foreign relations were conducted by an official known as the Grand Pensionary. In the temporary absence of an ambassador British interests were in the youthful but brilliant hands of the thirty-one-year-old Secretary of the Embassy, Matthew Prior, better known perhaps as a poet than a diplomatist.

As passport control officer, in addition to his other duties, Prior spent considerable time in endeavouring – not with invariable success – to check the illicit passenger traffic between Dutch and English ports, pursuing Jacobites in various guises and unravelling their secret communications which, as in more recent wars, assumed a variety of forms in a variety of hiding-places. For this purpose he naturally sought the collaboration of the Dutch authorities, and it is doubtful whether Law, who was believed to be sympathetic to the Jacobite cause, could have escaped their joint vigilance, even if he did not call at the Embassy on his arrival in The Hague to pay his respects to the Secretary. 'The Pensioner has given me the honour of a long audience', wrote Prior to Whitehall about the time of Law's arrival on the Continent, 'in order to our taking such methods as may most effectively locate this gang and hinder rogues, who really come from France to pass into England and wenches to bring letters in their stays ... or a little lower.'

According to J. P. Wood, Law's early nineteenth-century biographer who had access to certain materials which are not now available, the youthful fugitive from justice was actually employed for a time by the *chargé d'affaires* in secretarial duties.[1] If this were so, these duties must have been purely honorary, since Prior was extremely short of cash at this time and always complaining to Whitehall that his pay was many months in arrears. 'Hitherto I have borrowed and done pretty well,' he wrote at this period:

[1] He is stated to have officiated 'for some time as secretary to the British resident in Holland': J. P. Wood, *Life of John Law* (1824) at p. 11. This statement is not confirmed by any of the departmental correspondence in the Public Record Office.

'those who lent me money and are not yet paid have had the trouble on't, but for want of more such civil persons I begin to be a little troubled myself. There is a great correspondence between the stomach and the heart: she is out of humour commonly when one is hungry, and it is time to think what friends I have at Whitehall when Famine sets triumphant on the cheeks of my two footmen and the ribs of my two horses.' However he may have been employed in the Embassy Chancery, if indeed he was employed there at all, it is reasonably certain that Law spent his week-ends in the manner inimitably described by the poetic Prior.

While with labour assiduous due pleasure I mix
And in one day atone for the business of six,
In a little Dutch chaise on a Saturday night,
On my left hand my Horace, a nymph on my right:
No *mémoire* to compose, and no *Post-Boy* to move
That on Sunday may hinder the softness of love,
For her neither visits nor parties of tea,
Nor the long-winded cant of a dull refugee.
This night and the next shall be hers, shall be mine,
To good or ill fortune the third we resign:
Thus scorning the world, and superior to fate,
I drive on my car in professional state.

*　　*　　*

And is it enough for the joys of the day,
To think what Anacreon or Sappho would say?
When good Vandergoes and his provident *Vrow*,
As they gaze on my triumph, do freely allow,
That, search all the province, you'll find no man there is
So blest as the *Englischen Heer Secretáris*.

Unlike Prior, during working hours Law was more interested in finance than in politics. He seems to have lost little time in turning his footsteps in the direction of Amsterdam, which appeared as the financial counterpart of The Hague in the struggle against Louis XIV. For it was Amsterdam's famous bank which provided most of the sinews of war at this time.[1] This

---

[1] Cp. Matthew Prior writing in July 1696 to Whitehall: 'We expect you will either make war or peace in good earnest . . . If you intend war Mr.

remarkable corporation was not an ancient institution. It had been founded less than a century previously in order to provide a steady currency in which normal commercial dealings might be transacted. At the beginning of the seventeenth century Dutch traders (like English traders at the time of Law's first visit to the Continent) were suffering from two inconveniences. One was the defective state of their local coinage, much of which was of lighter weight than its face value, and the other was the circulation of masses of foreign coins of uncertain value. It was to remedy this state of affairs that the Bank of Amsterdam had been incorporated.

The bank conducted business on the following lines. Merchants used to bring all kinds of coins to the bank, and the bank would give them credit for their real as distinct from their nominal value. In other words they allowed the value of weight rather than the value which appeared in the inscriptions on the coins. The banker then locked up the coins and gave the merchant what virtually amounted to banknotes representing the coins. These banknotes were used to settle the bills of exchange when they matured and other business; and the notes were much sought after, since it was known that they represented a given number of perfect coins. In fact they came to be in such a demand that they usually were at a slight premium or *agio*, which the bank customarily charged a purchaser. In other words, the notes sold for a little more than the nominal value of the gold or silver they represented. People paid for the extra convenience of a note in much the same way as they do now for a cheque or postal order.

Law described the working of the bank in clear and characteristic language:

> This Bank . . . is a secure place where merchants may give in money and have credit to trade with. Besides the convenience of easier and quicker payments, the banks save the expense of bags and carriage, losses by bad money, and the money is safer than in the merchants' houses, for it is less liable to fire or robbery, the necessary measures being taken to prevent them.

Dykevelt has borrowed three millions Holland's money of Amsterdam at 5 per cent, the States being security for the interest and with this you are to besiege Dunkirk. Get to it as you can.' Hist. MSS. Comm: Bath Manuscripts, III, 81.

Merchants who have money in the Bank of Amsterdam, and people of other countries who deal with them, are not liable to the changes in the money, by its being alloyed or altered in the denomination. For the Bank receives no money but what's of value and is therefore called bank money, and though raised in current payments it goes for the value it was pledged for in bank payments. The *agio* of the Bank changes a quarter or half per cent as current money is more or less scarce.

With the object of inducing local merchants to open accounts with the bank, it was laid down by law that all bills of exchange above 100 pounds Flemish must be made payable at the bank. On the whole this legislation had succeeded in its purpose. The bank did not, however, discount bills or concern itself with bill broking. It could and did advance money on security to its customers, but 'overdrawing' was strictly prohibited under penalty of a fine of 3 per cent of the amount by which the customer's account was allowed to be overdrawn. Law noted that the directors could not honour all the banknotes issued without calling in all their loans, of whose advantage in promoting trade and industry he was at the same time strongly conscious.

So far as they lend they add to the money which brings a profit to the country by employing more people and extending trade; they add to the money to be lent, whereby it is easier borrowed and at less use [i.e. at lower interest], and the Bank has a benefit. But the Bank is less sure [i.e. secure], and though none suffer by it or are apprehensive of danger, its credit being good, yet if the whole demands were made or demands greater than the remaining money, they could not all be satisfied till the Bank had called in what sums were lent.

The elementary principle of banking expressed in the foregoing sentences may seem a commonplace today, but when Law first visited Amsterdam it was a novelty to most visitors from the British Isles. To the exercise of the bank's function in creating credit, with which to drive the wheels of trade and industry, Law was convinced that Holland owed the commercial supremacy in Europe which she enjoyed at this time. England and Scotland, on the other hand, had superior natural advantages to Holland, but their trade and industry languished. Indeed he was convinced that had Britain, France or Spain applied the same measures to promote trade as Holland had done, Holland would not have been inhabited.

It was in Holland at this time that Law began to work out certain fundamental ideas which were subsequently embodied in what was known as his 'system'. The cardinal feature lay in what the author considered to be the real meaning of money. What is money, he argued, but a simple exchange voucher for use in the purchase of goods and services? If that is so, why use a costly and inconvenient metal such as gold? 'Money', he wrote, 'is not the value *for* which goods are exchanged, but the value *by* which they are exchanged. The use of money is to buy goods and silver, while money is of no other use.' What then is the good of using metallic money except for small token payments? None, since any sort of paper could be used in the same way and much more cheaply.

Law used to illustrate the truth of his axiom in characteristic fashion. Whenever he went to the gaming-tables, he brought two bags with him. One contained gold and silver coins, and the other contained counters. The counters were employed to save him the inconvenience of using large quantities of coins. At the end of the evening's play the counters were presented to him by their holders and duly honoured.

2

In the spring of 1697 peace negotiations were begun in Ryswick, a village lying a mile or two out of The Hague on the road to Delft. Both sides were momentarily tired of the struggle and, in particular, Louis XIV required a breathing space. The declining health of the Spanish King Charles II, who had no near heir, adumbrated the question of the succession to that monarch's throne, and Louis felt that his own claims, which he secretly hoped to advance, would have little chance of realization if he were at war with Spain at Charles's death. He accordingly made offers to which William III and the rest of the allies eventually agreed. The preliminaries lasted throughout the summer and much time was wasted, as often happens at peace conferences, on trifling questions of protocol and etiquette. 'The chief business of Harly and Kaunitz', Macaulay wrote of the principal French and Austrian delegates in his *History of England*, 'was to watch each other's legs. Neither of them thought it consistent with the dignity of the Crown which he served to advance towards the other faster than the other advanced towards him. If therefore one of them perceived that he had inadvertently stepped forward too quick, he went back to the door, and the stately minuet began again. The ministers of Louis drew up a paper in their own language. The German statesmen protested against this innovation, this insult to the dignity of the Holy Roman Empire, this encroachment on the rights of independent nations, and would not know anything about the paper till it had been translated from good French into bad Latin.'

The Treaty of Ryswick was signed in the small hours of the morning of September 10, 1697. Matthew Prior, who had acted as secretary to the British delegation, was already on the way to London with the news. France lost all her territorial acquisitions during the past twenty years with the exception of Strasbourg, and Louis agreed to recognize William as King of England, promising at the same time to give no aid to any claimant to that throne – an undertaking which he was later to violate. An impressive mission was despatched to Paris headed by William's favourite minister, the Earl of Portland with the rank of Ambassador, who was joined shortly afterwards by the indispensable Mr. Secretary Prior. A crowd of Englishmen followed who had not had an opportunity of tasting the delights of the French capital for many years, among them several who were homosexually inclined. Wrote the famous Elizabeth Charlotte Duchess of Orleans at the time: 'Nothing is more ordinary in England than this unnatural vice . . . and all those who followed Lord Portland to Paris led a terrible life with the debauchees of Paris. Lord Westmoreland, Lord Raby and three or four others did not hesitate to make public what their inclinations were.' Portland's short embassy (it lasted less than six months) is said to have cost £80,000. His equipage was magnificent, and on the occasion of his formal entry into Paris he had six carriages, twelve led horses, twelve pages, fifty outriders and a great following of noblemen. John Law may well have been among those who witnessed this extraordinary spectacle, for he is known to have been in the capital about this time.

Though barely sixty the Grand Monarch of France had for most of the past forty years been his own first minister and the absolute ruler of his country, whose boundaries he had in a long series of military campaigns succeeded in considerably extending during this period. He was now living an extremely quiet and secluded life, being entirely governed by his former mistress Madame de Maintenon, whom he had secretly married soon after his wife's death fifteen years before. This extraordinary woman had been mainly instrumental in persuading Louis to conclude peace at Ryswick, and she seemed determined to prevent him from engaging in any future conflicts. 'Madame Maintenon', wrote Prior, 'is our friend and will keep the Peace, if possible *as she made it*, not out of any kindness she has for us, but from a notion that the King's engaging in business impairs his health. 'Tis incredible what power that woman has; everything goes through her hands, and Diana made much less a figure at Ephesus.' The profound religious influence, which Madame de Maintenon exercised upon Louis, produced a certain sombre atmosphere and made for a lack of gaiety at Court, which rendered the King much less popular with the aristocracy than with their social inferiors. 'The common people of this nation have a strange veneration for their King,' Prior remarked: 'it is certain he might have the last penny of them as well by their inclinations as his power *pour la gloire*. But the people of quality hate him to hell, and (as the French do things always to excess) there is nothing so extravagant as their expressions of this kind in an *auberge* over-night, though they dare as well be hanged as not rise at five the next morning to be at Versailles by eight.'

Prior was particularly struck by the King's personal vanity. 'The monarch as to his health is lusty enough, so he speaks a little like old Maynard,[1] and picks and shows his teeth with a good deal of affectation, being the vainest creature alive even to the least things. His house at Versailles is something the foolishest in the world; he is strutting in every panel and galloping over one's head in every ceiling, and if he turns to spit he must see himself

---

[1] Sir John Maynard, serjeant-at-law, for many years doyen of the English Bar. Born in the reign of Queen Elizabeth he lived to congratulate William III on his accession, and to the King's remark that he had outlived all the men of the law of his time he made the historic reply that 'he had like to have outlived the law itself if his Highness had not come over'. He died in 1690.

in person or his Viceregent the Sun with *Sufficit orbi* or *Nec pluribus impar*. I verily believe that there are of him statues, busts, bas reliefs and pictures above two hundred in the house and garden. In the meantime Madam Maintenon governs him as Roxalana did Solyman. He lives at Marly like an Eastern monarch, making waterworks and planting melons, and leaves his bashaws to ruin the land provided they are constant in bringing in their tribute.'

The King's younger brother, the Duke of Orleans, known as 'Monsieur' was a despicable creature. At one time 'Monsieur' had shown signs of military prowess, but for many years he had led a life of luxurious idleness, being entirely given over to his male favourites. The Duchess, 'Madame', as she was called at Court, had been a husky Rhine maiden when she had married Monsieur as his second wife more than a quarter of a century previously (his first wife Henrietta of England, whom he was accused of poisoning, had been a sister of Charles II), and she always remained a shrewd German *hausfrau* disliked but respected by her royal brother-in-law. To her gift for correspondence we owe one of the most penetrating and informative pictures ever painted in words of Louis XIV's remarkable Court. Of her husband she had no illusions. 'He cares for nothing but his young friends, and spends whole nights eating and drinking with them,' she wrote at this time. 'He also gives them enormous sums of money. Where they are concerned, nothing matters and nothing is too costly, although at the same time the children and I have scarcely the necessities of life. When I need chemises and sheets I have to beg for them for a very long time, but he gives La Carte [a prime favourite who was Captain of his Guards] ten thousand crowns to buy his linen in Flanders . . . Monsieur has had all the silver which came from the Palatinate melted and sold and has given the money to his minions. Every day new favourites are brought to him and he sells and pawns all his jewels in order to make them presents . . . Monsieur says publicly and does not try to hide it from either his daughter or me that he is getting old and has no time to lose, and that he does not intend to save anything but will use everything in order to amuse himself to the end.

Their only son Philip Duke of Chartres had recently celebrated his twenty-first birthday and was now enjoying the freedom of his own separate establishment in the late Cardinal Richelieu's palace in the heart of Paris, renamed the Palais Royal. This young man, who was destined to exercise a fateful influence in the life and fortunes of John Law, was both intelligent and industrious, but he already exhibited that love of dissipation which was later to make him notorious. 'My son behaves no better than his father,' wrote Madame, 'He gives all he possesses to his mistress . . . He also allows himself to be put upon by his lackeys, and is so terribly debauched that I am afraid in the long run it will cost him his life. He passes whole nights in orgies of debauchery and often does not go to bed until eight o'clock in the morning . . . He is not lacking in intelligence nor is he ignorant, and from childhood he has always had an inclination towards all that is good and suitable to his rank. But since he has been his own master and these wicked people have taken him up and made him hobnob with vulgar strumpets, his character and appearance have altered so much that you wouldn't recognize him any longer.' Although His Catholic Majesty was inclined to frown on behaviour of this kind, the position of the Duke of Chartres at Court was secured by his marriage to Mademoiselle de Blois, the King's legitimized daughter by his late mistress Madame de Montespan.

Gambling was also a popular pastime in the Palais Royal. One of the most ardent card-players named Boissière was a son of the celebrated courtesan Ninon de Lenclos. It might be said that gambling was bred in his bones, since the story went that his paternity was decided by the drawing of lots between two courtiers. It may have been over a game of lansquenet that Law first made the young Duke's acquaintance. Alternatively the Scotsman may have been introduced to the Palais Royal circle as a student of finance whom Chartres might possibly be interested to meet. It is certain that they did meet at this period in Paris. Law found Chartres charming, easy of access, possessed of a remarkable memory for facts and figures, and well informed in finance as well as politics and the arts. It is known that Law also met the Marquis de Chamillard, whom Louis XIV had placed in charge of the country's finances as Controller-General in 1699. Michel de Chamillard was a middle-aged mediocrity who owed his rise partly to the patronage of Madame de Maintenon and partly to his skill at billiards by which he was brought to the King's notice. On leaving Paris Law promised to keep in touch with both men.

3

While in France Law spent some time at St. Germains-en-Laye, where Louis XIV's generosity had assigned the exiled English King James II an estate and an allowance to maintain himself and the members of his Court who had followed him across the Channel at the Revolution. Any sympathies which the Scotsman may have had with the fallen monarch must assuredly have been dulled by the conditions which he found there. Although situated in the most delightful surroundings a few miles from the most attractive capital city on the Continent, the place was beset with an intolerable atmosphere of gloom and mutual recrimination. Like Louis, the ex-King of England had become intensely religious, and his suite was infested with priests who occupied all the best accommodation. Indeed the château strongly resembled a monastery, and there were no less than three places of worship within its walls. James indulged in the most severe spiritual exercises and mortified his flesh with such repeated fastings and floggings that eventually the courtiers and even the priests were obliged to interfere and restrict his austerities. In the words of his principal biographer, he had 'turned St. Germains into a sort of solitude'.

One August afternoon in 1698 the exiles emerged from their retreat and drove over to St. Cloud to attend the christening of the Duke of Chartres's second daughter. It is possible that Law was among those who made the journey from St. Germains to witness this spectacle, and James's lean features may have reminded him of his friend the Groom-Porter and lottery promoter as they did Mathew Prior, who has left a characteristic account of it. 'I saw King James and his Queen,' wrote Prior afterwards, 'and there was nothing so odd as to see the Duke of Berwick and Lord Middleton traversing the gallery on one side, and I and Lord Reay of the good Mackay brood on the other side, each looking on the other with an air of civility mixed with contempt. The gentlemen belonging to the Duke d'Orleans and Chartres were embarrassed enough to call him one moment "*Le Roy d'Angleterre*" to them and speak to me next of "*Le Roy Jacques*". It was, as most human things are, a farce ridiculous enough. King James looks mighty old and worn, and stoops in his shoulders

. . . You never saw such a strange figure as the old bully is, lean, worn and riv'led not unlike Neale the projector. The Queen looks very melancholy, but otherwise well enough. Their equipages are all very ragged and contemptible.'

Living in the neighbourhood of St. Germains at this time was an Englishwoman about Law's age who styled herself Lady Catherine Seignieur. Directly descended from Sir Thomas Boleyn, father of the celebrated Anne, second wife of Henry VIII, she was a sister of the titular Earl of Banbury and had married a Frenchman named Seignieur. Her brother Charles had been an immate of the King's Bench Prison at the same time as Law, and it is possible that he gave Law an introduction to Catherine. Her mother was a daughter of an Irish peer, Lord Sherard.

Charles Knollys, who claimed the Earldom of Banbury, had married ten years previously a woman named Elizabeth Lister. Almost immediately after the ceremony, which took place in the Nag's Head Coffee House in Covent Garden, the notorious Fleet prison parson, Dr. Cleaver officiating, Knollys deserted his bride in favour of another woman named Elizabeth Price, who is stated to have been employed in some capacity at the Court of St. Germains. They travelled about Europe for several years together and eventually went through a form of marriage at Verona in 1692. On Knollys's return to England he was challenged to a duel by his first wife's brother-in-law, who was unfortunately killed in the ensuing encounter. On being charged with murder Knollys had pleaded the privilege of trial before the House of Lords on the ground that he was the legitimate descendant of his grandfather William, who had been created Earl of Banbury by Charles I. There was no doubt that William Knollys had been raised to the peerage under this title in 1626 when he was eighty years of age. His wife had borne him no children for the past thirty years, but she then proceeded to produce two sons who each in turn claimed to succeed to the Banbury peerage. The second, who was the father of Catherine and Charles, was born in the Earl's eighty-fifth year. The paternity of both these sons was called in question, and as a result the House of Lords had decided that Charles Knollys had no right to the earldom. The trial was then moved to the Court of King's Bench where Knollys pleaded misnomer. After lengthy argument and delay, during part of which time Knollys was confined in the court prison,

Chief Justice Holt eventually declared the Lords' decision invalid and quashed the indictment. Meanwhile Knollys had appeared before the ecclesiastical Court of Delegates which, after a trial lasting over three years on the conflicting claims of Elizabeth Lister and Elizabeth Price, had decided in favour of the former on the ground that the latter unlike her opponent could be no worse off than before since she had borne Knollys no children: also unlike Elizabeth Lister she 'had been a player and mistress to several persons'.

Nothing is known of Monsieur Seignieur except that his wife appears to have got tired of him. Her meeting with Law, whether by chance or design, quickly led to friendship, soon turned to affection. The upshot of the matter was that they agreed to run away together to Italy. And so one day about the turn of the century she secretly left her husband's house and together with her lover posted off to the south.[1]

4

The travellers' immediate object-ive was Genoa, at that time an independent state with a national bank which rivalled that of Amsterdam in reputation. Their route lay through the Rhône valley and Switzerland. The valley like the rest of France was suffering from a most acute industrial and commercial depression at this time. The disastrous policy of Louis XIV fifteen years previously in revoking the celebrated Edict of Nantes, which had guaranteed the French Protestants liberty of religion, had now come to full fruition. The best artisans and craftsmen were to be found among the Huguenot element of the population and those who had not been sent to serve in the galleys had fled to neighbouring countries taking their tools and the secrets of their trades with them. The depression was

---

[1] In a letter dated May 12, 1783, to the Earl of Buchan, who was thinking of writing a monograph on Law, Horace Walpole states: 'I met the other day with an account in some French literary gazette, I forget which, of his having carried off the wife of another man.' See *Letters of Horace Walpole*, ed. Mrs. Paget Toynbee, XII, 448–449 (London, 1904). Walpole had several portraits of Law in his house at Strawberry Hill, including one by Rosalba in crayons whose whereabouts is now unknown.

intensified by lack of money in circulation. By contrast Switzerland, which had attracted many of the Huguenot refugees, seemed to be commercially and industrially flourishing.

Law and his companion stayed for a short while at Neuchâtel. This town and the surrounding district in the Jura mountains, though geographically part of Switzerland, did not then form part of the Swiss confederation. They constituted a sovereign principality, for whose rule Louis XIV's nephew the Prince of Conti was a claimant. François Louis de Bourbon, Prince of Conti, was engaged in pursuing his pretensions on the spot, and it is known that Law made his acquaintance there at this time. Conti was reported to be the lover of the Duchess of Chartres, who was his sister-in-law and also Louis XIV's daughter by Madame de Montespan; and, as she had recently seen Law in Paris, it is possible that she supplied him with the necessary introduction. The prince was about thirty-five, intelligent, well mannered and possessed of great ability. But he was also tainted with the prevailing vice of the time, for, in the words of 'Madame' the Duchess of Orleans, 'his love for his sister-in-law does not prevent him loving his pages as well'. Louis XIV disliked him and in order to get rid of him had recently tried to obtain the Polish throne for him. Conti's dilatory and apparently unwilling departure, due to his dislike of foregoing the Duchess's charms, cost him this Kingdom, since although he had been legally elected he had discovered on his arrival in Danzig that the Elector of Saxony was already in possession. His claim to the principality of Neuchâtel, though legally valid, was meeting with no better success. The Swiss declined to give him any military assistance in the face of the demands of the late ruler's sister who did indeed eventually acquire the principality. In spite of his preoccupations, however, Conti found time to receive Law and listen to his views on economics and finance, but like his kinsman the Duke of Chartres he could do no more than ask his visitor on taking his leave to write to him when he had any interesting ideas or proposals to communicate.

The Law *ménage* settled down in Genoa. Though no longer mistress of the Mediterranean and the trade with the East, this little republic was still an extremely rich state despite the severe bombardment by the French fleet, which her capital port had suffered some years previously for declining to acknowledge the suzerainty of Louis XIV. For generations her merchant bankers and shipowners had lent money to the Kings of Spain and had financed Spanish armies and fleets in both hemispheres. The war which broke out at this time – a renewal of the struggle between Louis XIV and his old enemies – closely concerned Spain, and consequently enabled fresh fortunes to be made in the counting houses and offices of Genoa. The intelligence which Law was able to pick up from the representatives of the various powers in Genoa, whom he took care to cultivate, induced him to speculate in foreign exchange and securities. These dealings soon began to yield a considerable profit to himself. 'Although the Italians are a very subtle cunning people,' wrote one who professed to know him well during Law's lifetime, 'he found cullies enough to pick up a great deal of money from; and it was here that he laid the first foundation of his fortune.'

From Genoa Law is stated to have taken himself and his mistress to the neighbouring republic of Venice where his good fortune continued. In a short time he is said to have been worth £20,000. If she was, like Genoa, no longer at the height of her commercial hegemony, Venice was still a rich independent state with a local bank which helped to provide the speculator with ample opportunities of personal enrichment. Law, we are told, was constantly to be found at the Rialto when the exchange was open for business. 'No merchant upon commission was punctualer, he observed the course of exchange all the world over, the manner of discounting bills at the Bank, the vast usefulness of paper credit, how gladly people parted with their money for paper, and how the profits accrued to the proprietors from this paper.' In the evenings he would gamble at lansquenet or faro or écarte. 'His incomparable readiness in numbers made him a perfect judge of the hazards and advantages of all plays, his serene temper without transport made him master of himself when fortune ran against or for him, so he generally came [out] a gainer, seldom a considerable loser.'

Meanwhile a fresh European conflict had been provoked by the thorny problem of the succession to the Spanish throne. Towards the close of the year 1700 the imbecile King of Spain had at length been gathered to his fathers. By his last will Charles II had bequeathed the throne to Louis XIV's grandson and his own grandnephew, Philip Duke of Anjou, and this dull and phlegmatic sprig of the House of Bourbon now ascended the throne as Philip V. His pretensions were disputed by the late monarch's other brother-in-law, Leopold II, Emperor of Austria, who claimed the heritage for his son the Archduke Charles. This development had, of course, been foreseen for some time in London, as well as The Hague, where it was felt that the trade of both countries was bound to suffer from the French and Spanish crowns being united in the same family and possibly under the same head. William III had accordingly devoted the closing years of his reign to reviving the coalition of powers which had fought France in the days before the Peace of Ryswick, and he had fully briefed his able lieutenant Marlborough in his designs for the continuance of the struggle against the seemingly indomitable Louis. A final fillip to British patriotism had been administered by the Grand Monarch's injudicious action in breaking the peace treaty by the proclamation of James Edward the 'Old Pretender' as King James III of England on his father's death at St. Germains in 1701. Already the French were in occupation of the Spanish Netherlands, while in Northern Italy a French force supported by Piedmontese and Spaniards prepared to stem the approach of the Austrians under Prince Eugène, whom Law doubtless saw on their way through Venetian territory. Eugène scored some preliminary successes and eventually captured the French Commander Marshal Villeroy during a surprise night attack on Cremona. In 1702 the struggle began in earnest with Marlborough's first campaign in the Netherlands.

Law's activities are impossible to describe with any precision at this time, since he wrote no letters during this period which are in existence. A curious reference in the Archives of the Ministry of Foreign Affairs in Paris to the incarceration of a certain 'Sr. Las', a foreigner, in April, 1701, suggests that John may have spent a week in a French prison at this time.[1] Unfortunately the offence is not stated and further details are lacking; but, if the delinquent can be identified with Law his arrest was probably because his papers were not in order. According to his own statement, he was in Piedmont during the spring of 1703 when

---

[1] The documents concerning this incident are quoted by A. Beljambe in his essay, *La Pronunciation du Nom de Jean Law le Financier*, in *Etudes Romanes*, Paris, 1891. There was a number of variants of Law's name in use in France including Las, Lass, and Lasse.

he gave the French ambassador in Turin the details of a scheme he had worked out for the revival of French industry in some of the districts through which he had passed on his way to Italy two or three years previously. In Turin Law secured another potential patron in the person of Duke Victor Amadeus, ruler of Savoy-Piedmont. This able but crafty character was at this time contemplating a change of sides in the European struggle. Family ties bound him to France. His wife was a sister of the Duke of Chartres. One of his daughters was married to one of Louis XIV's grandsons, the Duke of Burgundy, heir presumptive to the French throne, and another was married to the other grandson Philip, the new monarch of Spain. In spite of his French connections, however, Victor Amadeus had changed sides more than once in the earlier campaigns against Louis, and once again he found himself tired of the insolence which he had been obliged to suffer at his kinsmen's hands. His actions, it must be admitted, though cunning and calculated, were always designed to promote the welfare of his principality. Indeed any project with that end in view won his immediate sympathy. He consequently received Law kindly and gave him all the information he required as to the administration of his state and its resources.

Among other things Law was struck by the large numbers of French workers who, principally for religious reasons (for the Protestants in Savoy-Piedmont were undisturbed), were employed in the textile factories. He estimated there must be about 4,500 such workers who but for Louis XIV's stiff-necked obstinacy over the Edict of Nantes might have been enriching the country of their birth with the products of their labours. Law now devised a plan for the revival of industry in the Rhône valley. The districts of Lyonnais, Forez and Beaujolais were to have cloth and silk mills, flour mills and bakeries, and nursery gardens. No details of his scheme have survived, but no doubt they included some measure of religious toleration for Huguenot workers, as well as the creation of credit by the issue of paper money in the area. All that is known is that in April, 1703, Law handed a draft of his proposals to the French ambassador in Turin for transmission to the Marquis de Chamillard, Controller-General of Finance in France. Some time later he received a reply in which the French minister, while praising the scheme's merits, regretted that it could not be put into immediate execution by reason of the war.

It was hoped that it might be examined anew when peace had again been concluded in Europe.

The projector's thoughts now turned towards his native land. It was over ten years now since he had been in Scotland. His mother was still alive and living in Edinburgh, but she was getting on in age and he was anxious to see her before she died. Catherine Knollys, otherwise Seigneur, had lately presented him with a son if not an heir, and under the style of Lady Catherine Law he felt he could with safety return and present her to his friends and relations in Edinburgh. An additional reason for his return was that his succession to the family estates was now ensured. In the very month that John Law handed his industrial scheme to the French ambassador in Turin, his mother in Edinburgh made a will in which she entailed the property upon him and his heirs. Some months afterwards John Law set off for Scotland with his family, travelling, it is said, through Germany and Holland. In this event he must have seen something of Marlborough's campaign between the Rhine and the Meuse where the Anglo-Dutch forces were slowly gaining ground against the French. It appears to have been during the winter of 1703–1704 that Law finally reached his mother's house in Edinburgh.

5

The returning prodigal, it seems, settled down quietly with Catherine and their baby son at Lauriston, which his mother had put at their disposal to live in. He found the old lady in failing health, but the sight of her eldest and favourite boy, whom she had not seen for twelve years, gave her a new lease of life. What manner of reception she accorded her alleged daughter-in-law is not known, nor has it been established whether she ever knew that Catherine and John were not married. The effect of the entail which she had recently executed was, however, quite clear to John. His infant son, being illegitimate, would not be able under Scottish law to inherit the property.

Queen Anne now occupied the throne of England, and one of John Law's first acts was to address a petition to Her Majesty. He knew that, if he set foot in England, he was liable to arrest on the charge of having broken gaol, if not for murder, for the late

King had merely reprieved not pardoned him. 'Yet', he prayed, 'your petitioner is debarred from serving Your Majesty (as he is most desirous) in the just war wherein Your Majesty is now engaged.' He added that Mr. Robert Wilson, the Beau's brother who had brought the action of appeal of murder in the King's Bench, had agreed, thanks to the intercession of several of Law's influential friends in Scotland, to drop the proceedings. There is no doubt that the Queen examined his application for clemency as she was in the habit of considering personally all the petitions which her subjects thought fit to address to her. On this occasion she was advised not to accede to it by her Minister, the Tory Robert Harley, at that time Secretary of State for the Northern Department. Under date September 5, 1704, Harley accordingly endorsed the document with the ominous but decisive word 'Rejected'.[1]

Balked of his desire to serve the Queen in England, which he seems to have been anxious to do, Law determined to put his services at her disposal in another manner. So long as he remained in Scotland and so long as Scotland preserved her separate government, Law was safe from arrest for the offences he had committed south of the border. Scotland was then in the throes of a most acute trade depression, and it occurred to Law that he might do worse than formulate a scheme based on the experience and ideas which he had gained on the Continent. In the months immediately following the rejection of his petition for pardon he accordingly sat down and wrote an essay of some 40,000 words in length embodying his proposals for the revival of Scotland's economy. The work was completed early in 1705 and the manuscript was entrusted for publication to the Edinburgh firm of printers and publishers which was carrying on the business of the late Andrew Anderson. (Anderson had been an uncle of John Law's and King's Printer.)[2] Under the imprint of this firm the book was published anonymously, the author being simply

---

[1] The original petition is preserved among the Portland MSS. at Welbeck Abbey. In describing the petitioner as a resident of Scotland it clearly establishes that Law was living there in 1704, a fact which has sometimes been doubted. See Historical MSS. Commission, *Duke of Portland's MSS.*, VIII, 320 (London, 1907).

[2] Andrew Anderson married Agnes Campbell, a sister of Law's mother. In 1661 he was granted a forty-one years monopoly as King's Printer by Charles II. He died in 1676. Fairley in his *Lauriston Castle* (at p. 82 note) states that his shop was on the north side of the Cross.

described as 'a Scots gentleman'. Its full title was *Money and Trade considered with a proposal for supplying the Nation with Money*. The book immediately aroused interest in the Scottish capital, and in spite of its anonymity the authorship soon became known.[1]

Although Scotland and England had been united under the same crown since the beginning of the preceding century, each country had its separate government, Parliament and commercial arrangements. Scottish manufactured goods were subject to import duties on entering England and Scottish shippers were deprived of the benefits of the English Navigation Acts – that is a Scottish vessel could not carry foreign goods from the port of their country of origin to an English port. William Paterson, the founder of the Bank of England, had promoted a scheme to colonize the Isthmus of Panama with Scottish settlers, but this so-called Darien scheme had turned out a dismal failure. The colonists had been decimated by disease, starvation and the depredations of the Spaniards. At the same time the harvest in Scotland failed, and the country had an adverse trade balance, that with France alone amounting to £50,000 annually. Unemployment, poverty and scarcity of money in the hands of the majority of the population were matched by profligate extravagance on the part of a few favoured members with the means. These disasters produced a growing demand north of the Tweed for free trade between the two countries, but Queen Anne's English ministers preferred to shelve this question for the moment until the time was ripe for making an economic partnership the price of full political union.

At the end of the year 1704 an incident took place in Edinburgh which made a vivid impression on Law who witnessed it: he was to recur to it from time to time in his own economic writings and arguments and indeed he was one day to put its lesson into practice. His first publication contains a vivid description of it. The country's unfavourable trade balance had almost exhausted the supplies of gold and silver in the vaults of the Bank of Scotland. The bank had lately begun to print notes of the denomina-

[1] The original edition of this work is now extremely rare. There is a copy in the British Museum and another in the National Library of Scotland. A second edition, 'by Mr. John Law now Director of the Royal Bank of Paris', was published in London in 1720. The title pages of both editions are reproduced below facing p. 112.

tion of £1 sterling in order to meet small payments, and this measure would in all probability have enabled the Bank to continue business and meet any immediate and sudden liabilities had it not been for an unfortunate announcement that the government intended to revalue the coinage. Coins in circulation and in the bank consisted of crowns worth 5s. 6d. It was now proposed by the Privy Council that these should pass for 6s., this process being known as an 'augmentation' of money. This produced a sudden and severe run on the bank, since note-holders naturally wished to convert their notes into crowns at the old rate while there was still time. The run lasted three weeks and the result was that the bank was obliged temporarily to suspend payments and close its doors.[1] Law was of the opinion that it would have been wiser to have initiated the reverse process – in other words to announce a 'diminution' of the coin by declaring the crown to be worth only 5s. instead of 5s. 6d. 'If the Privy Council had lowered the Crown to 5s. and the other money in proportion,' he wrote, 'the occasion of the demand being removed, in all appearance money would have been returned to the bank.' Consequently, far from withdrawing coin from the bank's vaults, its customers would have hastened to bring in their crowns from all over the country while they could exchange them for notes at 5s. 6d. before the rate dropped. 'In a short time notes would have come in so fast that what money could have been got would not have answered the demand.' The lesson Law learned from this experience was that, when a bank of issue is in difficulties, the 'diminution' of the coinage of the realm is a useful expedient for attracting specie to its coffers. 'Augmentation', on the other hand, tends to drive money away from the banks and out of the country, or, as we should say to-day, to cause a flight of capital.

[1] Law described the incident as follows: 'The consumption of foreign goods and expense in England, being more than the export of goods did pay, the balance sent out in money lessened the credit of the Bank; for as credit is voluntary, it depends on the quantity of money in the country and increases or decreases with it. Coining notes of one pound supported the Bank by furnishing paper for small payments and thereby preventing a part of the demand for money. By these notes the Bank might have kept its credit till other methods had been taken to supply the country had not a report of raising the money occasioned an extraordinary demand, which in a few days exhausted the money in Bank and put a stop to payments.' *Money and Trade Considered* (ed. 1720), at p. 32.

Law was by no means alone in his endeavours to solve his country's economic ills. Scotland teemed with tracts and pamphlets, for the most part anonymous, in which a variety of remedies was proposed and controverted with equal vehemence. In the van was William Paterson who put forward a plan for a trading corporation which would revive the Darien scheme, encourage manufacturers, and relieve unemployment by financing public works undertakings.[1] Then there was Hugh Chamberlen whose acquaintance has also been made. After the ignominious collapse of his scheme for a Land Bank in London he had withdrawn to the Continent, but about 1700 he had appeared in Edinburgh where he had been pestering the Scottish Parliament with his plans. It will be remembered that the 'man-midwife', as he was popularly known, proposed to issue notes against landed estates up to the value of one hundred years' purchase. Law devoted a chapter of his book to Chamberlen's scheme; he had no difficulty in showing that at most an estate would not sell for more than twenty years' purchase, and consequently that notes should not be issued to the landowner, who pledged his estate with the bank, in excess of this figure. This is what he in fact himself proposed as an integral part of his own scheme in *Money and Trade*. As a result he was accused of appropriating Chamberlen's ideas for his own purposes. In the final version of his plan, which he drafted in abbreviated form for presentation to the Scottish Parliament, it will be seen that he discarded altogether the feature of a note issue based on landed security – a fact, it may be added, which is not generally known and which has been overlooked by most previous writers.

It must be admitted that Law's *Money and Trade* is far from light reading. Its reasoning is clear enough, but it is often so briefly stated that it is extremely difficult to follow. Adopting the words of a distinguished Scottish economist, the late Professor J. S. Nicholson, to a person not well versed in economic reasoning, it will be about as entertaining as a treatise on the differential calculus

[1] See *Proposals and Reasons for constituting a Council of Trade*, published anonymously in Edinburgh in 1701. A second edition of this work, which appeared in Glasgow in 1751, erroneously states Law to be the author. This error has unfortunately been repeated by subsequent writers, including the author of the article on Law in the *Dictionary of National Biography*. The evidence of Paterson's authorship has been conclusively proved by Saxe Bannister in *The Writings of William Paterson*, I, 1-4 (London, 1859).

is to a non-mathematical reader.[1] Nevertheless it is a thoroughly sincere work, evidently composed at fever heat, and there is nothing of the prospectus monger and 'projector' deluding the public about it, with which many critics have sought to invest Law and his monetary schemes. The book contains closely reasoned chapters on barter, the balance of trade, the precious metals, the growth of banking, credit and the advantages of a paper currency. At that time the workings of finance were a mystery to the majority of people, as indeed they still are to many, and there was a general deep-rooted mistrust of innovations designed to interfere with what were considered the immutable laws of the monetary science. Law had essentially the mind of an inventor. Novelty attracted him, and he flatly refused to accept views on his pet subject simply because they had been hallowed by long tradition. Old-fashioned merchants might regard gold as the sole form of wealth, but not so Law. On the other hand there was nothing of the simple-minded crank about him. He knew exactly what he wanted and he did not hesitate to reinforce his case with the most plausible language if the occasion demanded. As he expressed it in an interesting pen-portrait of himself which he wrote many years later, 'if at times he used specious arguments when he considered them a necessary road to the truth, it was with so fine an art that one found oneself brought suddenly into brilliant light without noticing that one had passed through darkness to get there'.

6

On June 28, 1705, the Scots Parliament met in Edinburgh to consider the overtures for a union which had at last been made with somewhat ill grace by the sister country. The representative of the Crown in this assembly, or Queen's Commissioner, as he was called, was the twenty-six-year-old Duke of Argyll, a high-spirited and impetuous young man, who had already served with distinction in the

[1] Nicholson's brilliant and readable essay on Law was the first real attempt at appreciation of the man and his 'system' to appear in England. It was originally delivered in the form of a lecture in Edinburgh in 1888 and later republished in the author's *Money and Monetary Problems.*

campaign in the Netherlands and was the possessor of singular rhetorical gifts, if no great depth of judgement. Horace Walpole described him as 'a patron of ingenious men', and it is known that John Law was one of the objects of his patronage.

The national or patriot party in the House was led by the veteran Andrew Fletcher of Saltoun, a picturesque character who had been sentenced to death for his complicity in the Monmouth rebellion in the reign of James II, had subsequently escaped to Europe where he had wandered about for several years in various disguises, and had fought the Turks in Hungary as a volunteer before returning to his native country as a supporter of William III. While in favour of free trade and an economic arrangement between the two countries, he and his party were opposed to complete political union. The most wholehearted supporters of the union proposals were a small compact group of members nicknamed by their opponents the '*Squadrone volante*' because they always acted and voted together in the assembly. They were led by the Marquess of Tweeddale, Argyll's predecessor as Commissioner, and included the Earl of Roxburghe, described as 'the best accomplished young man of quality in Europe', and George Baillie of Jerviswood, son of the celebrated patriot Robert Baillie who had been executed on a trumped-up charge of treason in Edinburgh twenty years before. The Jacobite members, on the other hand, were opposed to union in any shape or form. Most conspicuous among them, perhaps, was George Lockhart of Carnwath, on the authority of whose *Memoirs* we have it that John Law had by this time 'found a way quickly to get into my Lord Duke of Argyll's favour' and had also become 'very intimate' with the *Squadrone*.

In the speech which he delivered on the Queen's behalf at the opening of the session in Edinburgh's Parliament House, the Duke of Argyll earnestly recommended the assembled legislators to appoint commissioners to enter into negotiations for a Union with the English commissioners who had already been appointed for the purpose in London. A hot-tempered debate followed on the Address which then, as in the present United Parliament today, it was customary to move by way of dutiful thanks to the Throne. In the course of this discussion an amendment was moved and carried which provided that the House should first proceed to consider matters relating to trade and finance. This development provided Law with the opportunity he had been hoping for of bringing forward his own monetary proposals. The *Squadrone* were in complete agreement with them and they chose as their spokesman to present them George Baillie of Jerviswood who accordingly moved that 'Mr. Law's project . . . might be taken into consideration'. The document in which the author had embodied his proposals was thereupon ordered, in accordance with the usual parliamentary procedure, to lie upon the table of the House until its next meeting.[1]

'There need be no speeches', wrote Law in introducing his proposals, 'to show how much a sufficient stock of money, or a good fund of public credit, which is the same thing (money being but the counter of commerce), would be serviceable to the people and trade of the Kingdom, or how much it would tend to the honour and justice of the Queen and Parliament to pay off and clear the debts of the Government so long and so justly due to the Army and Civil List.' Briefly he proposed the establishment of a trading corporation or 'Commission of Trade' with power to issue notes bearing three per cent interest, such notes to pass for legal currency. One half of the directors or 'commissioners' was to consist of 'able and knowing merchants' and the other of 'nobility and barons', the whole board to be nominated by or with the approval of the Government. The notes would be employed by the corporation 'in erecting a fishery and in improving our manufactories; in a word . . . in setting the people of the nation to work on all things to which they can apply themselves, by buying up their goods with these notes and sending them abroad and there selling them to the best advantage'. The proceeds in foreign currency of these exports could be used in the foreign country to buy necessary goods for import into Scotland where they would be retailed at ten per cent profit to domestic purchasers who might pay for them with the corporation's notes. One half of the profits would be divided among the commissioners as remuneration and the other half would become a sinking fund for cancelling the notes. The government debt in respect of the

[1] *Two Overtures humbly offered by his Grace John Duke of Argyll Her Majesty's High Commissioner and the Right Honourable the Estates of Parliament*. There is a copy of this extremely rare tract in the National Library of Scotland. It has been reprinted by S. Bannister in *The Writings of William Paterson*, vol. II (London, 1859) at p. xliii *et seq.*, with Paterson's reply.

army and civil list was to be similarly liquidated by the issue of interest-bearing notes by the Treasury. The corporation notes were not, as Law had originally proposed in *Money and Trade*, to be based on the security of land, but rather on the country's power to produce goods and services – a revolutionary idea for those days and one which is sometimes still advanced in our own.

Dr. Chamberlen's Land Bank scheme had also been canvassed among the members. In moving that Law's scheme should be given further consideration by the House, Baillie of Jerviswood observed that 'in his opinion it was a more rational and practical scheme than that of Dr. Chamberlen'. On hearing this, Fletcher of Saltoun rose and proceeded to run down Law's scheme in no measured terms, calling it among other things 'a contrivance to enslave the nation'. He proposed that both Chamberlen and Law should be brought into the chamber 'there to reason and debate the matter so as the House might be better satisfied which of their proposals was the most practicable and advantageous'.

At this point the Duke of Roxburghe, a member of the *Squadrone*, intervened to say that he thought it 'very unfair to oblige a gentleman to come to the Bar without first knowing whether he himself was willing to appear in so public a manner especially since he had not dedicated his book to the Estates of Parliament or put his name to it'. This speaker added his opinion 'that Mr. Law, or any gentleman that had employed his time and thought for the good of his country, ought to be treated with good manners'.

This last remark so enraged Fletcher that he blurted out that 'if anybody taxed him of ill manners they were unmannerly and not he'.

Roxburghe rejoined with dignity that 'what he had spoken was not pointed at any particular member with a design to accuse him of want of manners, but was rather an appeal to the justice of the whole House how hard it would be to stage a gentleman for his generous endeavours without his consent'. However, he added, if Fletcher 'fancied himself struck at, he might if he pleased take it so'.

'I take it as I ought,' growled Fletcher from his seat.

It was clear to all who witnessed this scene that a challenge between the two members involved must inevitably ensue. For this reason, when the House rose, the Commissioner ordered both men to be confined under house arrest. Roxburghe readily acquiesced and remained at home, but Fletcher managed to slip away having first sent out a note to his adversary requesting a meeting on the sands at Leith, the usual venue for such encounters at that time. Fletcher was eventually run to earth in a tavern by one of the Commissioner's men who had been sent to look for him. However, he put the man off, saying he had done nothing to warrant arrest, that the whole affair was a mistake and that he would immediately wait upon the Commissioner to explain it. But instead of going to Holyrood he went off to Leith taking along a second in the coach with him. Meanwhile Roxburghe, chafing under his confinement, sent a message to Argyll who eventually agreed to release him. He then repaired straightaway to Leith where he found the irate Fletcher waiting for him at the appointed place about six o'clock in the evening. The seconds were for making up the matter in a friendly way, but Fletcher insisted on obtaining satisfaction for what he considered the affront offered him in Parliament.

Baillie of Jerviswood, who was acting as Roxburghe's second, stepped between the two principals and said that Roxburghe had 'a great weakness in his right leg so that he could hardly stand' and that therefore 'it was not to be expected that this quarrel could be decided by the sword'. Fletcher, having apparently anticipated this objection, immediately produced a case of pistols and in a very cavalier manner desired Lord Roxburghe to take his choice. Baillie went on to protest that his principal's disability equally incapacitated him from firing on foot. Whilst he was arguing and Fletcher becoming more and more impatient, a company of Horse Guards was suddenly seen approaching in the distance. The seconds realized that the troops must have been sent in search of their party by the Commissioner, and they thereupon eagerly seized the opportunity which this development provided them of saving their principals' honour. They both fired their pistols in the air, and the whole party returned together to Edinburgh escorted by the Guards.

A few days later, after tempers had had time to cool, Parliament resumed the debate on Law's scheme. It was soon clear that the sense of the House was against the proposals. A much more formidable and expert opponent than the impetuous Fletcher had in fact been working quietly against them. This was William

Paterson who had circularized members with a pamphlet in which he successfully (as it turned out) controverted Law's arguments. A pertinent political objection also was that the adoption of the scheme would place too much power in the hands of a small body of officials, or, in the words of the Jacobite Lockhart of Carnwath, 'it was so found that in process of time it brought all the estates of the Kingdom to depend on the government'. The upshot was that Law's project was rejected, it being agreed by the House that 'the forcing [of] any paper credit [on the country] by an Act of Parliament was unfit for this nation'.

The author's disappointment was naturally keen, but he plucked up heart again when he discovered that the details of his plan had been forwarded to London by one of Harley's confidential agents in Edinburgh and that it must come to the notice not only of the Secretary of State but also of Lord Treasurer Godolphin, the virtual Prime Minister. Law renewed his petition for pardon, offering at the same time to serve Her Majesty in Flanders at his own cost. His hopes were high indeed. "'Tis the part of every subject', he wrote, 'to save the ease and honour of the government and the good and prosperity of his country. He who has the happiness, by his endeavours, to do service to either, deserves to be encouraged by both: and even he who fails in his attempt, having done his best, merits the thanks of those to whom he has showed his good wishes.'

Queen Anne's rejection of the petition for a second time on her Minister's advice was not only an added disappointment to Law but, when taken in conjunction with the trend of political events in Scotland, it placed his personal security in jeopardy. A few weeks after the Scots Parliament had passed its vote against Law's financial scheme, the House finally agreed to the appointment of Commissioners to treat for union with England. Law realized that union itself was now only a question of time, and that the moment the measure had reached the statute book and the Scottish Government had ceased to exist as an independent entity he would be liable to immediate arrest and imprisonment. There seemed nothing for it, therefore, but to go abroad again. He accordingly told Catherine to pack up their belongings and get ready to embark for the Continent. Whilst waiting for a vessel he is said to have spent most of his time gambling and to have won an estate worth £1,200 a year from a certain Sir Andrew Ramsay.

The Law family appears to have left Edinburgh sometime in 1706. Besides the financier and his wife the party included their young son John and a baby daughter, called Mary Catherine, who had been born a year or two before in Scotland. In due course they all arrived safely in Brussels.

CHAPTER III

THE PROJECTOR

The easiest gateway through which to enter the Continent at this time was Belgium or the Spanish Netherlands, as Flanders and Brabant were then known, which were in the possession of the allies thanks to Marlborough's successful campaign in the early months of 1706. The future of these provinces, which had been under Spanish rule since early in the previous century, was naturally bound up with the acrimonious question of the Spanish succession, and the allies – in particular England and Holland – were determined to prevent their acquisition by a French prince. At the moment the prospects for France appeared bleak. Marlborough's crowning victory over the French forces at a village near Namur called Ramillies had been followed up by one of the most brilliant military pursuits of the age and had resulted in the withdrawal of Marshal Villeroy's troops behind their own frontier. Meanwhile in the south the Austrian commander Prince Eugène was engaged in driving the French out of Italy, a process which culminated in the complete rout of the French army before the walls of Turin.

The Laws' arrival in Brussels coincided with what was for France the darkest period in the Spanish Succession War. The country was nearing exhaustion and bankruptcy while her enemies were closing round her from every side. John Law accordingly determined that the moment was propitious to offer the French Government his credit scheme which had been turned down by his own country. By what means are unknown he succeeded in obtaining a safe conduct to enter France, and sometime early in 1707 he passed through the lines of the opposing armies and made his way unhindered to Paris. He found the country groaning under an intolerable burden of taxation, internal commerce virtually at a standstill, exports reduced almost to vanishing point, and the Treasury so depleted that the armies had neither regular pay, food nor clothing. Among the curious expedients for raising money was a tax on baptisms and marriages which, far from raising revenue, resulted in the poorer classes baptizing their children themselves and going through the ceremony of marriage before witnesses but without the assistance of a priest. This led to serious gaps if not complete stoppages among the registers of births and marriages in the country, not to mention a rapid rise in irregular unions and illegitimacy.

These disastrous conditions were in great measure due to the incompetence of the Marquis de Chamillard, under whose administration Louis XIV had unwisely united the departments of finance and war – two portfolios which should have absorbed the undivided energies of two men of genius at such a time. Louis's excuse was the repeated conflicts between the two departments in former times which he now wished to avoid. He refused to listen to Chamillard's protest that the double load was too heavy for one man to bear; and when at last the long-suffering but unintelligent minister wrote to the King that, if he were not speedily afforded some relief, everything would perish, Louis replied: '*Eh bien! Nous périrons ensemble.*' It was to this minister, the successful billiard player and favourite of the King's mistress, that Law was now obliged to address himself. He managed to obtain an audience with Chamillard before whom he laid a memorandum designed to show, in his own words, that 'the employment of a new kind of money may be better than gold or silver'. The proposed innovation was, of course, paper money which would be based on landed security; and the memorandum, in which he set out the lines on which it should be issued, closely followed his reasoning in *Money and Trade*, with particular application to France.[1]

But Chamillard was not convinced by these arguments. Indeed he did not understand them, nor did he apparently consider Law's

---

[1] The original MS. of this so-called *Mémoire pour prouver qu'une nouvelle espèce de monnaie peut être meilleure que l'or et l'argent* was discovered by Professor Paul Harsin in the Arsenal Library in Paris and published by him in his edition of Law's writings in 1934: John Law, *Œuvres complètes*, I, 195–214.

proposals worth while discussing either with his colleagues or the King. This supreme example of ministerial stupidity is reflected in a fragment of Law's correspondence which is preserved in the National Archives in Paris. 'The opinion seems to be that what I have proposed does not even merit discussion by the Council,' wrote Law on June 15, 1707. 'I am not surprised at this. A new kind of money with better qualifications than gold or silver does not appear feasible here in present conditions.' With this failure he added that there was nothing further to keep him in France and he prepared to continue his travels. Unfortunately he could not see the Duke of Chartres, who had been the only well-known Frenchman who had shown any signs either of under-standing or appreciation of monetary theories on the occasion of Law's previous visit. Chartres, who since his father's death was known as the Duke of Orleans, was away at the wars. But Law did arrange to see the Duke's secretary, the Abbé de Thesut, with whom no doubt he left some particulars of his proposal. According to Massillon, Bishop of Clermont, the Abbé introduced Law to Nicholas Desmarets, a nephew of Louis XIV's great minister Colbert and a former official in the finance ministry, who was destined soon to supersede the incompetent Chamillard.

It has been asserted that Law indulged in high play during this visit to Paris, particularly at the house of a prominent actress and courtesan named Duclos where the faro tables were always crowded. His winnings are said to have caused such jealousy that some spiteful-minded individuals made representations to the Marquis D'Argenson, head of the police, that this gambler and foreigner was an undesirable character and should be ordered to quit the city and the country forthwith. However, there is no evidence, as has been suggested, that Law was given twenty-four hours' notice in which to leave the capital. On the contrary it appears from the correspondence already quoted that he obtained a six-weeks extension of his passport to enable him to travel through the country by easy stages since it was in the middle of the hot weather. It is not impossible, however, as the contem-porary financial writer Marmont du Hautchamp suggests, that Law was required by the police commissioner to leave Paris on the ground that 'he was too familiar with the game he had intro-duced to this capital'. Before the end of the summer the Law family found themselves once again in Italy. They repaired first to

Genoa where John was able to renew his acquaintance with the municipal bank and write another treatise on his favourite topic.[1]

Nominally written for the information of the Prince of Conti the *Mémoire sur l'Usage des Monnaies*, which Law composed in Genoa, was really designed as an object lesson in political economy for any ruler who might be interested in improving his country's finances. Its sub-title read: 'The profit or loss for a prince or a state in altering the denomination of the coinage and in the augmentation or diminution of its value in relation to that of neighbouring states.' During his recent visit to France the author had been particularly struck with the catastrophic results produced by the ill-informed and arbitrary interference by the authorities in matters of trade and finance, which destroyed public confidence. In terms which it is unnecessary to recapitulate Law showed, for example, that a statutory prohibition of the export of specie was the reason best calculated to make it leave the country; that lowering the gold or silver content of the coinage was unfair to trade and in any event reacted prejudicially against the government, and that the price of commodities, whether raw materials, consumer goods or money on loan, should not be arbitrarily fixed by the government. 'Suppose I have money out on loan today in Genoa at 4 per cent, and ships with cargoes of specie are expected from Spain,' he argued. 'If the ships arrive safely, it is right that the interest should fall to 3 per cent. If they do not arrive, surely I ought to be permitted to make a profit and increase the rate of interest to 5 per cent?'

The Prince of Conti forwarded this interesting document to the Duke of Burgundy, eldest son of the Dauphin, but no one in Paris seems to have paid any attention to it.[2] It has been estimated that the depreciation of the currency and other arbitrary economic measures did more injury to France at this time than all the

---

[1] See *Histoire du Système des Finances sous la Minorité de Louis XV pendant les années 1719 et 1720*, I, 70–71. This work, which appeared in six volumes at The Hague in 1739, has always been attributed to the contemporary financial writer Marmont du Hautchamp. Professor Harsin, in the preface to his edition of Law's writings, has shown that either Law had a considerable hand in the composition of the *Histoire* or else du Hautchamp had before him many of Law's unpublished MSS. which he embodied in his text as he wrote it.

[2] It was first published by de Forbonnais in 1757: *Recherches et Considérations sur les Finances de France*, II, 542.

victories of Marlborough. Conditions were exacerbated during the winter of 1709 when the cold was the severest in living memory, bankers failed in considerable numbers, trade was at a standstill and the shops were empty of goods. Bowing to popular outcry Louis at last consented to sacrifice Chamillard. This genial but inefficient ignoramus was replaced by Nicholas Desmarets whose acquaintance there are reasons for supposing that Law had recently made in Paris. Though incomparably more able than his predecessor, the new minister could do little really effective with his country's finances while serving such an absolute master as Louis XIV. The King fervently believed that all the wealth of his subjects was his own, and when he took it he only took what by rights belonged to him.

2

Beyond the fact that he remained with his family in Italy, the exact course of Law's wanderings is unknown between the year 1707, when he was in Genoa, and the winter of 1711–1712, when he reappeared in Turin. No doubt he visited the principal Italian cities and frequented their gaming-tables, though whether, as has been stated, the considerable sums which he won in Genoa and Venice resulted in his being requested to depart immediately from the territories of these republics is open to question. According to the work attributed to Marmont du Hautchamp, Law cut a striking figure at the Carnival ball in Rome where he also won heavily at the tables. Also, while in Florence he is said to have become friendly with the Prince of Vendôme, Grand Prior of France, who borrowed a large sum of money from him which Law handed over 'with the best grace in the world'. Marmont du Hautchamp states that he won the largest sum of all at Genoa. But at the same time there is no doubt too that Law was busily engaged in working out schemes which later came to be known as his 'system'. The proposals which he laid before Duke Victor Amadeus, on entering Savoy-Piedmont in 1711, when taken in conjunction with those he had already submitted to the Marquis de Chamillard and the Prince of Conti, must dispose forever of the myth, which was later to gain much credence, that John Law was nothing more than a scheming adventurer who happened to be lucky at cards and dice.

What Law proposed to Victor Amadeus was an institution which united in itself the advantages of a trading corporation and a bank of issue to be incorporated under the style of the Bank of Turin. The bank could deal in all forms of real and personal property like any other trading company. It could also lend money on security at a fixed rate of interest to its customers, but it was not to be obliged to lend to the government. The basis of the bank's cash reserve was to consist of such specie and securities as were in the Ducal Treasury and for which the government was to accept in exchange notes payable on demand. The notes, which were thus freely convertible, were to be in denominations of 10, 100, and 1,000 lire, and they were all to bear the imprint of the royal arms. Taxes and other debts due to the Treasury were to be paid in notes of the bank. The forgery of notes was to be subject to the same penalties as the counterfeiting of specie. The bank was to have power to print notes 'for such sums as might be considered necessary for the good of trade'. In order to safe-guard against the danger of inflation and at the same time pre-serve the convertibility of the notes, it was expressly laid down that the proportionate reserve of cash to notes must never fall below 75 per cent – in other words, that the amount of specie held in the bank's vaults must never be less than three-quarters of the face value of the aggregate of notes in circulation at any given moment.

It will be seen that Law's proposal for the creation of a state bank in Savoy-Piedmont was of the soundest character, especially as regards the convertibility of the bank's notes. To suggest, as was later done by Law's enemies and repeated by a number of writers, that Victor Amadeus rejected the scheme on the ground that he was not rich enough to risk the ruin of his state is as palpably untrue as it is unfair to Law. It is true that the project was turned down – but this was due to a series of difficulties raised by the Duke's finance minister who most likely was jealous of the attentions that had been paid a foreigner. Law's phenomenal success as a gambler also rendered him suspect to the Duke's ministers. On the contrary Victor Amadeus was in favour of the objects of the proposed bank and he did his best to remove the obstacles in its way by bringing Law together with the obstructive minister. Writing to the Duke from Milan on March 6, 1712, Law thanked His Royal Highness for the kindness he had shown him, and in fact their correspondence continued on the most friendly terms. Victor Amadeus had advised Law that in his view the scheme would have the best chance of successful realization in France. Law pointed out that at the moment, for reasons which have already been seen, this was impracticable. In the meantime he would go to Holland where he had another project in view.[1]

During his stay in Turin Law had opened a current account with the Bank of Amsterdam, at which time he is said to have been worth about £100,000. In July, 1712, he bought a house in The Hague, described as one of the finest houses in that city, which he furnished with becoming splendour. His immediate object was nothing less than the promotion of a state lottery by persuading the various provinces of the Union to authorize the opening of subscription lists in return for a percentage of the takings. Law's old acquaintance Thomas Neale, the great lottery promoter in England, had died some years previously, and Law had somehow managed to obtain full details of his lotteries which he now proceeded to improve upon in his own project. It has been alleged that M. Hornbeck, Pensionary of Rotterdam, who was 'also a nice calculator', discovered that Law made a profit of 200,000 guilders out of the lotteries he had promoted and that in consequence the promoter was privately advised to leave the country. However that may be, John Law is known to have left The Hague in the summer of 1713 taking the bulk of his fortune with him. For the third time he posted off to France.

A number of significant events had occurred since the occasion of his last visit four years previously. In the first place Louis had succeeded in coming to terms with all his adversaries with the exception of Austria. This was largely made possible by the change of political parties in England where a Tory government, determined to conclude hostilities in Europe, had come into power. Peace had in fact been signed in the Dutch provincial capital of Utrecht a few weeks before Law left Holland. The ostensible cause of the long struggle was settled by leaving the Bourbon Philip on the Spanish throne on condition that the

---

[1] According to du Hautchamp (*Histoire* I, 71), on leaving Turin Law went to Vienna where he proposed his scheme to the Emperor, but no evidence has been found to corroborate this.

crowns of Spain and France should never be united. But if France had emerged with relatively few territorial losses she was at the end of her resources and virtually bankrupt. Secondly, the aged French monarch had suffered a severe personal loss in the deaths of the Dauphin and the latter's son, the Duke of Burgundy, and the Duke's eldest son which had occurred within a few months of each other. The Dauphin died of smallpox, while his son and grandson were suspected of having been poisoned.

This meant that the heir to the kingdom of France was Louis XIV's great-grandson Louis Duke of Anjou who was then a baby. Furthermore, since the infant's mother was dead, it seemed likely that on his accession to the throne the office of regent would devolve upon his nearest male relative. This was Philip Duke of Orleans, formerly known as the Duke of Chartres, who had now returned from campaigning in Spain and had resumed his old life of debauchery in the Palais Royal. He had grown extremely unpopular and his enemies openly accused him of all sorts of crimes including an unnatural love for his daughter, the Duchess of Berri, not to mention the murder of the Dauphin, the Duke of Burgundy and his son.

These stories about Orleans were without foundation, but they increased the Duke's unpopularity and for the time being prevented him from playing any part in public life. Law is known to have reached Paris before the end of 1713 when he appears to have had some conversations in the Palais Royal. With Desmarets, who had succeeded the unfortunate Chamillard at the Finance Ministry, he did not fare so well. He wrote for an interview with the minister on December 24, being anxious, as he put it, to discuss a proposal which he hoped would appeal to the minister 'being for the service of the King and the advantage of his subjects'. Desmarets endorsed this application with the words *'Quand il viendra, je lui parlerai,'* and as sometimes happens in government offices the letter was filed away without the writer being informed of the decision which had been taken on it. At all events Law returned to the charge three weeks later with a further letter – dated January 11, 1714 – in which he repeated his request, adding that his affairs obliged him to leave Paris shortly. So as to remind the minister of the writer's identity, the letter was signed 'John Law, *écossais*'. Apparently this likewise produced no effect, since Law departed for Holland almost immediately.

Law had kept on his house at The Hague where it seems that Catherine and his children were expecting him. About two months after his return he received some news which led him to retrace his steps to the French capital, this time taking his family with him. It appears that he was invited to go to Paris to discuss his banking scheme with Desmarets. Whatever the nature of the news Law received at this time, he was sufficiently encouraged to buy a house in the heart of the capital and settle down there with his family. His new home was one of the gracious buildings in that most fashionable of Paris squares, the Place Vendôme, or the Place Louis-le-Grand, as it was then called. According to Saint-Simon it was the Duke of Orleans who prevailed upon Desmarets to send the message which brought the financier back to Paris. Meanwhile Victor Amadeus, to whom the Peace of Utrecht had given the islands of Sicily and Sardinia, in addition to Savoy and Piedmont with the title of King, had written to Law for assistance in organizing the finances of his enlarged dominions.

Law had several long meetings with the Controller-General in the course of which he developed his proposal for a state bank to be formed on similar lines to what he had already proposed to Victor Amadeus. Desmarets listened attentively and promised to consider it carefully. Profiting by the relations he had thus established with the minister, Law then proceeded to request a personal favour.

He had a lot of trunks and chests containing clothes and furnishings in The Hague which he had sent for. As they might easily go astray at the customs in Rouen, he asked that they might be passed through the barriers there unopened and forwarded on to his house in the Place Vendôme. But the minister, who had formed quite an esteem for his visitor, felt that this was going a little too far. Desmarets pointed out that the passing of belongings through the customs duty-free was a privilege accorded to ambassadors 'by virtue of their public character', and then only by grace. However, if Law wished it, he was ready to give orders that the articles should be brought to the Customs House in Paris and there opened in Law's presence. This incident, trivial as it may appear, throws an interesting side-light on Law's character. It shows that he rated himself as a person of consequence and he expected to be taken by the authorities at his face value.

While he was waiting to hear from the finance minister, and at the same time wondering whether he should accept Victor Amadeus's invitation, an important event occurred across the Channel in London which caused Law to ponder still more. Queen Anne, who had twice refused him the benefit of her royal clemency, died on August 1, and the Whig supporters of her Hanoverian successor George I came into power in Whitehall. There was now a strong chance that the ban, under which Law had lain for twenty years, might now be lifted, so he wrote off to all the Scottish nobility of his acquaintance including the Dukes of Argyll and Roxburghe. In due course these noblemen 'were pleased to give him their assurances that they would intercede with the King for his pardon'. Among those whose good offices Law solicited in this manner was the Earl of Stair. It was, therefore, with more than ordinary interest that Law heard, towards the end of 1714, that Stair was to be the next British minister at the court of Louis XIV.

3

Britain's diplomatic representative in Paris at this time was the poet Matthew Prior under whom Law is stated to have served in a supernumerary capacity when Prior was secretary of the embassy at The Hague twenty years before. The poet had been sent to take charge of the preliminary negotiations to the Treaty of Utrecht which were signed on behalf of Great Britain by Prior towards the end of 1712 and were popularly known as 'Matt's Peace': he had stayed on in the French capital with the rank of plenipotentiary. But his association with the Tory party leaders, particularly Bolingbroke, made his recall inevitable after Queen Anne's death.

At the time of his appointment John Dalrymple, Earl of Stair, was forty-one years of age and thus two years younger than the financier. Like Law he was a Scotsman and a native of Edinburgh. Indeed they had several other tastes in common, including a love of wine, women and high play. The Edinburgh drawing-rooms were still buzzing with talk of the spectacular marriage which he had contracted. To compel his would-be bride, a widow who had sworn she would never remarry, to accede to his wishes, he had concealed himself in her bedroom and in the event obliged her to go to the altar to save her reputation. This good woman, it may be added in the words of Stair's official biographer, 'exercised by gentle methods a favourable influence upon Stair, particularly in restraining within the bounds of temperance his convivial indulgence in wine'. It is possible that the two men first met in their youth about the time of the celebrated massacre of Glencoe in 1692 for which Stair's father has always been held responsible, or alternatively they may have first come across each other during the debates in the Scottish Parliament which preceded the Act of Union. Stair was among the Scottish noblemen whom Law petitioned to intercede with the new English king for his pardon, and it is significant too that Law should have been the first person the minister received on reaching the British embassy. 'Wednesday January 23 at night, arrived in Paris,' Stair noted in his journal. 'Saw nobody that night but Mr. Law.'

During their conversation on the night of Stair's arrival in the French capital Law brought up the question of his own position and future. He was desperately anxious for an opportunity of putting his ideas on banking and credit into practice, and he explained that he was ready to use the considerable fortune he had acquired in the course of his travels as a basis for his operations. He told the minister of the invitation he had received from Victor Amadeus and showed him the latter's letters which Stair admitted were 'very obliging and pressing'. He would prefer to serve his own country, if Stair would arrange it with the government in London, and he suggested he might formulate plans for the liquidation of the country's floating debt. Stair promised to put forward this suggestion to James Stanhope, then Secretary of State for the Southern Department, and indeed he kept his word. 'There is a countryman of mine named Law of whom you have no doubt often heard,' he wrote to Stanhope. 'He is a man of very good sense, and who has a head fit for calculations of all kinds to an extent beyond anybody . . . Could not such a man be useful in devising some plan for paying off the national debts? If you think so, it will be easy to make him come . . . I would not venture to speak thus to you of this man had I not known him for a long time as a person of as good sense as I ever knew in my life, of very solid good sense and very useful, and in the matters he takes himself up with certainly the cleverest man that is.'

Stair also wrote to Lord Halifax, the brilliant First Commissioner of the Treasury,[1] who had formerly been accredited in a diplomatic post to the United Provinces. 'I had the honour to know Mr. Law a little at The Hague', replied Halifax, 'and have by me some papers of his sent to Lord Godolphin out of Scotland, by which I have a great esteem of his abilities and am extreme fond of having his assistance in the Revenue. I have spoken to the King and some of his ministers about him, but there appears some difficulty in his case and in the way of having him brought over.' This view was repeated by Stanhope some weeks later. On April 30 the Secretary of State wrote to Stair: 'Though I have not hitherto in my returns to your lordship's letters taken notice of what you have writ to me once or twice concerning Mr. Law, yet I did not fail to lay it before the King. I am now to tell your lordship that I find a disposition to comply with what your lordship proposes, though at the same time it has met and does meet with opposition, and I believe it will be no hard matter for him to guess from whence it proceeds.' The allusion here seems to be to Robert Wilson and his friends at Court and in the City who were unwilling that such a task should be entrusted to a convicted murderer and gaol-breaker, even should a complete pardon be forthcoming from the Crown.

But Law had got tired of waiting. Before Stanhope's letter reached the British embassy in Paris Law was busy discussing with Desmarets a scheme he had in mind for paying off the French national debt which now amounted to 1,000 million livres.[2] Much of this debt consisted of irredeemable bonds, and it seemed impossible that the French government would ever be able to meet it. At that time the government was paying its bond-holders 7 per cent. The finance minister proposed the drastic expedient of converting the existing stock to a 4 per cent loan, at the same time raising the necessary sum for interest and redemption by way of a lottery. Law warmly opposed this project. 'If such a considerable or drastic reduction in the rate of interest were really necessary for the good of the state or the administration of the King's affairs', he told the minister, 'it would give me greater satisfaction to reduce my own personal expenditure rather than to continue

---

[1] Broadly speaking the First Commissioner of the Treasury corresponded to the Chancellor of the Exchequer in present times; he was in effect finance minister.

[2] At that time the rate of exchange was about 14 livres to the £.

to enjoy what my holding at present yields. But I fear that any savings which His Majesty may effect through this reduction will be more than counterbalanced by the bad effect which it will have on trade. If the same ends can be achieved by the means I propose, it seems to me that it would be more acceptable to the King than the adoption of this extremity, that it would yield his subjects a higher rate of interest and at the same time would make for a better opinion of France in the eyes of foreign countries.'

Briefly Law's scheme was to reduce the interest to 5 per cent, and with the 2 per cent saved to redeem the stock gradually, a process which he undertook to complete within twenty-five years. This method of paying off the national debt he urged was infinitely preferable than recourse to a lottery. It would, of course, be facilitated by the stimulus to trade which he was certain would take place if he was also allowed to conduct a banking business as well on behalf of His Majesty. The bank was to be a state institution and to be operated on lines similar to those he had proposed to King Victor Amadeus in Turin. 'Surely,' he argued, 'an artisan or bourgeois who goes to the Town Hall to be paid his *rente* and is put off to the next day, uncertain what he will receive then, would much rather be given bank-notes which he could cash by simply walking fifteen yards?' At the same time Law was careful to impress upon the Minister his personal disinterestedness. His own affairs were such that there was no need for him to risk either his reputation or his fortune unless he were certain of the success of his scheme. In proof of his good faith Law offered not only to defray the cost of the conversion operation out of his own pocket, but also to present 500,000 livres to the poor if its execution did not work out entirely in accordance with his proposals. He thus undertook to restore French credit and to establish it on a higher level and a more advantageous footing than was enjoyed by either Great Britain or Holland. Paris, he admitted, could never become a great centre of commerce since the Seine was not then navigable from the sea to the city, but if his projects were realized, he was sure the capital could occupy a foremost place in the world of money and foreign exchange business. Finally, he urged that the fact of his alien nationality should not be allowed to militate against his scheme and render it suspect. He pointed out that he had established himself and his family in Paris and furthermore that he had invested the bulk of his fortune in French municipal and state holdings. He had always had a strong inclination and liking for France. His ambition was to serve such a great monarch as Louis XIV and to be of use to the whole French people. As he put it, 'aims such as these, rather than personal interest, were the motives which inspired him to work'.

The French finance minister, who was as much struck by the zeal with which their author expressed himself as with the proposals themselves, promised to lay the debt project before the King. In the meantime he requested Law to let him have full details of the banking scheme. There seems to have been some delay about this – partly due no doubt to the time which it took Law to work out the details as applicable to France and possibly also to an attack of some illness which confined Law to his room at this time. At all events it was not until the middle of July that Law took his coach and, bearing his draft scheme of a state bank in writing (*Mémoire sur les Banques*), drove down to Marly where the minister was staying with the rest of the court. Meanwhile its details had become known among the principal private bankers in Paris, and they were far from being sanguine as to the prospects of Law's bank. 'I saw Bernard', wrote Stair of one of them[1] in his journal during this month. 'He told me the Council would refuse Law's project, there being no foundation for the bank he proposes in a country where everything depends on the King's pleasure.'

Law followed up his *Mémoire* with a detailed outline of the proposed bank's constitution and two letters explaining its working and refuting anticipated objections to it. He even drafted the letters patent authorizing its creation which he fervently hoped the King would sign and publish. The bank's charter as a royal bank was to run in the first instance for a term of twenty years with Law as managing director. In the meantime business was to be conducted in Law's house in the Place Vendôme until more suitable premises could be found. In other particulars the scheme closely resembled his previous proposal to King Victor Amadeus. The notes, which the bank were empowered to issue, were to be payable on demand and, following the custom of the Bank of

[1] Samuel Bernard (c. 1651–1739), well-known French banker, is said to have acquired a fortune of 33 millions during Chamillard's tenure of the finance ministry. He lent considerable sums to Louis XIV who flattered him outrageously to secure his loans.

Amsterdam which had impressed Law for many years, to represent specie of a *given weight on the particular date of issue*. The notes (*écus de banque*) were to be in denominations of 1,000, 100 and 10 crowns (*écus*)[1] and to be of different sizes so as to safeguard against false change being given. There was to be a cash reserve of 10 million crowns with the customary precautions against overissue of notes. The bank was therefore to be operated on strictly orthodox lines.

Neither the banking nor the national debt project seems to have reached the Council chamber. They were, however, placed by Desmarets before the King. That bigoted monarch, instead of enquiring into their merits, simply asked whether Monsieur Law was a Catholic. On being informed he was not, Louis XIV roundly declared that he would have nothing whatever to do with a heretic who was obviously 'not to be trusted'.

4

The refusal of King Louis XIV to consider Law's financial plans was one of the last public acts of the Grand Monarch's long reign. Some members of the English colony in Paris, including, it is said, the new minister, had made bets that Louis would not survive the first day of September. 'If I continue to eat with my present hearty appetite', the King had laughingly explained in June, 'I shall make the English lose their money.' But he was wrong. His last illness overtook him at Versailles in the hot days of August. He hurriedly made a will in which he appointed a Council of Regency to act during his great-grandson's minority, at the same time naming the Duke of Maine, his favourite bastard son, as in charge of the boy Louis's education and the military forces attached to his person. The actual regency would by birth devolve upon the Duke of Orleans, but the dying monarch seems to have hoped to curtail the Regent's powers in this way. Then, fortified by all the customary rites of the Church, Louis XIV passed away towards ten o'clock in the morning of September 1, 1715. Had he lived four days longer he would have celebrated his seventy-seventh birthday.

On the day following the King's death the French Parliament,

[1] An *écu* was worth 5 livres or about 7 shillings in English money.

which was a purely formal legislative body, assembled to hear the reading of Louis's will. Orleans promptly took charge of the proceedings and got himself confirmed Regent with plenary powers to act for the infant Louis XV. The provisions in favour of the Duke of Maine, which formed a codicil to the will, were brushed aside in spite of the royal bastard's attempt to retain his functions. Some concessions were made to the Parliament's prestige by restoring its ancient right of remonstrance when royal edicts were presented for registration, as well as making the Secretaries of State subject in matters of policy to specially constituted councils or departmental committees; but in effect the Regent's authority over the Kingdom was as absolute as the Grand Monarch's had ever been. In addition Orleans was empowered to choose the members of the Council of Regency, which thus not unnaturally came to consist of his particular friends. One of the Regent's first administrative acts was to dismiss Desmarets from the finance ministry.

The post of Controller-General of Finance was offered to the Duke of Saint-Simon who had been one of the Regent's staunchest adherents through all changes of fortune. Fortunately for the country Saint-Simon declined the offer. Though he was a shrewd observer and an incomparable narrator of happenings at Court, as his writings show, he had no capacity for business affairs – indeed he admitted that he had never mastered even the elementary rules of arithmetic. He did, however, accept nomination to the Regency Council. The portfolio of finance was thereupon offered to and accepted by one of Saint-Simon's bitterest enemies, the thirty-seven-year-old Duke of Noailles, whom the chronicler described as 'the most exact, the most faithful, the most perfect copy of the serpent which beguiled Eve and destroyed the happiness of the race that humanity has been able to produce'. This diatribe, like others on those whom Saint-Simon hated, was by no means wholly merited. The new minister, with whom Law now had to deal, was an average second-rate soldier and politician, amiable, cultured and industrious. His prime failing was that he tried to please everybody, which often made him appear ridiculous as well as insincere. In all departmental business he was guided by Rouillé du Coudray, an old and experienced state councillor and financier, who united vast erudition with consummate debauchery.

The desperate condition of the nation's finances was speedily apparent even to Noailles's limited intelligence. 'We have found matters in a more terrible state than can be described,' he wrote to Madame de Maintenon a few days after taking over from Desmarets, 'both the King and his subjects ruined, nothing paid for several years past, and confidence entirely gone.' Besides the national debt of nearly 3,500 million livres there was an annual deficit on the budget of about 80 millions. No one was disposed to lend the government money while the mode of collecting revenue through the media of tax-farmers was as unjust as it was wasteful. By obtaining advances on future taxes to meet current expenses the government frequently anticipated the revenue of several years. Double entry book-keeping had not then been introduced by the finance ministry, so that no one knew the full extent of the government debt or precisely how it was made up. In some provinces the people flatly refused to pay taxes which increased the government's indebtedness to its officials. Many of the country's ministers and agents abroad had not received their regular salaries for years. To cut the cord which would remove this staggering burden of debt the Council of Regency seriously considered the extreme step of declaring the state bankrupt and thus at one stroke wiping the national slate clean of all its liabilities.

Noailles said it would take eleven years to balance the country's budget. But Orleans needed more expeditious measures. During the weeks immediately following Louis XIV's death, the Regent, who had to some extent been caught unawares by this momentous event, was kept extremely busy attending to the numerous arrangements necessary to establish his government on the footing which he required. A month elapsed before he found time to see Law, whom the change of rulers had naturally made more anxious than ever to realize his favourite project. Meanwhile the Scotsman had been cultivating the Regent's more intimate advisers, particularly the wily old Abbé Dubois who had formerly been the Regent's tutor and had now moved into the Palais Royal at his master's request. The Abbé, who was prompted more by motives of personal greed than any marked patriotic feeling, undertook to push the banking scheme with the Regent. All the papers which Law had drawn up in such detail for Desmarets were now laid before the Regent, to whom the idea of a state bank appealed strongly. After several private conversations with the financier, Orleans told Law to explain his project informally to Noailles and Rouillé du Coudray and gave orders that it should be referred officially to the Finance Council for its examination and report. Amelot, the Minister of Commerce, and D'Aguesseau, the Procurator-General, were also to be consulted, as their departments would be particularly affected.

There now followed for Law an exacting round of meetings and conferences. Although Dubois is said to have found the financier's accent disagreeable, he is admitted on all sides to have spoken tolerably good French – 'better than most Englishman generally, do', as the Regent's mother 'Madame' put it. The discussions opened in Noailles's house in the first days of October. During the next week the financier explained the working of the proposed state bank to the various ministers and counsellors concerned. Towards the middle of the month the matter was raised at a meeting of the Regency Council, and for a day or two prospects looked favourable for Law. But opposition was brewing rapidly. Noailles and Rouillé du Coudray, who suspected anyone in whom the Regent showed particular interest, determined to unite against the scheme, and they were supported by Amelot and D'Aguesseau. Rouillé set about collecting all the unfavourable views he could from the merchants and bankers of his acquaintance which included the wealthy and influential Bernard. Law went into the merits of all the objections which were raised and sent written replies to their authors, but when the Finance Council formally met to consider his project he knew that the feeling of the body was against it and in spite of the Regent's private support he suspected his efforts had been in vain.

The decisive meeting took place on October 24, 1715. Law was present along with thirteen leading representatives of the merchants and bankers in the country. Again he described his project with all the eloquence and persuasiveness that he could command. As usual he was careful to stress the need of preserving strictly an adequate proportionate reserve of cash in the bank to notes in circulation. The Regent, who presided on this occasion, then asked the other visitors for their views. Only four were in favour, one was for it at a future date, while the remaining eight headed by Bernard opposed. Then came the turn of the councillors. One or two like Noailles were inclined to hedge, but the majority spoke against, giving various reasons for their attitude. Some said that the public would not repose any confidence in the scheme, others that the opposition on the part of the merchants was bound to ensure its failure.

Finally the Regent said that he had personally been convinced of the soundness and wisdom of the project, but in view of the opinions expressed in the Council chamber he felt that the project must be dropped. As the meeting broke up he gave orders for a public announcement to be made to this effect.

Naturally Law was disappointed, but he refused to be down-hearted and he determined to persevere. One day about this time he happened to be talking to a group in the Palais Royal which included the Abbé Dubois. Someone mentioned the philosopher's stone. To the surprise of all present Law said he had discovered it.

'I can tell you my secret,' continued the financier. 'It is to make gold out of paper.'

'With paper,' the Abbé sneered sceptically. 'It's all very well to say that, but when shall we see this masterpiece?'

Law looked at his questioner and replied gravely: 'In about three or four years.'

5

While Law set about devising a different line of approach towards the realization of his scheme, the opposition he had met with from the members of the Finance Council was gradually offset by the harsh policy they inflicted on the public. Although the degrading proposal to declare a general state of bankruptcy was rejected, fortunately for the national honour, the means of retrenchment which were in fact employed were far from honest and in their attempt to curry favour with the people palpably unjust. At the same time the trade and industry of the country remained stagnant. The first measure was the compulsory conversion of all state securities from 7 per cent to 4 per cent interest-bearing after the scrip had been submitted to a commission appointed for the purpose – a process known as the *visa*. The new securities were known as state-notes (*billets d'état*). In his discussions with Noailles's predecessor, Desmarets, it will be remembered that Law had strongly opposed such a drastic reduction. The effect, as the Scotsman had foreseen, was immediately evident in the Paris money market. The price of the new stock fell sharply and was eventually quoted at 80 per cent discount.

The economies which followed, although they reduced the state's indebtedness, in no way assisted in the revival of national prosperity. Over 1,500 business houses had recently failed, money was extremely scarce and even bills of exchange had largely ceased to circulate, merchants being unwilling either to draw or accept these instruments, since a sudden change in the value of the coinage might well spell the merchants' ruin when the bills fell due. Salaries and pensions of government officials were now heavily cut and the coinage underwent a further devaluation, being reissued at nearly half of its previous intrinsic value. Most severe reform of all was the creation of a special tribunal with extensive powers to investigate and punish any financial or revenue offences suspected of having been committed since the year 1689. All merchants and men of business were required to produce the most minute balance sheets showing their profits during the previous twenty-seven years. Tax collectors, revenue officers, and government contractors and other petty officials were similarly called upon to give an exact account of their transactions during this period. False returns were punishable by a life term in the galleys for men and nine years' banishment for women, accompanied in both cases by confiscation of property. To assist the court in its proceedings informers were encouraged to come forward by the promise of a fifth of any fines or confiscations levied as well as a substantial proportion of any property concealed. From the decisions of the so-called Chamber of Justice there was no appeal.

This arbitrary innovation provoked a veritable reign of terror throughout France besides paving the way for the extortion of blackmail on a hitherto unprecedented scale. Servants threatened to expose their masters, mistresses their lovers and even children their parents if their lips were not promptly sealed with gold. Vigilance was exercised to prevent suspected offenders from leaving the country in a manner reminiscent of subsequent dictatorships; postmasters were forbidden to supply native travellers with chaises or horses, while revenue officials incurred the penalty of death if they travelled further than a league from their usual places of residence. However, as often happens with enquiries of this kind, the majority of those caught by the judicial net were the smaller fry, while the real rogues and thieves escaped. The inquisition conducted with such rigour yielded much less than was expected, although nearly 4,500 prosecutions took place in the course of twelve months, yielding 400 million livres. Samuel Bernard assessed himself voluntarily at 9 millions and the other leading merchant bankers followed suit in proportion, each fearful of being denounced by his fellows for paying too little. The court's activities tended more and more to extract forced loans from anyone in comfortable circumstances, all being assessed on the theory that they had made too much in the way of profits.

Such were the uncomfortable conditions prevailing throughout France as John Law worked on a revision of his plans during the months immediately following the rejection of his project of a state bank. In spite of this set-back the rumour persisted throughout the winter in Paris that the government was going to put bank-notes into circulation, and deputations of merchants prepared to approach the Regent on the subject. What Law now proposed was a private bank operated on the joint stock principle. He was prepared himself to subscribe a great part of the capital and in any event to defray the initial overhead expenses. The issue of notes was to be carefully regulated, but Law maintained that the resulting increase in the circulation of currency was bound to have a beneficial effect on trade, as well as re-establishing confidence by the creation of money of a fixed value. The remittance of money from one province to another, he urged, would be facilitated, while foreign merchants and shippers would know where they stood when they entered into contracts which stipulated payment in 'bank money'. Finally, he repeated the offer he had previously made of presenting a sum of 500,000 livres to charity should the project fail.

Orleans was completely won over by these arguments. Indeed he required little conviction, since he had had the wisdom to appreciate the original plan's merits. The Regent now proceeded to buttonhole each member of the Finance Council in private and he let it be known that Law would shortly submit his banking scheme in a revised form when he trusted that it would enjoy a unanimous passage by the board. The Regency Councillors were similarly spoken to. Everyone thus approached signified his agreement except curiously enough the Duke of Saint-Simon, who knew nothing and cared less about finance but who in his objections laid his finger on the weak spot in the scheme. Such a bank as was proposed, Saint-Simon argued, might be an excellent institution under a republic or under a constitutional monarchy such as England where the national finances were subject to an overriding measure of popular control. In a country like France, which enjoyed the absolute rule of a single individual, the operation of the bank might have the most pernicious consequences since such charges as were incurred by a costly mismanaged war, the rapacity of a royal mistress or favourite, or the luxury and extravagances of the King, 'might soon exhaust the bank and ruin all the holders of notes'. Orleans, however, maintained that the ruler would have such a strong personal interest in the bank's success that he would never permit such a contingency to intefere with its operation.

On May 1, 1716, the Finance Council assembled to consider the new scheme. The Regent, who had canvassed each member beforehand, anticipated no opposition. It was explained that the bank, which was to be restricted to the exercise of purely banking functions, would be incorporated as a private joint stock company with a capital of six million livres (about £300,000 sterling), consisting of 1,200 shares of 1,000 écus (£250) each.[1] Any member of the public could subscribe for shares without restriction as to amount, and shareholders of foreign nationality would not be liable to have their holdings attached or confiscated in time of war. Law was to be the managing director, while general policy would be in the hands of shareholders who would normally meet twice yearly. Voting power was to be on the basis of one vote for every five shares held with no shareholders to have more than thirty votes. Notes which the bank had power to issue would be dated and cashable on demand by the bearer 'in coin of the weight and denomination of that day'. Depositors would receive notes in return for the specie they lodged with the bank cashiers. The penalty for altering or counterfeiting the notes was death. Transfers of sums from the account of one customer to another were to be effected by means of bills resembling modern cheques. As soon as the capital figure stated had been subscribed, the bank would

---

[1] The fact that three-quarters of this sum were payable in *billets d'état* at the lowest market rate and only one quarter in cash reduced the effective capital to approximately 3,300,300 livres.

be ready to commence business in Law's house in the Place Vendôme where several rooms on the ground floor were being fitted up as offices.

The bank's charter which was read to the Council by Noailles set out these conditions clearly and it was immediately approved by the Council, as the Regent intended that it should. Orders were then given that it should be published in the form of a royal edict, which was done on the following day. The Regent added that at the managing director's invitation he had consented to become patron of the bank which would be known as the *Banque Générale*. A day later the project passed the Regency Council, only Saint-Simon dissenting.

At long last John Law was to have the chance for which he had dreamed and hoped and striven for upwards of twenty years past. The bank was the first great milestone on the road towards the goal he had set himself – the financial and commercial rehabilitation of his adopted country.

On the other projects which were revolving in his mind he determined for the moment to keep silent. Only to the Abbé Dubois did he give any hint of them as he handed over 30,000 *écus* worth of bank shares in return for that wily cleric's service in smoothing the way in the Palais Royal.

'M. l'Abbé,' he said, 'become my partner, and in three years you will be able to buy the city of Paris.'

Dubois thought for a moment as he pocketed the gift. 'No,' he replied. 'I have too much to lose.'

CHAPTER IV

THE BANKER

The royal edict in the shape of letters-patent authorizing the incorporation of Law's *Banque Générale* was published on May 2, 1716. Simultaneously copies were sent to the French Parliament with a peremptory request from the Regent for its immediate registration. This the Parliament accorded somewhat grudgingly, its members adding, as they did so, a supplication that 'the said Law shall be empowered to take charge of the said bank only after he shall have first obtained letters of naturalization if it pleases His Majesty to grant them'. The requisite letters were despatched to the Parliament a few days later showing that the bank's managing director had now become a citizen of France. These formalities occupied several weeks, and a further delay was caused by the difficulty which Law experienced in laying hands on a press to print the bank's notes, so that it was not until the beginning of June that the new bank opened its doors for business in the director's house in the Place Vendôme.[1]

At first the public was inclined to be sceptical of such a novel institution as a bank of issue, and it regarded the bank's notes with suspicion. Indeed many men and women in France had never seen a bank-note. It was the first time in French history that bank-notes had been put into circulation in the country, and there were still only five other states in the world in which this ingenious

---

[1] Only one quarter of the capital was paid up, viz. 1,500,000 livres, and of this sum only one quarter in specie, the remainder in *billets d'état*. The bank's initial cash capital was, therefore, 375,000 livres (less than £27,000), a slender enough sum considering the ambitious objects Law had in mind.

medium of exchange and instrument of credit was employed.[1] Law was branded in the local newspapers as an adventurer, *écossais et grand jacobite*, and as late as the end of July, after the bank had been in operation for two months, one of these journals asserted that the bank was only spoken of in Paris as a joke and almost everyone laughed at it. But this situation began gradually and perceptibly to change, as Law exerted every effort to capture general confidence. So as to attract business it was announced that the bank would effect remittances to any part of the country on behalf of its customers without charge. At the same time the Regent lodged a million livres with the bank, this large sum in specie being unloaded and counted out in the bank's offices as ostentatiously as possible. Before the summer was over the bank's daily deposits of specie were shown to exceed its outgoing payments, trade and industry began to benefit, the bank's discount rate was reduced, and the Duke of Noailles was moved to declare that 'nothing more useful could have been achieved than the establishment of the *Banque Générale*'. At this time bills up to 30,000 livres were discounted in favour of a single individual. Thus the bank's notes, which constituted a currency safe in form and convenient in use, came to be sought after alike by natives of the country and foreigners who realized that their value could not be altered by royal edict. Before the end of the year the bank's increased business made it necessary to move into larger premises; these were provided by the spacious Hôtel d'Avaux in the Rue Sainte Avoie.

So favourably impressed was the Regent by these developments that, in response to pressure from Law, he caused his finance minister to send a circular letter to all provincial *intendants*, as the senior revenue officials in the country districts were called, instructing them to see that all collectors of taxes made their remittances to Paris in notes of the bank, and also to accept notes in exchange for any specie they had in their treasuries. This letter, which was dated October 7, 1716, was the first sign of government intervention in the bank's affairs. As events turned out, the instruction proved to be premature, since the bank was not prepared immediately to furnish notes fast enough for so extended a use, while the tax receivers took advantage of it to hold back remittances. This led to a modification of the original instruction.

[1] Sweden, Genoa, Venice, Holland, Great Britain.

Tax collectors were henceforth directed to remit as hitherto, pending the full establishment of the bank's credit arrangements, but to continue to exchange for specie any notes which were presented to them. The succeeding months witnessed a marked increase in the note circulation, so that when, on April 10, 1717, the Council issued the decree which ordered that the notes should be accepted in payment of all taxes and other royal revenues throughout the realm and which has usually been regarded as the beginning of official intervention, in reality complete legislative effect was simply being given to a practice which had been current for some time in various parts of the country. The practice was, however, not accepted without considerable opposition in certain provinces, notably Bordeaux, and the Regent was obliged to step in and punish a number of recalcitrant tax collectors before the notes could be said to enjoy general currency.[1]

Other individual opposition was a constant source of worry and irritation to Law. The most acute thorn in his flesh was the finance minister Noailles, who became extremely jealous of the bank and its successful director and whose necessary departmental assistance was only secured at the Regent's urgent bidding and only with considerable reluctance on the part of the minister. Partly to counterbalance this covert opposition Law proceeded to cultivate Saint-Simon who, though he had spoken against the bank at the Regency Council, was an implacable enemy of the finance minister and as a councillor and confidant of the Regent might be expected at least not to obstruct the bank now that it had become an established legal institution. At the Regent's request Saint-Simon received Law alone at his house once a week when the gossip of the day as well as the bank's affairs were discussed with a candour which grew with each meeting. 'I soon knew that if Law had desired these regular visits to my house', wrote Saint-Simon later, 'it was not because he expected to make me a skilful financier, but because like a man of good sense – and he had a good deal – he wished to enlist a servitor of the Regent who had the best post in his confidence and who long since had been in a position to speak to him of everything and everybody

[1] The obstructive and tyrannical conduct of Courson, the Intendant of Bordeaux, in refusing to carry out his instructions was one of the many causes of dispute between Saint-Simon and Noailles and was partly responsible for the latter's eventual dismissal.

with the greatest liberty.' At their first meeting Saint-Simon, in spite of his ignorance of finance which he was always ready to proclaim, stressed the overriding importance of preserving the convertibility of the bank's notes and, according to his own account, he repeated this injunction on numerous subsequent occasions, so that in examining the bank's weekly balance sheet, as they customarily did together, Law was always able to show that he was more than ready to meet any normal demands of note-holders for coin. These weekly visits worked out in the way Law had hoped. 'The bank being in action and flourishing, I believed it my duty to support it,' admitted his host afterwards. 'I lent myself, therefore, to the suggestions Law put forward and soon we spoke to each other with a confidence I never had reason to regret.'

The alliance which Law succeeded in establishing with one of the Regent's most intimate and influential advisers was to bear fruit in the struggle for political power in which the banker was shortly to find himself involved. Meanwhile, in spite of the confidence which the bank had gained in the country at large, its director was at times hard put to it to sustain its credit. Private as well as political influences continued to work against it and Law had to keep constantly on the watch for his opponents' deliberately conceived efforts to break his bank. Bills drawn on the bank for large sums – instruments equivalent to modern cheques – would be accumulated by the payees and then suddenly presented without previous warning. One morning two men appeared at the bank and asked to see the director. On being shown into Law's office these individuals produced notes to the value of nearly five million livres and demanded immediate payment in cash. Law not unnaturally turned pale and requested twenty-four hours in which to collect such a considerable amount of specie. His interlocutors observed maliciously that the notes were supposed to be payable immediately on demand and that it was surely lowering the bank's reputation to ask for time to pay so trifling a sum. However, they agreed to the twenty-four hours, 'but not a minute longer', they added. As soon as these two unpleasant visitors had departed Law hurried to the finance ministry where he put the facts before Noailles, explaining that although the bank was quite solvent it would be impossible within such a short period to meet the notes from the bank's cash reserve. The minister, who, in spite of his personal jealousies towards the director, was only too well aware of the government's interest in upholding the bank's credit, saw the point and agreed that the government must come to the rescue. He thereupon gave orders that the desired amount of specie should be obtained from the state treasury and in this way the two malicious noteholders were paid in full within the agreed time limit. However, the mediocre and intriguing finance minister's days in office were numbered, as also were those of the chancellor D'Aguesseau, his colleague on the Regency Council who was likewise engaged in working against Law. Both men were warned by the Regent that, if they declined to co-operate with Law, they would have to resign their portfolios. They took no heed until the beginning of 1718 when the blow fell. They were both summarily dismissed and the offices were united in the Chief of Police M. D'Argenson whom Orleans hoped would prove a more pliant tool in the matter of financial policy.

At the end of two years the *Banque Générale* had weathered all storms, and its managing director could look back with some satisfaction on a record of solid and sustained achievement. 'Never before,' he said, 'was an enterprise of this kind established at such a difficult period.' Now the three principal objectives, which Law had set out to attain on the incorporation of the bank, had all been reached. So he told the Regent in a report on the bank's history which he prepared at this time. First, commercial confidence had been largely restored in the kingdom. Secondly, means had been provided for the natives and foreigners alike to deposit funds with complete security, and thirdly, the notes of the bank were now tantamount to universal bills of exchange which circulated freely throughout France and were also known abroad. Under Law's judicious management the bank's own fortunes as well as those of the country had prospered. At the end of 1717 the bank was able to pay the shareholders a half-yearly dividend of 7 per cent; it had already reduced its commercial bill discount rate from 6 to 4 per cent as money became more plentiful. All the same, Law made it clear to Orleans that he was still beset with many difficulties and that he must count on the Regent's continued support to keep him and his bank afloat in the tempestuous sea of local politics and petty jealousies of Paris. 'It is to be hoped,' he added, 'that His Royal Highness will exercise his authority to remove

these difficulties which certain individuals, while full of good
intentions but still in a state of darkness, might otherwise be able
to put in the way of carrying on this project.'

2

While the General Bank made
headway, its director's personal position was not rendered by any
means easy from the character and behaviour of the head of the
government with whom he had constantly to deal and on whose
support the bank almost entirely depended. The Regent had a
quick brain and a lively intellect; he readily appreciated Law's
financial arguments – indeed Law used to say that the only two
public figures who thoroughly understood his theories on credit
were Orleans and King Victor Amadeus – and in dismissing
Noailles and D'Aguesseau he showed a laudable determination to
remove existing obstacles in the way of their implementation. On
the other hand, although he rose early and often worked from
six in the morning until eight in the evening, he wasted a great
deal of time in public as well as in private. His audiences were too
prolonged and too easily granted, partly through an unfortunate
desire to play off one individual against another, and partly
through a tendency to immerse himself in much unnecessary
detail. His familiarity and readiness of access were often abused
and led to unpardonable liberties being taken by those who had
little or no respect for him. In the evenings he surrendered himself
shamelessly to the most reckless dissipation, and no matter of
state, however pressing, was allowed to interrupt his orgies.

His mother, who was in a good position to observe his activities, has left a faithful account of him at this time. 'My son is no
longer a youth of twenty, he is a man of forty-two years', she
wrote, 'so Paris cannot forgive him for running off to balls after
women in such a hair-brained fashion when he has all the affairs
of state on his shoulders . . . He is quite incapable of loving
passionately and of being attached to the same person for long.
On the other hand, his manners are not polite and seductive
enough for him to expect to make himself loved. He is very
indiscreet and tells everything that happens to him. I have told
him a hundred times that I am very much surprised that women

are so foolish as to run after him, they should rather flee from him. He begins to laugh and says, "You don't know the loose women of to-day. It gives them great pleasure to tell how I lay with them" ... He has an accursed mistress who drinks like a fish and is unfaithful to him, but, since she never asks him for anything, he is not jealous of her. He spends whole nights in that wicked society, and stays at the table until three or four o'clock in the morning, which is very bad for his health. I am terrified lest he get something worse with all these goings on. Heaven preserve him!'

The notorious supper parties in the Palais Royal, which took place nightly, were usually comprised of a dozen or so boon companions, whom the Regent called his *roués*, and a few specially chosen women who invariably included his immodest daughter the Duchess of Berri and a group of singers and dancers from the opera. As a rule the servants were dismissed and the guests helped themselves to the dishes. On these occasions all pretence to decency was abandoned. There was abundant wit and still more vulgarity. At one session the judgment of Paris was re-enacted with a lack of costume which was entirely classical. Madame de Parabère, the Regent's 'accursed mistress', represented Juno, and the Duchess of Berri played the part of Venus. Everyone present is said to have been intoxicated, while the licence became more unbridled as the night wore on. There was never an evening in which the Regent did not get stupidly drunk and he expected the guests to follow his example. 'The company drank as much as they could, inflamed themselves, said the filthiest things without stint, uttered impieties with emulation, and when they had made a good deal of noise and were very drunk they went to bed to recommence the same proceedings next day,' so wrote Saint-Simon who strongly disapproved of their activities. 'From the moment when supper was ready, business, no matter of what importance, no matter whether private or national, was entirely banished from view. Until the next morning everybody and everything were compelled to wait.'

It is scarcely surprising that his round of debauchery, kept up as it was night after night without intermission, should have begun to show itself in the Regent's features long before Law established his bank. In 1716 he injured one of his eyes while playing tennis and, although expressly warned by his doctors, he continued his immoderate potations with results as unfortunate for his temper as his sight. His appearance grew bloated and at his first audiences in the morning he was sometimes so stupefied that he signed any papers before him without question. All that can be said for the Regent Orleans in this connection is that his indiscretions were confined to his private relations: never in his wildest and most inebriated moments did he divulge any state secret to mistress or *roué*. 'Look in your glass,' he said to one female guest who ventured upon an enquiry of this kind, 'and see if so pretty a face was made to talk politics.'

The banker could not at any time be counted a member of this debauched circle, although he had an interesting link with it. One night a woman appeared in a state of nature in the antechamber to the Regent's bedroom where she mounted a pedestal in the pretended pose of the goddess of love. As the duke reeled through the room at a late hour besotted with wine and lust, this striking figure suddenly sank into his surprised but by no means reluctant arms. Thus began a liaison which was not without significance for Law, since, when the Regent tired of this lady's affections (as he fairly rapidly did), he either passed her on to the financier or else Law appropriated her for himself. The female in question was the thirty-five-year-old Claudine Alexandrine Guerin de Tencin, who had once been a nun but had later violated her vows and fled from her convent to the delights of the Regent's Paris. More recently she had been the mistress of one Chevalier Destouches to whom she had borne a son who, though abandoned in the city streets as a foundling, was destined to grow up into a mathematician and philosopher of European fame under the name of Jean d'Alembert. When not actively engaged in pursuing the art of love the frail Madame de Tencin could be found presiding over an agreeable salon in her house in the Faubourg St. Honoré, much frequented by artists and men of letters, and it was here that Law cultivated her acquaintance. This association, as will duly appear, was to have important consequences for the bank director.

With the exception of this liaison and one other which, astonishing as it may seem, he was to develop with the Regent's sexagenarian mother 'Madame', Law remained faithful to his Catherine, to whom at this time nobody suspected that he was not married. The principal contemporary chroniclers all pay tribute to their simple and regular mode of living which remained

Lauriston Castle.
From an engraving by W. Miller

Philip Duke of Orleans
Regent of France

unspoiled by riches and success. 'There was in his home more order and cleanliness than luxury,' declared the contemporary social historian Duclos. 'Tall, well built, with a pleasant and agreeable face, much intelligence, of remarkable politeness, with haughtiness without insolence,' was how this writer described the banker at this time, while Catherine was 'an English woman of quality, of a haughty character, which the manners of our little and great dames soon rendered impertinent.' This opinion is confirmed by that most acute of observers, the Duke of Saint-Simon. 'Law was a Scotchman, of very doubtful birth,' wrote Saint-Simon, 'tall and well made, of agreeable face and aspect, gallant and on very good terms with the ladies of all the countries he had travelled in. His wife was not his wife; she was of a good English family and well connected, had followed Law for love, had had a son and daughter by him, passed for his wife and bore his name without being married to him . . . She had one eye and the top of one cheek covered by an ugly mark as of wine; otherwise she was well made, proud, impertinent in her conversation and in her manners, receiving compliments, giving next to none, paying but few visits, these rare and selected, and exercising authority in her household. I know not whether her credit over her husband was great, but he appeared full of regard, of care, and of respect for her.'

Sincerest of all compliments to Law's character was likewise uttered by Saint-Simon. 'There was neither avarice nor roguery in his composition,' said this critic. 'He was a gentle, good, respectable man whom excess of credit and fortune had not spoiled, and whose department, equipages, table and furniture could not scandalize anyone.'

3

One day at Marly, not long after Louis XIV's death, the Regent, in the course of a conversation with Law, remarked that thanks to the financier's overtures he was beginning to see a way out of the formidable difficulties which confronted the country.

'Sire,' rejoined Law, 'my bank is not the only one of my ideas not the greatest. I will create something which will surprise

Europe by the changes it will bring about in favour of France – changes more profound than have resulted from the discovery of the Indies or the introduction of credit.' In addition to the restoration of order in the nation's finances, the projector went on, agriculture, trade and commerce would be expanded, the royal revenues increased and the national debt extinguished without any injury to the state's creditors. These benefits were to be obtained through the medium of a vast trading corporation which should have a fleet of sixty ships and a capital of at least 22,000,000 livres at its disposal. In short Law declared that once internal credit had been re-established, he could make France the greatest commercial nation in the world. 'Your Highness's regency well employed will suffice to increase the population of the country to 30 millions and the royal revenues to 300 millions . . . France will thus become the retreat of the happy and the refuge of the unfortunate.'[1]

The idea of a trading company as an instrument of colonization to the pecuniary advantage of the mother country was no novelty in France, but unlike its British counterpart the French corporation had never proved a conspicuous success. Louis XIV's ministers had founded such companies to develop French interests in different parts of the world including the West Indies, Canada, North Africa and China. Towards the close of the seventeenth century two Frenchmen called Marquette and La Salle had penetrated nearly a thousand miles up the fertile valley of the river Mississippi, the vast territory through which this waterway flowed being appropriated by the French monarch and renamed Louisiana after himself. In 1712 a wealthy financier named Antoine Crozat had obtained from Louis an exclusive monopoly of trade with this territory for fifteen years on condition that he peopled the new colony with forty French emigrants annually and paid certain taxes to the royal treasury. By this time the concession had come to extend three thousand miles upstream and to include all the territory lying between the Alleghanies on the east and the Rocky Mountains on the west – in other words, the present states of Louisiana, Mississippi, Arkansas, Missouri,

---

[1] These ideas were developed in an interesting essay entitled *Réetablissement du Commerce* which Law wrote in the summer of 1715. The only copy known to have survived was given by Law to the French philosopher Montesquieu, when the two men met in Venice in 1782, and is now in the *Bibliothèque Nationale* in Paris.

Illinois, Iowa, Wisconsin and Minnesota – in fact it extended from the Gulf of Mexico to the French establishments in Canada. Over this enormous area, rich in agricultural and mineral resources but as yet for the most part uninhabited save by roving bands of Indians, the French King now exercised a vague and shadowy dominion.

Disputes which he had with the local French governor added to the taxes demanded of him determined Crozat to sell out at the end of five years, or rather to surrender his privileges to the King. It was here that Law stepped in. According to the banker's own statement, it was Noailles (not yet dismissed from the finance ministry) who first proposed to float a company for the purpose of taking over Crozat's moribund interests. The company was to have a capital of two million livres. Law laughed when he heard of this paltry figure and immediately went to the minister and offered to subscribe the whole amount himself. Next day Noailles told Law, if he could guarantee to produce a million annually by way of interest, that is at 4 per cent, he would agree to a capital of 25 millions with Law as managing director. This is what in fact happened, except that the amount of the authorized capital was eventually multiplied by four. On September 6, 1717, Parliament registered the royal edict which created the Company of the West (*Compagnie d'Occident*), as the new venture was called. A week later the Regent announced the names of the members of the board of directors. It was seen that Law's headed the list.

By its charter the company was granted the monopoly of trade with Louisiana and the absolute control of the internal affairs of the colony, both for a period of twenty-five years. All minerals discovered during the term of the concession were to belong to the company. It could arm and equip vessels of war, the property of the colonists was exempt from taxation, and real estate in the colony could be freely alienated. The only condition which the company undertook to observe was the importation of six thousand white and at least three thousand coloured settlers to the territory. The company's capital was to consist of shares of 500 livres each to be subscribed in state bonds (*billets d'état*). The latter on being paid up were to be converted into perpetual annuities (*rentes*) carrying interest at 4 per cent, while the original bonds were to be burned. This feature was a characteristic stroke

99

of genius on Law's part, since it was designed to relieve the government of nearly one half of the floating debt, while the shareholders would receive the same rate of interest as they had for their bonds and at the same time enjoy the profits, which it was hoped would soon accrue in abundance, from the development of the colony.

The nominal amount of the capital, which was fixed towards the end of 1717 at 100 million livres, represented an unprecedented sum for those days. However, the real amount was very much less than this figure; since state-bonds were at a discount of about sixty per cent in the market: this meant that the real value of the paid-up capital was only about one-third of its nominal amount. Furthermore the bulk of the company's assets, instead of being cash invested in ships and warehouses and so on, really consisted of dubious government obligations. The four million livres due by way of interest for the first year was to be set aside as working capital, and this sum in fact constituted the company's sole liquid assets. As usual Law was sanguine and optimistic: there seems no doubt that he believed that the extended use of his bank-notes would enable business to be created and capital expenditure induced by the aid of credit. Meanwhile the subscription lists remained open for several months, and the stock was subscribed very slowly. The Company of the West did not at first catch on with the public. Indeed for nearly two years its shares were quoted below par.

4

The year 1717, which saw the beginning of his Mississippi project, witnessed two other incidents involving the financier in the country of his adoption. The first of these was the acquisition by the French crown of the largest and finest jewel the world had ever seen. The other was the visit to the French court, for the first time in history, of a Russian Emperor.

In 1701, Thomas Pitt, grandfather of the first Earl of Chatham, had been Governor of the English East India Company's settlement of Fort St. George in Madras, and while in India he had acquired from a native merchant an uncut diamond of prodigious size. The stone, for which Pitt paid over £20,000, weighed 410 carats in its uncut state. Its history was curious. According to one account it was formerly one of the eyes of the famous Hindu idol Juggernaut at Chandernagore. Another version has it that it was stolen by a slave worker in the Parteal mines of the Great Mogul who managed to secrete it in a wound in his leg and at the same time to reach the coast, in the words of an English paraphrase of the passage in which Saint-Simon describes the episode, 'without being subjected to the rigid and not very delicate ordeal that all persons not above suspicion by their name or their occupation are compelled to submit to ere leaving the country'. The slave is supposed in turn to have had the gem stolen from him by an English sea-captain who disposed of it for £1,000 to the merchant from whom Pitt had eventually purchased it. The Governor, who by reason of his priceless acquisition came to be known as 'Diamond Pitt,' had sent it by one of his sons to England where it was cut with great skill at a cost of £5,000, the weight being reduced in the process by about 75 carats, but leaving what was generally agreed to be the finest diamond in existence. 'It is of the size of a greengage plum,' wrote Saint-Simon, 'nearly round, of a thickness which corresponds with its volume – free from all spot, speck or blemish, of admirable water, and weighs more than 500 grains.'

This amazing stone had not been without embarrassment to its owner. Pitt had known little rest while it was in his possession and had undertaken many travels, usually in disguise, in a vain endeavour to sell it. In 1714 he had come to Fontainebleau and had offered it to Louis XIV, but the price demanded had been too much for the Grand Monarch. In 1717 Pitt again visited France, this time with his two sons – Robert, father of the future Earl of Chatham, and Thomas, shortly to be created Lord Londonderry – and the party made Law's acquaintance. They had with them a replica of the jewel which Pitt gave Law, who brought it to the Regent with a proposition for the purchase of the original on behalf of the King. Again the price proved a stumbling block. Orleans was afraid of the blame which he might incur if he authorized such a purchase at a time of economic scarcity when many French citizens were in want of the necessities of life. Undismayed, Law brought the model to Saint-Simon who, when he saw it, consented to tackle the Regent again with the argument that 'it was not consistent with the greatness of a King of France to be repelled from the purchase of an inestimable jewel unique of its kind in the world by the mere consideration of price, and that the greater the number of potentates who had not dared to think of it, the greater ought to be his care not to let it escape him'. Saint-Simon kept his word and went to the Palais Royal. To the Regent's objection he replied that His Highness 'ought not to regard the greatest King in Europe as he would a private gentleman who would be very reprehensible if he threw away 100,000 livres on a fine diamond while he owed many debts which he could not pay; that he must consider the honour of the crown and not lose the occasion of obtaining a priceless diamond which would efface the lustre of all others in Europe; that it was a glory for his regency which would last for ever; and that, whatever might be the state of the finances, the saving effected by the refusal of the jewel would not much relieve them, for it would be scarcely perceptible.'

This line of reasoning made a noticeable impression on the Regent's mind. Meanwhile Law kept warning Pitt in the strongest language of the loss he would suffer if he were to cut up the diamond into a number of pieces with the result that at last the owner reduced his price to 2,000,000 livres, or, in English money, about £135,000. It was at this figure that the gem changed hands and became part of the French crown jewels, being renamed the 'Regent'. 'I much applauded myself', noted Saint-Simon at the time, 'for having induced the Regent to make so illustrious a purchase.' Indeed the purchase itself was a relatively simple transaction. Payment was more difficult. The details were left to Law to arrange. This he did on the best terms he could obtain from the former owner. Until the capital sum could be raised Pitt was to receive the interest on the purchase money, and as security, he was to have other jewels to the value of the full amount.[1]

While France's leading banker was engaged in these negotiations, the Tsar Peter the Great arrived in Paris on a state visit. For Law and everyone else who either saw or came into contact with the famed ruler of Muscovy, the six weeks which Peter spent in the Kingdom in the summer of 1717 were unforgettable. In his middle forties – he was just a year younger than Law – this

[1] The diamond, which was valued in 1791 at nearly half a million pounds sterling, was stolen with the other French crown jewels during the Revolution, but it was subsequently recovered and is now in the Louvre.

spectacular figure, whose rage could be cyclonic and whose in-humanity barbarous, had opened a window in the Baltic capital named after him through which his country's inhabitants for the first time in their history were forced to look towards the west. In his endeavour to acquire all the advantages of modern science for Russia, Peter had travelled over Europe, on one occasion working incognito as a shipbuilder in Holland. He had expressed a desire to come to France during the reign of Louis XIV, but that monarch, probably for reasons of domestic economy, had politely declined to receive him. The Regent, however, had no such scruples, and in due course the Tsar and his suite reached the French capital, where a whole hotel was allotted for their accommodation.

In characteristic fashion Peter declared that the grand bed-chamber assigned to him was much too grand, and as soon as he had seen it he insisted on his simple camp bed, which accom-panied him on all his travels, being put up in a small dressing-room adjoining. His behaviour at table excited general astonish-ment. 'What he ate and drank at his two regular meals is incon-ceivable', noted Saint-Simon, 'without reckoning the beer, lemonade and other drinks he swallowed between these repasts, his suite following his example – a bottle or two of beer, as many more of wine, and occasionally liqueurs afterwards; at the end of the meal strong drinks such as brandy, as much sometimes as a quart. This was about the usual quantity at each meal.' His interest in everything he saw coupled with an air of easy familiarity made him on the whole a popular visitor. At one army barracks, for example, which he visited, he tasted the soldiers' soup and wine, drank their healths, slapped them on the shoulders and called them comrades. He went to call on Madame de Maintenon, but that harridan, anticipating his curiosity, had gone to bed behind closed curtains. Peter, on entering her chamber, first drew the window curtains and then the bed curtains. Then he looked at the occupant of the 'four-poster' for a moment, let the curtains drop and left the room without uttering a word. Only at Versailles did his conduct occasion a little scandal. Here the Tsar and his suite spent a night in the palace apartments formerly occupied by the late King's mistress. A number of ladies of easy virtue were imported for the delectation of the party with results that, un-fortunately for certain members of it, soon became painfully evident. It is reported that Peter submitted with good grace to the medical treatment which his surrender to Venus had rendered necessary and was agreeably surprised at the moderate size of the fee which was charged.

Indeed Peter's inquisitiveness was seemingly insatiable. 'The Tsar excited admiration by his extreme curiosity, always bearing upon his views of government, trade, instruction, police, and this curiosity, embraced everything, disdained nothing in the smallest degree useful,' so observed Saint-Simon. 'It was marked and enlightened, esteeming only what merited to be esteemed, and exhibited in a clear light the intelligence, justness and ready appreciation of his mind.' Such a novel institution as the first bank of issue in the country naturally did not escape the Tsar's roving eye, and he displayed the deepest interest in the operations of the *Banque Générale* and its director. As usual, he asked innumerable questions, and he enquired into every aspect of the bank's working from the manufacture of notes to the fixing of the discount rate.

Peter left France well satisfied with what he had found there, though he expressed surprise at the luxury on all sides and he foretold that one day it would bring ruin on the country. What impressed him more was Law's bank and, as we shall see, he was not to forget it.

5

Marc René D'Argenson, the new finance minister, was sixty-five years old at the time of his appointment to succeed the obstructive mediocrity Noailles at the beginning of 1718. His severe features, accentuated by a long term of office as head of the police, confirmed the impression which he was at pains to give that nothing escaped his vigilant and penetrating eye. He had indeed proved an able policeman, for he enjoyed being kept busy in the confidence of the great, so that he became somewhat put out when he discovered that in his new office there was nothing for him to do – the condition of acceptance being that his official mantle should simply serve as a cloak for Law's operations behind which the banker's policy should be carried out. Afraid lest the secret of his advancement should be detected by the public, D'Argenson invented a comic role for himself. He pretended to be overwhelmed with business, and was seen immersed in a sea of papers and dictating simultaneously to four secretaries. He would drive ostentatiously through the streets to his office in the evening in a lighted carriage and would make appointments at all hours of the night, taking care to be inaccessible by day when in fact he was sleeping in his house.

If the new minister had confined himself to this ridiculous charade and left Law to get on with his projects of financial reform, the arrangement might have proceeded smoothly and satisfactorily for all concerned. Unfortunately D'Argenson was seized with a desire to show off further. He became profoundly jealous of the attention which Law had excited in the Regent's council and circle by his method, already described, of liquidating half the national debt through the medium of his Company of the West. Knowing next to nothing of public finance D'Argenson sought advice from others who were likewise jealous of the foreigner's success. As a result the minister came forward with an astonishing counter-measure – nothing less than the extinction of the debt at one stroke. This was to be achieved by the tried and unpopular method of depreciating the coinage; 48 livres in specie weighing 9 ounces plus 12 state-bonds (*billets d'état*) were to be received by the Treasury in exchange for 60 livres of the coinage which weighed only 8 ounces. By this 'augmentation' the livre would be devalued by one-sixth while *billets d'état* would be absorbed at the same time. To Law this process savoured of sharp dealing; indeed he had always been opposed to 'augmentation' since the days, many years before, when he had seen it followed with disastrous results in Scotland. However, as a private citizen he was in no position to object to it, particularly as the convertibility of his banknotes was unaffected.

The decree authorizing the execution of D'Argenson's revaluation of the coinage was published by the Council in May, 1718. As a money measure it was not considered necessary to send it to the Parliament for registration, there being only one precedent in the past when such a measure was thus submitted, and then only out of courtesy. Parliament reacted by requesting the Regent to suspend the decree. When Orleans refused, the assembly passed an edict forbidding the execution of the decree on the ground that it was prejudicial to the state, to commerce and to the fortunes of individuals. To this the Regent retaliated by abrogating the

Parliament's edict and prohibiting its printing and posting; at the same time he ordered the enforcement of the Council's decree. The unpopularity which any measure of monetary devaluation naturally incurred was, in this instance, directed by the Parliament against Law who was somewhat unfairly held responsible for it by that body. At all events Parliament now attacked the bank and its director. By an edict dated August 12, 1718, Parliament ordered the bank to keep within its charter; at the same time revenue officials were forbidden to deposit their balances in the bank, and foreigners whether naturalized or not were peremptorily admonished not to meddle in its affairs.

The publication of this edict brought to a head the friction which had been growing for some time between the Regent and Parliament. Unlike the English assembly the French Parliament was essentially a judicial body whose duties included the formal registration of royal edicts. In the past it had claimed a right of remonstrance, but this had been suppressed by Louis XIV to be somewhat unwisely revived by the Regent on taking over the reins of government. 'Our parliamentary gentlemen began as humbly as those of England,' wrote Saint-Simon, who hated them, 'and though their assembly was but a simple court of justice, limited in its jurisdiction by the other courts of the realm to judge disputes between private people, yet by dint of hammering on the word parliament they believed themselves not less important than their English brethren who form the legislative assembly and represent all the nation.' There is no doubt that the French Parliament had come to attribute to itself real as apart from formal legislative functions. A clash with the Regent was, therefore, inevitable.

Not content with publishing their edict, the Parliament appointed a secret commission to enquire into the circumstances of the obnoxious financial decree. A number of witnesses were examined and evidence collected on the strength of which it was intended to arrest Law and execute him before the Regent should have time to intervene. Fortunately for Law this intention was reported to the Palais Royal. A council of war was hurriedly held in Saint-Simon's house to decide what should be done.

Law's life being in peril, it was agreed that the safety of the financier must be the prime consideration. Law himself was present at this gathering but seemed uncertain as to the best course to pursue. According to Saint-Simon he looked more dead than alive and at one stage in the discussion he broke down in tears. Flight was out of the question, since, although he had a safe conduct from the Regent, Orleans' signature would not be worth the paper it was written on if anyone connected with the Parliament should succeed in laying hands on the banker as he traversed the streets of the city between his house and the bank. If Law were taken in this manner, it would probably be too late to send a detachment of guards to force an entry into the *Palais de Justice*, the Parliamentary headquarters – 'frightful', mused Saint-Simon, 'if instead of Law, only his suspended corpse had been found!' In the end it was agreed that to ensure his personal safety Law should take up his quarters in the Palais Royal. This suggestion was acted upon immediately. 'He might have been kept in safety at the Bank,' remarked Saint-Simon afterwards, 'but I thought the Palais Royal would be better; also that his retirement there would create more effect and induce the Regent to hold firm to his purpose, besides allowing His Royal Highness to see the financier whenever he pleased.'

As events turned out the extraordinary measures for Law's protection did not last long. The Regent had determined on a bold stroke to silence the Parliament for good and during the next fortnight preparations were hurried forward in secret. This was the summoning of a special meeting of Parliament known as a Bed of Justice (*Lit de Justice*) at which the King presided and personally directed the Parliament to approve any measures he thought fit. It was necessary to organize the occasion secretly, sending out invitations as if for an ordinary meeting, since it was thought that if it were known that a Bed of Justice were intended many members would decline to attend and others might prevail upon the King to change his mind. The King's objection to the heat was made the excuse for holding the session in the Tuileries palace.

The coup was brought off according to plan on the morning of August 25. As soon as the 'parliamentary gentlemen' had taken their places in the assembly, guards were posted round the building and throughout the grounds of the palace to prevent any of the members from leaving. Even those who desired to withdraw momentarily in order to relieve the necessities of nature were kept under strict observation during this operation. In this quasi-comic atmosphere the Bed of Justice was held and the King's wishes made known from the steps of the throne. By royal command the sixty-nine members of Parliament present in their red robes were adjured to keep within strict bounds of authority – in effect their right of remonstrance was annulled and their power broken. They had the good sense to accept the situation with a becoming air of resignation. Henceforth the Regent was to have little further trouble from them.

The director of the *Banque Générale* had had a harrowing escape, but the incident had revealed one thing to him. He felt that he could depend on the Regent not to sacrifice him to popular clamour, no matter how pressing and vociferous it might become. He knew now more or less where he stood. 'Monsieur Law is worthy of praise on account of his cleverness, but it must be confessed that he is detested in this country,' wrote the Regent's mother shortly after the decisive Bed of Justice had taken place. 'My son is charmed by his cleverness in business.'

6

If the effectual suppression of the Parliament had removed a dangerous threat to Law's life, it had also removed a serious obstacle in the way of D'Argenson pursuing his own financial schemes which, as we have seen, were motivated by intense jealousy of the successful banker. The minister now cast about for means to promote a rival undertaking which would ruin both the *Banque Générale* and the *Compagnie d'Occident*. He found them in the persons of four brothers named Paris, sons of a poor innkeeper in Dauphiné, who had enriched themselves during the late war when they had obtained an army contract to provision the troops. As private bankers the Paris brothers had more recently been entrusted with the execution of the hated *visa* or inspection of individual accounts, so that they possessed an intimate and detailed knowledge of all revenue matters.

As has also been seen, tax collecting was farmed out to individual collectors who paid a lump sum for the privilege, recouping themselves as best they could in the process of collection. A new finance minister was in the habit of renewing these leases to the tax-farmers when he assumed office, since he invariably received a handsome money perquisite for this mark of official favour. On this occasion the Paris brothers had secured the leases in return for the payment of an annual sum of 48 million livres, the leases being nominally held by their agent, a man named Lambert, who was in fact D'Argenson's valet. The brothers then proceeded to form a company to farm the taxes with a capital equivalent to that of the Company of the West (100 millions). Like Law's venture too the shares were to be paid for in state bonds which, as discredited government obligations, stood at a heavy discount, and they were to bear interest at 4 per cent. The total amount of the share capital was offered by the promoters as security for the annual payment under the lease, which the Treasury could not well refuse to accept seeing that the security in question emanated from itself. The shareholders were to participate in any profits or losses made, and the company's books were thrown open for subscription by the public.

Just as Law's projects had by this time come to be known popularly as 'The System', so the tax-farming venture sponsored by D'Argenson and the Paris brothers received the nickname of 'The Anti-System'. In reality the latter was a dangerous rival to Law's companies. The Anti-System's profits seemed better assured than those from the projected development of the Mississippi region, and unlike the Company of the West there was no reservation of the first year's share dividends as working capital. The Paris brothers were known to be shrewd men of business and energetic capitalists who would unquestionably strive hard to make their project yield handsome returns. Law realized that the Anti-System, while operating to the pecuniary advantage of its promoters and the shareholders, would be disastrous for the country at large were it allowed to develop unhindered. Somehow, he determined, it must be countered, for it must never be forgotten that Law always endeavoured to associate the state with his enterprises. In this instance the problem was far from easy, particularly since the shares of the tax-farming company had found greater favour with the public and were being more eagerly subscribed than those of the Company of the West.

First, it seemed to Law that other more powerful methods must be found to attract the public to his colonial scheme. To this end he induced the Regent to increase the trading concessions which the Mississippi company enjoyed. The monopoly of the manufacture and sale of tobacco was made over to the company for four million livres yearly, for fifteen years.[1] A little later the French African trading corporation, the Company of Senegal, was acquired and absorbed together with all its assets and other stock in trade. But in spite of these additional advantages the Mississippi company's shares still remained below par.

Secondly, Law proceeded to use the Anti-System as an instrument for obtaining a change in the bank's constitution which he had advocated for some time. This was its conversion from a private into a state institution. Such a change, it will be remembered, he had proposed in his original scheme which had been rejected by the Regency Council shortly after Louis XIV's death. For over a year, he had argued with the Regent that the *Banque Générale* had become a repository for royal funds to such an extent that it was anomalous that its administration should continue to be in the hands of private individuals as the directors and shareholders were. A series of conferences was held in the Palais Royal from which D'Argenson was excluded until the last when the decision was finally taken. As from January 1, 1719, the *Banque Générale* was to cease to be a private corporation and was to become a government concern under the title of *Banque Royale*, to be administered in the name and under the authority of King Louis XV. The original shareholders were paid off in full – in specie – a profitable form of compensation for them since they had subscribed their holdings in state bonds, of which capital only a quarter had been fully paid up. In short, the bank was nationalized. But Law remained director, in which office he was confirmed by royal edict. At the same time branches of the bank were declared established in a number of provincial towns – Lyons, Rochelle, Tours, Orleans and Amiens – but it was significant that none of these possessed a local Parliament, like Marseilles, for instance, where otherwise hostile demonstrations against the bank might have been stimulated.

The government likewise became responsible for the bank's note issue in circulation which at the time of the nationalization edict stood at about 12,000,000 livres.[2] To facilitate arrangements for

[1] Although said to be twice what the previous *concessionaire* had paid, this relatively low sum shows how small was the use of tobacco at that time.

[2] This figure, which I accept, is that given by the French economist

a substantial increase in the note issue which the government now had in view, an extremely important and significant difference was introduced which affected the convertibility of the notes. Hitherto the notes had been payable in bank money (*écus de banque*) 'of the weight and standard of the day'. In future notes were to be payable either in this currency or else in current coins (*livres tournois*) which were subject to arbitrary changes in value due to the recoinage which the government carried out from time to time. Although theoretically given the choice between the two forms of specie when exchanging their notes, the public in practice were obliged to take *livres tournois*. Thus instead of being based on specie of fixed and unvarying value the notes were subject to changes in value dependent on the fluctuations of the current coinage. At the same time the first step was taken towards the achievement of an inconvertible paper currency. By royal edict all payments above 600 livres were to be made in gold or notes – not silver. As there was very little gold in the country at the time, this amounted to an enforced circulation of the notes.

It seems clear from a study of contemporary authorities and documents that Law, far from having these changes forced on him by a despotic ruler as has sometimes been supposed, was himself the warmest advocate of the new form of currency and other accompanying measures. He was so thoroughly convinced of the superior merits of paper to metal that, now confidence in the bank's notes had become more widespread, he felt that further wonders in the shape of financial and commercial rehabilitation could be achieved by making the use of the notes virtually compulsory and at the same time pursuing a policy of gentle inflation. Doubts as to the bank's credit having been removed, he could thus afford to abandon the old form of note in favour of an instrument capable of enjoying a much greater circulation. In April, 1719, an edict was issued by which it was sought to fix the

---

Eugène Daire in his introduction to his edition of Law's writings, published in his *Economistes-Financiers du XVIII Siècle* (1843), rather than the higher figure of 51 million or more given by Levasseur and other writers. For the somewhat intricate line of reasoning by which Daire is believed to have arrived at 12 million, the interested reader should consult the able and informative article, 'An Historical Study of Law's System', by Andrew McFarland Davis in *The Quarterly Journal of Economics*, vol. I (Boston, Mass., 1883), at p. 312.

value of the notes by exempting them from any 'augmentations' or 'diminutions' which the coinage of the realm might undergo. It has been stated by the contemporary Forbonnais and other writers that Law was opposed to this exemption, not wishing the bank's notes on their face to possess any features which would make them preferable to coin. However, the fact remains that he was to adapt this new feature of the notes to his own purposes – in other words, applying the lesson he had learned many years previously in Scotland, he was to utilize the announcement of impending 'diminutions' to attract specie to the bank in exchange for notes.

Law had now achieved a position of some consequence as well as notoriety in the country with which he had entirely identified all his personal interests and ambitions. By a series of skilful manœuvres he had succeeded in establishing a place for himself in French banking and commerce as well as at court. The time had now come for him to stimulate public interest in his schemes on an extended scale. He hoped to make the people of France both rich and happy. This object he realized could be better promoted on the vast scale he had in view by state control of finance and industry rather than by private enterprise. In the endeavour, which was now beginning, he must be considered far in advance of his age.

Money and Trade

CONSIDERED,

WITH A

PROPOSAL

For Supplying the NATION with MONEY.

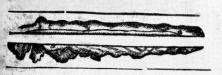

EDINBURGH,

Printed by the Heirs and Successors of *Andrew Anderson*, Printer to the Queens most Excellent Majesty, *Anno* DOM. 1705.

Title Pages of First and Second Editions of *Money and Trade Considered*

MONEY

AND

TRADE

CONSIDER'D;

WITH A

PROPOSAL

For SUPPLYING the

NATION with MONEY.

By Mr. JOHN LAW, *now Director of the Royal Bank at* Paris.

The SECOND EDITION.

LONDON:

Printed for *W. Lewis*, near the *Piazza* in *Russel-Street, Covent-Garden.* 1720.

John Law and Lady Catherine Law.
From contemporary anonymous engravings

CHAPTER V

THE DIRECTOR

By the spring of 1719 the Company of the West had been in existence for eighteen months, but its shares had never at any time during this period risen to par. Although they stood higher than the *billets d'état* in the market, they were nevertheless at a considerable discount in terms of current money. Indeed it was the aim of the brothers Paris and the other promoters and protagonists of the Anti-System to keep them in that condition indefinitely. It was now becoming abundantly clear to Law that he must adopt some bold course of action if he was to succeed in gaining the interest of the man-in-the-street in his ambitious colonial scheme. The card which he now proceeded to play was designed to captivate the public imagination completely, and it was as novel as it was daring for those times. He purchased the right to 'call' for two hundred shares of the Company at par in six months' time, the 500-livre shares then being at a discount of approximately 50 per cent. That is to say, in six months he undertook to pay their holders 100,000 livres, the par value of the shares, although their market value was only about 50,000 livres at the time of his offer. Furthermore he deposited a sum of 40,000 livres as earnest of his good faith which was to be forfeited if he failed to take up the shares at the agreed date.

This action on Law's part, which obtained the widest publicity, introduced to the French stock market for the first time in its history what is generally known today as dealings in futures. In the France of that day they were known as *primes* or *policies*. Such transactions had been known to London brokers for some years but were entirely novel to the French. Law's object, of course, was to promote speculative dealings in the Company's shares and thereby attract public attention to the concern. In the event he fully succeeded. The shares gradually rose to par, and before all Law's contracts had matured they were worth ten times their par value. Law's apparent recklessness reaped a liberal reward for his own pocket and enhanced his personal reputation.[1] Indeed as a stockjobbing operation it has been seldom if ever equalled in the history of speculation. To a people inexperienced in the methods of stockjobbing, however, Law now began to assume in the eyes of the public the qualities of a wizard wielding a magical power in finance. People argued that if the Director-General of the Company made such a purchase it was because he possessed advance information of the Company's potential profits and the further privileges it must shortly receive from the government of the Regent and Louis XV.

But in promoting the Company's welfare Law did not trust solely to the effect of the 'calls' which he had purchased. He had already secured tobacco and other commercial monopolies for the concern: to these were now added, by favour of the Regent, the two remaining French trading corporations of substance which had not yet been absorbed in the Mississippi Scheme – the East India Company and the China Company – whose property and commercial rights were transferred to Law's company. The Company of the West was now renamed the Company of the Indies, but to contemporaries as to posterity it continued to be known as the Mississippi Company. For this tremendous undertaking Law painted a future in the rosiest of colours. An enormous capital united in one vast corporation, which controlled the markets of the world and whose ships sailed the seven seas, was bound, he argued, to produce results commensurate with the magnitude of the undertaking. He likewise predicted enormous profits which, he pointed out, when distributed among the multiple body of shareholders, must enrich a great part of the

---

[1] On January 3, 1720, the younger Count D'Argenson wrote: 'My father has just relinquished the portfolio of finance, which has been placed in the hands of M. Lass [*sic*] under the title of Controller-General. He only lacked the title, all the administration of the office having been in his hands for the past few months, and it only remained for my father to surrender a title which had become quite bereft of any official duties.' See Comte E. de Barthelemy, *Les Correspondants de la Marquise de Balleroy*, II, 99 (Paris, 1883).

community. It is true that no business corporation at any time in previous history had such possibilities in view as this company. America, Africa, Asia, India, and China were all within its vast field of monopolistic enterprise, and there is no doubt that its commercial prospects were boundless. What was needed in the management of this huge corporation was public confidence and the slow and steady development and building up of business. Unfortunately these qualities were not destined to be combined in relatively satisfactory quantities.

Fresh capital was necessary for the new venture, and to this end the government authorized the issue of 50,000 shares of the par value of 500 livres for public subscription. The shares were offered for sale at a premium of 10 per cent and were made payable in twenty monthly instalments of 5 per cent each. On depositing the amount of the premium and one monthly payment anyone could receive an allotment. In other words, the price per 500-livre share was 550 livres, and by paying 75 livres in cash the investor was allotted a single share. Before the second monthly payment was due the price of the shares had advanced to 1,000 livres with the result that on his original cash investment of 75 livres the specu-lator who sold out netted a profit of 450 livres or 600 per cent.[1] On the other hand, the investor who purchased his share at a single cash payment received a bonus of 10 per cent, and this attractive device added to the amounts derived from the initial monthly payments placed a sum of more than 25 millions in specie in Law's hands.

Perplexed by these operations which it did not understand, Parliament refused to register the edict which authorized the incorporation of the new company. This refusal impeded the Company's business for several weeks, but eventually on June 17, 1719, the Regency Council published a decree giving it the force of law notwithstanding the opposition of Parliament. A few days later another decree was published, inspired by the fact that the price of the shares in the old company (the Company of the West), although steadily rising, was still not advancing fast enough for Law's desire. By this new decree Law provided that for each

---

[1] By deducting the amount of the 19 remaining monthly payments (i.e. 475 livres) from 1,000, the speculator received 525 livres per share, which, allowing for the 75 livres he had originally put down, left him with a profit of 450 livres.

single share in the new company every intending purchaser must henceforth possess four shares in the old. Thus in order to obtain ten shares in the Company of the Indies it was now necessary to possess forty in the Company of the West. The old shares were soon popularly known as 'mothers' (*mères*) and the new ones as 'daughters' (*filles*). The effect of the new decree was precisely as Law had anticipated. There was an immediate run on the old shares which sent up their market value by leaps and bounds. The issue of the *filles* was soon over-subscribed, while the *mères* continued to change hands in an ever rising market and indeed were sought for almost at any price.

Meanwhile the Company obtained further commercial advantages from the government. The exclusive rights of farming the Alsatian salt mines and trading with the Barbary States were followed by the grant of the profits of the royal mint for a term of nine years. To furnish the 50 million livres which the King demanded in return for the right of coinage a further issue of 50,000 shares was made at 1,000 livres per share, although their par value was 500 livres. Like the *filles* the purchase price of these latest shares was payable in instalments, but in order to subscribe the investor was required to possess four *mères* and one *fille* for each new share allotted. Shares of this issue became known as grand-daughters (*petites-filles*), and now that something approaching a frenzy of speculation had seized the French public, these young ladies were soon in more eager demand than had been the case with their parents whose value of course they served to enhance. Throughout the summer of 1719 the price of all the Mississippi stock rose with bewildering rapidity, and shares which had been quoted at 1,000 livres in July touched five times that amount by September.

It was at this time that Law embarked on a new series of speculative operations, which was to crown the success of his System. It will be remembered that the Paris brothers, promoters of the Anti-System, had in the previous year obtained for their nominee Lambert, former valet of the minister D'Argenson, the contract for the collection of all the taxes in the realm in return for an annual payment of $48\frac{1}{2}$ millions. Law now undertook to pay 52 millions if the contract were transferred to the Company of the Indies, and at the same time to lend the King 1,200 millions in order to liquidate all the state's debts. On these terms Lambert's contract was cancelled and the Company became responsible for the collection of all the royal revenues and virtually the sole creditors of the government. Thus the Anti-System was overthrown and Law took a sweet revenge on his enemies. In order to raise the agreed 1,200 millions (subsequently increased to 1,500 millions when it was ascertained that the original sum stipulated was insufficient to extinguish the whole of the government's liabilities), the Company was authorized to issue 300,000 shares of 500 livres each in the shape of 3 per cent annuities (*rentes*). Payment for the *cinq-cents*, as this further issue was known, was to be in ten monthly instalments, of which the first was payable in cash and the remainder in state-notes (*billets d'état*). Thus, too, the old *rentiers* suddenly found themselves deprived of practically all outlets for investment except those which led up to the 'System'.

It was now announced that the capital of the Company was complete and that no further issues would be made. In point of fact a final unauthorized issue of 24,000 shares was made almost immediately afterwards. This brought the total issue to 624,000 shares of a nominal value of 312 millions but, owing to all the shares being sold at a premium, except those in the original Company of the West, of an actual value nearly six times that amount, approximately 1,800 millions. With receipts estimated at 82 million livres yearly the Company might have paid a dividend of 130 livres on each 500-livre share, or 16 per cent, a most handsome dividend in ordinary circumstances. But for the multitude of investors, who had paid 5,000 livres a share, this would only represent a dividend of a fraction over $1\frac{1}{2}$ per cent, and Law was determined that the Company should declare a dividend of at least 200 livres per share, or 4 per cent in these abnormal circumstances. In his desire to enrich the vast community of small investors by this means, he was led further to excite, by various manœuvres and manipulations of the market, the stockjobbing fever which was already rapidly and dangerously raising the temperature of the French body commercial. In this manner his name was to become inseparably linked with what must surely rank as the greatest speculative mania of all time.

2

Besides the methods already described, speculation in the shares of the Company of the Indies received a strong impetus from the glowing reports of conditions in the Mississippi region which by this time were enjoying a wide circulation. The attractions of the colony were dexterously 'puffed' among all sections of the vast credulous and gullible French public. Louisiana, as the area was now beginning to be called, was represented as a veritable Paradise, whose savage inhabitants both male and female invariably welcomed their new masters with every mark of respect and affection. The natives were depicted as kneeling before a Jesuit priest and crying out for baptism, although one of these religious missionaries in fact declared that they were quite ready to be baptized ten times a day for a glass of brandy. There were mountains full of gold and silver and other precious minerals, lumps of which the natives, knowing nothing of their true value, were ready to exchange for such European manufactures as knives, looking-glasses and of course alcohol. It was also reported that far up the Arkansas river was an enormous emerald rock of fabulous value, and an expedition was promptly fitted out to survey it. (The expedition journeyed seven hundred miles upstream but failed to find any emeralds.) A contemporary map showed many mines which today, nearly two and a half centuries later, remain undiscovered. One contemporary writer, at the height of the boom in the Company's shares, declared that Louisiana was an island, and another pamphleteer of the time, who wrote for the benefit of the ladies of Louis XV's court, asserted, doubtless not without some justification, that few of them probably knew whether Mississippi was a continent, an island or a river.

The truth was that Louisiana was as yet a scarcely habitable desert, the area near the Mississippi's mouth being ravaged by yellow fever and the territory of its upper reaches by various Indian tribes. However, some conscientious attempts at colonization were made at this time, and settlements were granted by the Company to various prominent Frenchmen on condition that they populated them with immigrants. Law himself took a reservation in Arkansas and despatched thither a colony of Germans which he had recruited in the Rhenish Palatinate. But these means were found to provide an insufficient number of colonists, and so recourse was had to the methods of the press-gang. By an edict of June, 1719, vagabonds, tramps and domestic servants, who remained out of employment for longer than four days, could all be transported to the Mississippi. At the same time the hospitals and prisons were combed for prostitutes, since there was an acute shortage of women in the new colony, and it was felt that the fertility of the race might be encouraged by the importation of groups of these unfortunate females. The first boat-load which arrived in Louisiana was eagerly seized upon by the male colonists on the spot, and after they had been inspected to the satisfaction of their future husbands its contents were carried off satisfactorily to the marriage bed, although a dispute between two claimants for the hand of the last woman to be disembarked was only with difficulty resolved by lot in preference to armed encounter. The prospective wives, whose favours were thus so eagerly desired, in most cases turned out disappointingly since they were quite unsuited to the primitive conditions of colonial life, so that subsequent cargoes were disposed of much less rapidly than the first. Still, most of them did eventually find homes of a kind.

Complaints were received by the directors of the Company of the loose methods of life as well as venereal diseases introduced into Louisiana by the latest immigrants, and it was decided in future to send out married colonists. Here again the arrangements were carried out with more haste than discretion on the part of the authorities responsible. In September, 1719, 180 brides were married at a mass wedding to as many young men who had just been released from prison. Contrary to the previous practice the girls were allowed to choose their husbands, and after the ceremony the couples marched through the streets of Paris in circumstances which fairly astonished the onlookers. Each partner was bound to his fellow by an iron chain, but whether this precaution was adopted to prevent possible escapes, or merely to emphasize the nature of the unions which had just been solemnized, it is impossible to determine. In subsequent spectacles of a similar character chains of flowers were, with somewhat better taste, substituted for those of iron, while Law personally selected a number of young men and maidens of good character from one hospital and promised them each a dowry if they would undertake to commence a new life together in Louisiana. But the capital continued for some time to be treated to the scarcely edifying spectacle of *'demoiselles de moyenne vertu'*, as the chronicler Buvat described them, bedecked with ribbons and cockades, being driven in carts through the city preparatory to their departure for the New World. Travelling conditions were far from comfortable for the emigrants on the road to the port of embarkation as well as on board ship, and they were often barbarously treated, being shut up at night like cattle and given little or no food to sustain them on the journey. It is scarcely surprising that the numbers of casualties in such circumstances should have been alarmingly high.

The most objectionable feature of this enforced exodus, which amounted to deportation, was the opportunities which it provided to evil-minded individuals for the gratification of personal and family jealousies and animosities. Unscrupulous members of all classes of the community showed remarkable eagerness to rid themselves of inconvenient relatives, and the authorities were inundated with requests for the removal to the Mississippi of allegedly delinquent brothers and sisters, children and even spouses. Wives accused their husbands of being vagabonds and vice versa, and petty officials were frequently bribed to sign the necessary declarations. Squads of archers dressed in blue uniforms and known as the 'Mississippi gangsters' (*bandouliers du Mississippi*) roamed the countryside as well as the streets of towns and villages, in search of likely recruits for colonial service, and there is no doubt that numbers of harmless citizens were apprehended and shipped across the ocean as a result of the depredations of these press-gangs. The process culminated in the case of a Paris butcher named Quoniam, which caused a grave scandal in the capital and led to the *'bandouliers'* being placed under police supervision.

The butcher Quoniam, a man ripe in years and rich in substance, had the misfortune to be married to a young and good-looking woman who consoled herself in the traditional manner for her husband's lack of interest in her as a wife. Indeed her ways were so caressing that she had a host of lovers who were in the habit of coming to 'roast their love', as the saying went, at her husband's shop. One night, seeing her husband asleep before the fire, the frail Madame Quoniam admitted a particular satin-coated gallant, who was her favourite of the moment, and conducted him upstairs to her bedroom. Hearing a noise which woke him from his slumber and thinking that his wife had retired for the night, the worthy Quoniam went up to join her. On entering the room his eyes fell on the gallant whom he immediately took to be a burglar or perhaps worse. His first impulse was to run to the window and shout: 'Thieves! Murder!' He then ran downstairs to the front door still shouting and intending, as he thought, to summon the watch. At this moment the Mississippi press-gang happened to be passing along the street outside, and hearing cries of 'Thief!' within, they proceeded to surround the house, determined to arrest the supposed delinquent. By this time the cries had been vigorously echoed by Madame Quoniam and her lover, who realized at Madame's prompting that his only hope of escape from his unfortunate predicament was a pretended zeal for the prosecution of justice. The result was that when the butcher opened the door he was taken to be the thief and immediately seized by the gang. When Madame and the gallant appeared, both clad only in their underwear, the faithless wife profusely thanked the gang for apprehending a dangerous night marauder, pointing to the butcher's knife which hung from Quoniam's belt as evidence of his evil intentions. 'A moment later,' she added, nodding in the direction of her lover who had picked up a basting ladle, 'my husband would have put him on the fire.' To the accompaniment of peals of laughter from the deceitful lover and his mistress the unfortunate butcher, still slightly dazed and somewhat bewildered at this turn of events, was dragged away to the Châtelet prison. No heed was paid to his repeated protests, and in a short time he found himself on the way to the Mississippi.

To John Law must be attributed a share in the responsibility for the errors and injustices which accompanied these early attempts at colonization in Louisiana. But for one significant colonial feature, however he deserves credit. In 1719, on Law's instructions, the foundations of a new town were laid on a wide bend of the Mississippi river, just over a hundred miles from its mouth. The work was carried out by twenty-four convicted salt smugglers under the supervision of the colony's governor, Jean Baptiste Lemoyne, Sieur de Bienville. For some years the settlement remained little more than a collection of miserable wooden cabins in a malarial swamp infested with snakes and alligators.

But Law boldly predicted an imperial future for it. His foresight was amply justified, since today it ranks in size of population among the first dozen cities of the United States. The financier decided to name the new town after his patron and the patron of the Mississippi Company, and it has remained as perhaps the sole tangible memorial of the Regent's indolent and sybaritic rule – New Orleans.

3

For the Paris headquarters of the Mississippi Company Law had purchased the magnificent Mazarin Palace, lying between the Rue de Richelieu and the Rue Neuve-des-Petits-Champs, from the descendants of Louis XIII's great cardinal-minister. The price paid for this property is stated to have been one million livres. He also acquired six houses in the adjacent Rue Vivienne which he intended should become the premises of a large bourse or stock exchange as well as for the General Post Office. About the same time he transferred the *Banque Royale* from the hotel which it had occupied for the past three years in the Rue Sainte Avoie to a more luxurious establishment in the Rue de Richelieu, known as the Hôtel de Nevers. Extensive structural alterations were carried out by a well-known architect of the time named Mollet so as to suit these buildings to their new requirements, while the interior decoration was undertaken by Antonio Pellegrini, brother-in-law of the celebrated Rosalba. In the event the new premises came to cover a considerable area which corresponds approximately to the large square and surrounding buildings occupied today by the National Library of France.

It was from the spacious offices in the Rue Vivienne that the later and more spectacular issues of Mississippi stock were made. The final 324,000 shares, nominally offered at 5,000 livres each, were really put up for auction. Wild scenes ensued as a result of this proceeding. As soon as an issue had been announced a solid phalanx of anxious and impatient subscribers would form outside the issuing office staggering under the weight of the bags which they brought with them. They would spend whole days and nights there in their eagerness to exchange their money for the shares of the Company, and they remained seemingly undeterred by hunger and thirst and lack of sleep. Then, as soon as the news was given out that the last share in the issue had been allotted, the crowd would suddenly break up and melt away in a few moments, the unsatisfied hurrying off to bargain with their more fortunate fellows on the subscription list. Needless to add, this vast increase of stock was accompanied by a corresponding currency inflation, and during the latter half of the year 1719, when the rage for speculation was at its height in Paris, the bank issued notes to the face value of over 800 million livres. In other words, in order to float the new issues Law resorted to unbridled inflation.

The speculative dealings in the Mississippi Company's stock, which became notorious at this time, were carried on in a different district of the town. In the old medieval quarter between Rue St. Martin and the Rue St. Denis there lay a narrow street, not more than 150 yards long by five or six wide, called the Rue Quincampoix, which for many years had fulfilled the functions of an exchange. Since the days of Louis XIV this alley had been the recognized centre of transactions in state bonds, annuities and other securities. It now became the scene of the most fantastic operations ever recorded in the history of stockjobbing. It was here that the Mississippi shares changed hands at ever rising prices, and enormous profits were made daily by the more fortunate speculators. Early in the Mississippi boom it became necessary to enclose each end of the street by gates and to restrict commercial business to the hours of daylight, so that the inhabitants of the neighbourhood might sleep at night undisturbed by the cries of jobbers and brokers. One of the gates was reserved for the nobility and persons of quality and the other for the general public, but once inside all distinctions of rank were lost in the motley crowd of speculators shouting, gesticulating, waving papers and counting out money. Punctually at eight o'clock each morning the gates were opened to the roll of drums and the mob admitted; all vehicles were excluded and everyone was obliged to enter on foot. Princes, priests and doctors of the Sorbonne rubbed shoulders with shopkeepers and confidence tricksters.

The prevailing frenzy encouraged speculation of a subsidiary character. Fabulous rents were demanded and willingly paid for rooms in the Rue Quincampoix's few houses – some fetching as much as 400 livres a month. Every square inch from cellars to attics was occupied by the Mississippians, as the share dealers were

popularly known, and enterprising landlords even erected wooden
hutches on the roofs for the convenience of these lucrative
tenants. Most business, however, was transacted in the open high-
way by the interested parties, and even here those who could
facilitate this intercourse by the most trifling services reaped
rich rewards. A cobbler is said to have earned 200 livres a day
from supplying pens and paper to passers-by, allowing them to
sit down and settle their business in his booth. Others derived
handsome profits by letting out their backs as desks. A hunchback
is said to have netted no less than 150,000 livres from this ingenious use of his hump, while a soldier who possessed unusually
broad shoulders is said similarly to have made sufficient to enable
him to obtain his discharge from the army and purchase a pretty
estate in the country, whither he retired to spend his remaining
days in comfort. Caterers likewise cleared enormous sums from the
sale of their provisions. One speculator, having just disposed of
some shares at a considerable profit, is reported to have paid 200
livres (£14) for a partridge. Foreigners as well as provincials
flocked to the capital in search of fortunes and seats in stage
coaches from such cities as Brussels, Strasbourg and Bordeaux
were engaged up to two months in advance. Needless to say, a
lively business went on in coach tickets.

This amazing 'bull' market developed in the summer of 1719
and continued until the spring of the following year; 500-livre
shares, which were quoted at par in May, 1719, were sold for
5,000 livres in September and by the end of the year fetched
15,000 livres. Since the market was uncontrolled by any rules of
business, fluctuations were naturally much more violent than in
latter-day speculations, and there is no doubt that the Mississippi
market did on occasion react with extreme violence during this
period, although no official record of transactions was maintained. The story is told of the Regent's physician Chirac who
learned, while on his way to see a female patient, that the price of
the Mississippi stock was dropping. He could think of nothing
else, and even while holding the lady's pulse was heard to exclaim:
'My God, it falls! It falls!' much to the consternation of the patient
and her family whom the doctor was compelled to reassure that
she was not, as they all thought, on the point of death. When the
shares recovered they invariably rose to a higher price than any
at which they had been quoted hitherto. While shares commonly

sold for 15,000 livres at the height of the boom, there is authority
for the statement that they did sometimes change hands at prices
in excess of this figure; 20,000 livres is said to have been paid
by one speculator, and this exceptional figure probably constituted the record, showing as it does an advance of 4,000 per
cent on the price at par. When the astonishing rise in the price of
shares generally is considered, it will be seen that 20,000 livres of
shares purchased in 1718 would have realized nearly 2 millions
a year later. Towards the end of 1719 many speculators made
1,000 per cent on their investments inside a month.

In this fantastic period immense fortunes were acquired, sometimes at little risk or even at no risk at all. Agents who were sent
to dispose of shares at the latest quotation would wait until the
shares had risen so many points, then conclude their purchase and
pocket the difference. According to one story, a servant who was
sent by his master to sell shares at 8,000 had no difficulty in
finding a purchaser at 10,000, and proceeded himself to speculate
with the profit he had made on this deal. In a few days he
was reputed to be worth a million. Another individual who was
given some money to pay a debt bought some shares with money
in the afternoon and then went to dine in a restaurant near the
Rue Quincampoix. After he had finished his meal he discovered
that the price of shares had advanced by 11 per cent; he sold out
at a profit of 40,000, discharged the debt and kept the surplus.
Other stories were equally amazing. A valet is said to have made
fifty millions and a boot-black forty. Many of the successful
speculators invested their profits in precious stones. 'Large quantities of diamonds and jewels have been sent to Paris from England,' noted the Regent's mother at this time, 'and people who
have gained enormously on the shares buy without bargaining.'
One night a lady, who went to the opera, discovered her cook
in the next box clothed in the most costly dress and covered with
diamonds. 'Well, what about it?' exclaimed the cook in response
to her mistress's incredulous stare. 'I have become rich and I
dress up out of my wealth. I owe nothing to anyone. I like
dressing up, so I dress up. That hurts no one. What objection
can you have to that?'

In this fantastic age it was a commonplace for servants to
become as rich and indeed richer than their masters and mistresses.
The story is told of one coachman, who became wealthy as the

result of his visits to the Rue Quincampoix, retiring from service and engaging a coach of his own. The first time it drove up for him, however, he forgot his new role and inadvertently mounted the box in his old position. Law's own coachman was enriched in this way, and appeared one morning before his master to whom he presented two possible successors. 'But I only require one of them,' said Law. 'Of course,' replied the quondam coachman who now appeared resplendent in a nobleman's clothes. 'The other I shall engage myself.'

One of the largest fortunes was made by a poor widow from the provinces named Chaumont. In 1717 she came to Paris in order to collect a debt. Her debtor could only offer her state bonds, which were then standing at a heavy discount. She accepted the offer in despair, feeling it was better than nothing. She immediately exchanged the bonds for Mississippi stock and when she sold out her holding three years later she was worth 100 millions. At Ivery, where she bought a château, the hospitality which she dispensed became almost proverbial. An ox, two calves, six sheep and innumerable fowls are said to have been consumed daily by a multitude of friends and servants, while champagne and burgundy flowed without restraint.

One feature of this seemingly fabulous era is worthy of record. A new word made its appearance in the French language, a word on everybody's lips which has now passed into our own tongue – millionaire – originally used to describe the fortunate 'Mississippian'. As the individual responsible for its origin John Law himself must be regarded as the first of a long line of millionaires. But the tangible benefits of his 'system' were not confined to a single class of persons; they were spread over the whole community. 'What rank of people and what profession has not shared in the riches that have arisen from the new System?' asked its author at this time. 'Lands and houses are at double, nay, treble the value to the seller, and will increase considerably in revenue to the purchaser. The military and civil officers receive their pensions or salaries, which they had lost all hopes of. The merchants and workmen have not enough to answer the demand of the buyers. The common people, and even those who by the meanness of their fortune can scarcely be ranked in any class, all of them in short find a way of life to thrive and enrich themselves.' Of course, as in other times and countries, much of the wealth of the Mississippi millionaire was illusory. 'It is inconceivable what immense wealth there is in France now,' wrote the perplexed Dowager Duchess of Orleans at the end of 1719. 'Everybody speaks in millions. I don't understand it at all, but I see clearly that the god Mammon reigns as an absolute monarch in Paris.'

4

The colossal boom in the shares of the Mississippi Company made its Director-General the most sought after and courted man in France. People would jostle each other in crowds simply to gain a glimpse of him. Lord Stair, the British ambassador, recorded how he saw hundreds of people of quality besieging the front of Law's house in the Place Vendôme, although the door was shut fast to all comers. According to Saint-Simon several succeeded in forcing an entry through the door, others got into the gardens at the back and entered through the windows, while the most enterprising spirits climbed on to the roof and dropped down the chimney into the master's study. 'Law is so run after that he has no rest day or night,' wrote the Regent's mother. 'A duchess kissed his hands before everyone, and if duchesses kiss his hands, what parts of him won't the other ladies salute?' In fact, as the Duchess of Orleans added in somewhat coarser language, if Law desired it, the women of France would willingly kiss his arse.

While the fortunate few who managed to gain admission to Law's house were content to wait for hours in the great man's antechamber in expectation of a few moments' audience, others resorted to a variety of subterfuges to realize their one aim and desire. One night, when the financier was dining out, a lady who had failed to obtain an invitation to the same dinner, stationed herself outside the house where the meal was taking place and made her coachman and footman shout 'Fire!' Everyone ran out of the house to see the supposed conflagration, including Law, but as soon as the persevering false-alarmist had sprung from her carriage to buttonhole him, he saw through the ruse and promptly disappeared. Another woman made her coachman deliberately upset the coach with herself inside it in the Place Vendôme, and when Law, who witnessed what he thought to be a genuine accident, had come to her assistance, she confessed that it was a ruse designed to procure an interview with him and the allotment of some stock. Other females abandoned all feelings of decency and delicacy in the pursuit of riches. On one occasion, when he had received several ladies in the course of a long day's interviews, he begged to be excused for a few minutes in order to attend to an urgent call of nature. '*Oh, si ce n'est que cela,*' they replied, '*cela ne fait rien. Pissez toujours, et écoutez-vous!*' In the result Law was obliged to relieve himself on the spot, while the ladies continued to converse with him throughout the operation.

An amusing incident occurred in the course of some crowded gathering when a woman approached Law for an allotment of shares. '*Faites-moi un concession,*' was what she intended to say. '*Ah, Monsieur,*' she said by a droll slip of the tongue, '*faites-moi, ie vous en prie, une conception.*'

Law found some difficulty in preserving his composure at this seeming request from a suitor to make her pregnant. '*Madame,*' he replied with a smile and a touch of characteristic wit, '*vous venez trop tard. Il n'y pas moyen à présent!*'

English and particularly Scottish visitors to the French capital at this time were amazed and delighted at the deference being universally shown to one of their fellow countrymen. That observant traveller, Lady Mary Wortley Montagu, has recorded this in one of her letters from Paris at this time. 'I must say I saw nothing in France that delighted me so much', she wrote on October 16, 1719, 'as to see an Englishman (at least a Briton) absolute at Paris; I mean Mr. Law, who treats their dukes and peers extremely *de haut en bas* and is treated by them with the utmost submission and respect.' Another visitor, the Earl of Islay, brother of Law's old friend the Duke of Argyll, was passed through the crowded antechamber without having to wait, as befitted a Scottish nobleman, and received in the inner sanctum. The financier was seen to be seated at his writing-table composing what his caller took to be despatches of the utmost importance. Somewhat to his surprise Lord Islay was informed, in answer to a query on the subject, that this was not so and that the financier was merely writing to the gardener at Lauriston with regard to the planting of some cabbages at a particular corner of the kitchen garden. When the epistle was finished, Law asked the visitor to play a hand of piquet, and the two men sat down to a game, which lasted a considerable time, before his Lordship departed and Law gave orders for his other callers, who had been waiting outside all this while, to be admitted.

Many suitors endeavoured to enlist Law's interest in their own pet commercial schemes. Among them was an old Irish friend of the financier's youth, jovial Dick Steele. They had first become acquainted when both had been young men about London town frequenting the coffee houses in St. James's. Steele had also fought a duel, but with happier results than the 'Beau' Wilson affray. He too had achieved a measure of success in life, having been elected a Member of Parliament, and received a knighthood, while his plays, which ran at Drury Lane Theatre, and the essays which he contributed to *The Tatler* and *The Spectator*, had permanently enriched the literature of England. But, like other politicians and men of letters, Sir Richard Steele had been induced to put money into an undertaking, whose advantages were more apparent than real, and he now attempted to persuade the Scotsman to take up the project in France. 'I believe you may have heard my name mentioned since I had the honour to converse with you', he wrote to Law on August 12, 1719, 'and therefore will not suppose you will have wholly forgot me. With this hope I enter upon the business of this letter with the less preface, and at once inform you that the King has given me his letters patent for the sole use of an invention for bringing fish alive and in good health, wherever taken, to any other part however distant. It is well known how ill Paris and other parts of France are supplied with that commodity, and it will soon occur to you what great advantage may be made of such a privilege given by the King of France for his dominions.'

This remarkable invention consisted of a floating pool or pond which Steele had, as he put it, 'under a great deal of ridicule and contempt of the greater, the unthinking part of the world', succeeded in embodying in a sloop of sixty-one tons. 'The thing itself is a service to the world in general and a merit to the whole species of men,' he continued, 'and not only to this or any other nation; and therefore I presume it is a request grounded upon the law of nature, that every country should distinguish those from whom they receive benefit without regard to the places of abode or nativity or the soil to which they are born subjects. You have too enlarged a view, and the prince whom you serve has too well shown (by his just regard and favour to you) the same magnanimity, to need much discourse on this occasion.' Steele concluded by begging Law and his brother William to become partners in what promised to be a most lucrative business. But he was not very sanguine of such distinguished patronage. 'Whatever befalls this application,' Steele added, 'I wish your great and noble genius the continuance of prosperous adventures.'

In truth John Law was far too occupied as the hero of the hour in France to waste time in such a dubious project as Dick Steele's 'fish pool'. 'He pays the late King's dreadful debts and lessens taxation,' wrote 'Madame' to a friend, 'thus lightening the burden which is weighing down the people. Wood costs only half what it did, and the import duties on wine, meat and everything consumed in Paris has been abolished. This causes great joy amongst the people, as you can easily imagine.' On November 25, 1719, Law paid a visit to the Rue Quincampoix in the company of several noblemen and their ladies and there he received an ovation such as had been seldom accorded to a reigning sovereign. This episode was the occasion of a practical joke perpetrated by the financial wizard of popular imagination for the diversion of his companions. From the window of his coach Law threw handfuls of golden guineas and other coins bearing the effigy of the English king William III to the surrounding multitude. '*Vive le roi et Monseigneur Law*,' people shouted from all sides. While courtiers and speculators struggled and grovelled on the ground for this booty, one of Law's party, who was stationed at an upper window in a nearby house, deposited several buckets full of water on top of the undignified scramblers below, who were soon, remarked the chronicler Buvat who witnessed the scene, 'in a condition which can be imagined'.

Law's personal profits from the current speculation, which he and his agents did everything within their power to encourage, were far from inconsiderable. What he did not reinvest in the Company, he laid out in the acquisition of real and personal estate in France. He also gave away vast sums to charity. His enemies were later to assert that he had 'deposited' large amounts in the banking houses of Amsterdam and Hamburg, but such allegations were entirely false. With the exception of one estate in Scotland, whose purchase was never completed, all his dealings of this kind were confined to the country of his adoption. Here, it must be admitted, his purchases were on an extremely prodigal scale. He bought over twenty landed properties in different parts of France at prices ranging from 90,000 livres to over a million. A number of these, such as the estate of Effiat in Auvergne, carried with it the title of marquis. Other acquisitions included a quantity of jewels, a library of some 45,000 volumes, a wine-cellar, and the place of King's Secretary – this latter office he purchased solely for the sake of the privileges of nobility attached to it. His private household and manner of living, though considerably enlarged, continued for the most part in the frugal Scottish tradition. Saint-Simon, as we have seen already, failed to find any traces of avarice in his character, and on the whole he considered him unspoiled by the great access of riches and reputation which his successful business operations had gained for him. One particularly coveted distinction he received at this time in the shape of his election to the French Academy, of which celebrated body he became a member in December, 1719.

Catherine and the children were likewise courted, and everyone from the highest in the land danced attendance upon them. Cardinal Bentivoglio, the papal nuncio, unbent so far as 'to play at dolls' with Law's daughter, while her brother was (not without some opposition on the part of the more conservative courtiers) invited to dance in a quadrille with the king. Both children received a number of advantageous offers of marriage, all of which, however, their parents refused.

That Law was anxious to obtain a measure of political power in his own hands there is little reason to doubt, but any political ambitions he may have had were for means of maintaining the success of the System rather than for mere love of power for its own sake. Lord Stair, who quarrelled with him at this time, complained to the Regent of his presumption and insolence. The Regent, whose admiration for Law's financial genius was beginning to wane a little, agreed that he had such a high opinion of his own abilities and such a contempt for the abilities of others as made him difficult for most ministers and officials to work with. The Regent went on to say that he knew him to be a man whose head had been turned by his vanity and unbounded ambition and that nothing would satisfy him now but to be absolute master. Orleans then admitted that, though he was bound to employ Law in the nation's finances, he was determined he should not be listened to in political affairs. Stair believed that the Regent said what he really thought, 'but with all that', the ambassador was obliged to admit, 'a great master of the treasury like Law is first minister wherever he is'.

The origin of Stair's difference with Law, which was to have a fatal effect upon the ambassador's diplomatic career, may be traced to the latter declining an opportunity to purchase a substantial block of Mississippi shares in the summer of 1719. 'I did not think it became the King's ambassador to give countenance to such a thing', Stair virtuously declared, 'or an example to others to withdraw their effects from England to put them into the stocks here, which would have been readily followed by many.' This refusal prompted Law to expatiate upon French prosperity and the fact that it depended to a large extent upon himself and his policy. From this moment Stair was convinced that Law was determined to become the first minister of France, and to place the country of his adoption above all others. 'He in all his discourse pretends he will set France much higher than ever she was before and put her in a condition to give the law to all Europe; that he can ruin the trade and credit of England and Holland whenever he pleases; that he can break our bank whenever he has a mind, and our East India Company. He said publicly the other day at his own table, when Lord Londonderry was present, that there was but one great kingdom in Europe, and one great town, and that was France and Paris.' The financier's guest on this occasion was Lord Londonderry, a son of Thomas Pitt with whom Law had recently negotiated the sale of the Regent Diamond. According to Stair, Law told him that he would force down the price of the British East India Company stock, and, as proof of his 'bear' intentions, he undertook to sell Londonderry £100,000 of the stock in twelve months' time at 11 per cent below the current price. 'You may imagine', wrote Stair afterwards to the English ministers in Whitehall, 'what we have to apprehend from a man of this temper, who makes no scruple to declare such views and who will have all the power and all the credit at this court.'

It is significant that, with one comprehensible exception, Law refused any honours and distinctions from sources outside France. When the Abbé Dubois, for example, offered to persuade King George I to send him the patent of a dukedom together with the Order of the Garter, he would not hear of it. He likewise turned down an offer of the rulership of the rich marble-producing duchy of Massa-Carrara in northern Italy, which seems to have been made at the instigation of the Austrian Emperor Charles VI. Another petty kingdom which he declined was the small island of Tabarca off the North African coast which was put at his disposal apparently by the Bey of Tunis and whither he might have retired in later years.

The only foreign distinction which he consented to receive at this time was the freedom of his native Edinburgh voted him by the city fathers. They were prompted to do this, as they readily admitted, not only by reason of the fact that the financier had been born in the shadow of St. Giles and was descended from the most respected burgesses, but also because of his 'making such a figure in the world as reflects honour not only upon this city but upon the Scots nation'. The charter was conveyed to him in a handsome gold casket, which also contained the most flattering inscription in Latin, by the hand of Robert Neilson, son of Edinburgh's Lord Provost. This service so recommended Neilson that Law subsequently appointed him his private secretary.[1] Having expressed the wish that some of those abilities which had proved so useful to France might sometime be employed to the advantage of his native country which knew not how to profit by the genius which it produced, this remarkable testimonial concluded with a happy comparison of the financier's achievements. 'To recover the dispersed coin of a nation, to retrieve its sagging trade, to ease it of oppresive taxes, to introduce new manufactures and relieve the indigent in the most generous manner, are actions so much more worthy of being recorded to posterity than the conquest of the most famous warriors, as doing good to mankind is better than destroying them.'

5

Although he held no political office, Law was in such a powerful position, as Director-General of the Company of the Indies as well as of the Royal Bank, that

[1] According to Wood (*Life of John Law* at p. 158) Neilson later went to Holland and there learned the art of linen bleaching which he was subsequently the first to introduce into Scotland.

he could virtually compel the Regency Council to implement the various measures of economic reform which he had in mind. Accordingly, in the autumn of 1719, when the Mississippi boom was at its height, he introduced a series of economic reforms, which was designed greatly to benefit the country and at the same time to enhance its author's personal popularity with the inhabitants. His first object was to establish unity and equality in national taxation instead of innumerable arbitrary imposts which were prodigiously expensive to collect. His idea was a single tax or 'royal tithe' (*denier royal*) based on income, to which everyone in the community should be liable. In consequence numerous petty offices extending to every branch of the country's economic life were abolished to the satisfaction of all except their holders, an operation which resulted in a considerable saving to the treasury. In Paris alone there were hundreds of cloth measurers, tallow controllers, hay trussers, coal measurers, meat inspectors and examiners of every commodity from wine barrels to pigs' tongues. In expropriating this useless bureaucratic horde Law earned the deep gratitude of the French people, since the fees which these officials were entitled to charge by virtue of their offices added greatly to the prices which consumers were obliged to pay for the commodities concerned. As a result of Law's activities the retail prices of coal, wood, fish, corn, meat, poultry, eggs and other household necessaries were reduced by one-third.

But this was not the only amelioration of revenue. The duties on the transport of grain and foodstuffs from one province to another were abolished. The freeing of the hemp trade from similar restrictions was designed to afford an outlet for agriculture as well as to encourage spinning and weaving, which formed the main occupations of the poorer classes. Instead of receiving 4 per cent for their *rentes* held by the Mississippi Company, investors in state annuities henceforth received 3 per cent, the difference being applied to the tax reductions already described.[1] At the

---

[1] This debt conversion operation was bitterly opposed by Parliament, many of whose members were *rentiers*. Law, however, aimed at liquidating the *rentier* class which, since he was fundamentally a state socialist, he considered to be parasites. 'The easiness with which private persons found to purchase with a small sum a revenue sufficient for their purpose, because it brought them a great interest', he wrote in defence of the conversion, 'induced them to live in idleness and deprived the State of the service they might have done it in some useful profession, had they been obliged to

same time various public works projects were commenced at Law's instigation, notably the construction of barracks, canals and bridges. Hitherto citizens had been obliged to have troops billeted on them, and the provision of barracks constituted a much needed and popular relief. Nor was the commercial value of canals and bridges lost on Law. With one canal he even hoped to turn Paris into a port. 'They are working at a canal at Elboeuf', wrote the chronicler Buvat at this time, 'by means of which they expect to make the tide of the sea flow up the Seine to within a short distance of Paris, so as to render the river more navigable from that side and to carry goods on it at all times in abundance and less dear.'

There was seemingly no end to the benefits which flowed from the miraculous 'system'. The University of Paris was endowed with a portion of the revenues from the Post Office, ecclesiastical bodies were encouraged to sell their lands which had long been out of cultivation so that agriculture and the community at large might further benefit, arrangements were made for the migration of able-bodied beggars to the colonies, and a scheme of public assistance was introduced for the relief of the genuinely needy. In fact, it was proposed 'to establish hospitals at every six leagues where these poor people should be received, fed and taken care of by the inhabitants of the district, they being obliged to contribute according to each one's means'.

It was now generally expected that Law's signal services would be rewarded by some noteworthy mark of official recognition. There remained, however, one obstacle in the way of his employment in any public office. Although a naturalized French citizen the Director-General was still a Protestant and as such disqualified from holding any government appointment. His conversion being thus a condition precedent to his holding office, Law accordingly prepared to abjure the faith of his forefathers. The operation of receiving the financier into the Catholic Church was, on the advice of Dubois, entrusted to the Abbé Tencin whose sister, it will be remembered, was Dubois's mistress and is believed to have stood in the same relation to the proselyte. At all events Madame de Tencin appears to have acted as a willing intermediary in the

---

work. From hence commerce, which is the soul of the State, decayed . . .'
See *The Present State of the French Revenues and Trade* (London, 1720) at p. 22.

matter. Catherine Law suspected that she had a greater hand in the process than the Abbé, and this suspicion may have strengthened her decision not to follow the example of her husband and her children. According to 'Madame', the Duchess of Orleans, she was very much upset about the whole business. But this did not prevent its completion. It was originally intended that the formal ceremony of reception should take place in Paris, but the venue was changed to the neighbouring town of Melun when it became known that, if the ceremony were held in the capital, it might be disturbed by masquerades and other foolery on the part of the convert's ill-wishers. The public profession of the Roman Catholic faith was made at Melun on September 17, 1719. Law repeated the process less ostentatiously two months later in his parish church in Paris, the Abbé Tencin again officiating. For his services the Abbé is said to have received from the convert shares in the Mississippi Company to the value of 100,000 livres.

For Law, as it had been for the French King Henry IV two centuries previously, Paris was worth a mass, and in acting as they did both men were no doubt inspired by similar motives. But it cannot readily be admitted that Law's conversion and the circumstances attending it reflected much credit on any of the parties concerned. The notorious Abbé Tencin, who benefited to such an extent financially, was a man of scandalous morals; he was later convicted of simony and condemned to pay a large fine by the Parliament. The incident, although it enabled Law to gratify his ambition by opening the way to cabinet office, provoked by considerable opposition from his wife, who stoutly refused to follow his example. This was doubly unfortunate for the financier, since Catherine's husband Mr. Seigneur had recently died; and, but for Law's change of faith, it seems certain that they would have seized this opportunity to legalize their union by getting married, now that they were free to do so. Catherine, it appears, refused to join herself in matrimony with an apostate. As will be seen, they never did get married and, although Catherine continued to use his name and pass as his wife, she had no legal right to do so. As a general topic of conversation Law's conversion provided his enemies with a weapon of which they did not scruple to make full use. Lord Stair, in particular, went out of his way to attack Law, denouncing him both to the British Government and to the French Regent as a Jacobite, to whom all supporters of the Stuart Pretender's cause now looked for encouragement and support in their plans. This totally unfounded charge was to set the seal on Stair's diplomatic career. It is true that the Chevalier de St. George, as the late James II's son was known, had appealed to Law as 'a good Scotsman and faithful servant of the Regent', but the financier had refused to commit himself to any course of action calculated to jeopardize the alliance already existing between the governments of Louis XV and George I.

It was thus by no means all sunshine for John Law as his fortune neared its height, and storm clouds kept gathering on the horizon. More and more of the financier's enemies renewed their activities. About this time a plot was discovered to kill him. The circumstances are obscure, and Saint-Simon, who is the authority for this statement, does not elaborate it except to add that a guard of sixteen soldiers was assigned to Law for the protection of his person and household. A similar guard was provided for Law's younger brother William, who had come over from London shortly before this to assist in the management of the bank. Not much is known about William Law apart from the fact that he was four years younger than John; he had been a working goldsmith in Edinburgh, and later, after his migration to London, had at his brother's request acted as the bank's agent in the City. Besides a wife and considerable commercial knowledge William Law had brought with him to France numbers of craftsmen and artificers, particularly clock and watchmakers from Birmingham, whose arts and crafts the elder brother was anxious to introduce into the country of his adoption.

Animosity against the two brothers, even to the point of murder, may well have been encouraged by D'Argenson, whose retention of the office of Controller-General of Finance was a constant source of irritation to John Law and his friends, although the financier had succeeded in arrogating to himself most of the minister's official functions in the field of finance. D'Argenson, who also held the office of Keeper of the Seals, now began to experience the insecurity of his position. He knew, furthermore, that he was far from popular in the country. But he was also a man of good sense and a certain knowledge of the world, which he had acquired in the course of his long career as Chief of Police. He realized that if he persisted in clinging to the finance ministry he would probably end by losing not only that portfolio but the Seals as well. He thereupon took the hint and intimated his willingness to surrender the portfolio of finance. At last the road was open to the realization of Law's greatest ambition.

To silence any doubts which remained as to his change of faith, Law received the sacrament in the parish church of St. Roch in Paris on Christmas Day, 1719. At the same time he was appointed an honorary churchwarden, and, to mark the occasion suitably, he presented 500,000 livres to the church's building fund. His liberality at this time was indeed seemingly boundless. 'He is not avaricious', wrote the Regent's mother at this time, 'and gives lots of alms that are never talked about. He also gives away large sums of money and helps many poor people.'

As for his Catholicism he bore it lightly. With the frail Madame de Tencin, who claimed most of the credit for his conversion, he was altogether frank.

'Now that you belong to our communion,' she said to him, 'you can be saved . . .'

He interrupted her before she could finish her sentence.

'What is the good of saving myself?' he enquired with cynical jocularity. 'I am satisfied with having saved France.'

CHAPTER VI

THE MINISTER

One day early in January, 1720, Law's carriage was seen to drive into the royal palace of the Tuileries. During previous visits, when the financier had called on the King, he had been allowed to drive across the great courtyard to the entrance of the palace itself. On this occasion the carriage was stopped by the guard at the outer gates, while Law got out and was obliged to traverse the courtyard on foot. This incident, which was witnessed by the chronicler Buvat, gave rise to various conjectures and, since trifles of this kind often bore a sinister significance, it was thought by some that the financier might have in some measure fallen from favour. In fact the reverse was true. Law was graciously received by the youthful monarch simply to confirm a decision already made by the Regency Council and publicly announced the same evening. On that day – January 5, 1720 – John Law was appointed Controller-General of Finance for the Kingdom of France.

As has been seen, for some months past Law had been effectually exercising the power and functions of a finance minister, since D'Argenson, the nominal holder of the office, was to all intents and purposes a cypher. Nevertheless D'Argenson's ultimate surrender of his portfolio into Law's hands, though its political effect was little more than formal, created quite a stir in the country. The appointment of a foreigner, even though he had become naturalized, to such a high and powerful office in the state was unprecedented in French history. It provoked a considerable amount of hostile feeling, particularly among those, such as Saint-Simon, who distrusted 'the system'. But then, as Saint-

Simon put it, Frenchmen grow accustomed in time to everything, and the majority consoled themselves with the fact that they were no longer subject to D'Argenson's piquant humour and his strange hours of business.

To his credit Law declined to touch either the salary or the perquisites of his new office. But the saving to the Treasury was more than offset by the pensions and other pecuniary favours which the Regent at this time thought fit to shower on courtiers and favourites. The object of this largesse was doubtless to placate unfavourable criticism of the recent appointment, but it was an extravagance which filled the minister himself with uneasiness. Law still kept up his weekly meetings with Saint-Simon, and, being pressed during one conversation at this time, he reluctantly admitted that Orleans 'was ruining everything by his prodigality'. Were it not for the Regent's seemingly endless demands, Law went on, the bank had sufficient resources to meet all contingencies. As things were, however, the printing presses could not turn out notes fast enough; and this tremendous inflation, added to the prevalent rage for speculation in the Mississippi stock which had seized the whole country, unless checked, was bound sooner or later to lead to disaster, if the mania for buying should give way to a corresponding mania for selling and note-holders should endeavour to exchange their notes for specie. But in spite of his professed interest for the public purse, Saint-Simon was no better than the rest of the courtiers. He saw no reason why he should not share in the general enrichment, and without telling Law he went to the Regent and asked that the salary attached to a sinecure office which he held should be increased to 12,000 livres a year. He records in his memoirs that his request was granted at once.

To the outside observer, the stupendous Mississippi boom showed no signs of decline, let alone collapse. At the time of Law's appointment as Controller-General original 500-livre shares were reported to be changing hands at 18,000 livres each. A few days before, a general meeting of the Company had approved the Director-General's proposal to fix the dividends for the ensuing year in anticipation at 40 per cent of the par value of the shares; but, in view of their greatly enhanced market value, this nominally large dividend amounted in practice to little more than one per cent of the value which the public put on them. It is unnecessary to analyse Law's statement of the Company's business except to note that the profits, which he anticipated with characteristic optimism, could only have been yielded after years of patient and successful development of the Mississippi area. Notwithstanding these figures, whose significance was not lost upon the sagacious investor, speculators continued to buy for a rise, but they were for the most part made up of that numerous but deluded section of the community which does not rush to buy until the real as distinct from the apparent top of the boom has been passed. The prudent and experienced operators were already beginning to sell out and seek other fields for their investments.

The speculators, who had the foresight to realize their holdings, now invested in other commodities with the profits they had made. Comparatively few transferred their money abroad – they were chiefly foreigners. Most people, including Law himself, invested their profits inside France. The result, of course, was a rapid upward move in the prices of all such commodities in demand for this purpose. Land and houses were obvious objects of investment, and when they were unobtainable recourse was had to jewels, plate, furniture, horses, carriages and works of art. Commoner forms of merchandise were also invested in, including groceries, dry goods and even books. One enterprising stock-jobber, for instance, bought up an entire edition of Bayle's Dictionary. Far-seeing holders of bank-notes likewise began to exchange their paper for coin.[1] Foremost among the latter was

---

[1] Law endeavoured without success to counteract this tendency by exposing its folly in the French press. On March 11, 1720, he wrote with his usual cogent reasoning in the *Mercure de France*: 'Most people, surprised at their own gain, thought they might turn it into heaps of gold and silver, which they call realizing. They did not consider that the advanced price of stocks did not so much represent current money as capital funds . . . But this truth becomes palpable by the surprising height the stocks rose to, for they actually surpassed in value all the gold and silver which will ever be in the Kingdom. Here some will not fail to object that therefore they look upon these stocks to be but an imaginary and chimerical estate and that they were in the right to improve the happy moment of parting with them. I answer the houses of Paris taken together as a capital stock surpass perhaps in value all the specie in the Kingdom. The lands of France are worth more than all the gold which still lies hid in the mines of Peru. Have then the houses and lands for this reason nothing but a chimerical value? Upon this reflexion, which I suggest to the most part of those who never made any reflexion in their lives, I would ask will they all come to a resolution in one day to realize all their lands and

Louis Armand, Prince de Conti, son of Law's former patron. He had made enormous sums through speculation aided, it is said, by advance information from Law, but for some reason – probably because the Controller-General no longer yielded to his persistent demands for 'tips' – he now turned against him and proceeded to do everything he could to injure Law and his concerns. He began by sending three wagons to the bank which were what he estimated would be required to transport the gold which he proposed to obtain in exchange for his considerable note holding. So as not to impair public confidence Law dared not refuse this embarrassing claim, but as soon as he had satisfied it he hurried off to complain to the Regent. Orleans sent for the prince and reprimanded him, but legally he could not prevent him from keeping the specie. In revenge Conti spread the most damaging rumours about Law which he could collect or invent.

The Controller-General now found himself called upon to take a vital decision. The 'system' was in danger, and in seeking to preserve it he felt he had to choose between supporting the notes of the bank and the shares of the Company. The notes, which now enjoyed legal currency throughout the kingdom, were in the hands of all classes of the community and they enjoyed the backing of the government. The shares, on the other hand, were possessed by a relatively small section of the community which had purchased them largely in the hope of private gain. In the beginning he decided that he must support the notes, and his decision was embodied in a statesmanlike decree, which was published on February 24, 1720. This decree provided, first, that for purposes of control and administration the bank and the Company should be amalgamated; secondly, that in no circumstances should the combined institution be compelled to make advances by way

---

convert them into money? If such a frenzy should take place, it would reduce the most considerable houses and lands to nothing, and then those stupid sellers will want buyers. What is it that keeps up lands to their lawful value, how high soever but that they are not sold to realize them? Nobody sells them but to retrieve their affairs; the possessors commonly content themselves with the revenues which they produce, and they are therefore very rarely offered for sale, and when they are there's always as many buyers as sellers. Men ought, then, with regard to shares to think after the same manner and order as they do with respect to their estates. They seem unwilling to do it themselves, and there is nothing so difficult as to convince a multitude of their true interest and make them pursue it.'

of loans to the King; thirdly, that there should be no issues of notes except on the authority of a decree of the Council when requested by a general meeting of shareholders; and finally, that the Company's office should be closed to all dealings in its shares. By this piece of legislation Law considered it better that public confidence in the notes should be maintained, and inflation checked, while letting the price of the shares gradually drop.

Unfortunately for the Controller-General he was persuaded to reverse this policy less than a fortnight later. On March 5 a decree was published reopening the Company's office for the purchase and sale of shares, while the price was arbitrarily fixed at 9,000 livres a share. That is to say, the government undertook to pay 9,000 livres in bank-notes for each share any individual holder wished to dispose of. The consequent rush to sell showed that the shares were considerably overvalued at this figure while the attempt to 'peg' the price at 9,000 made wild inflation inevitable. During the next two months the note issue was increased by the enormous sum of 1,500 million livres, which went into circulation in payment of shares. The same edict, in an attempt to check speculation, prohibited all further dealings in futures or *primes*.

There is no doubt that the decree of March 5 really involved the 'system's' ruin. Opinions have long been divided as to the extent of the Controller-General's responsibility for this fatal measure. The nineteenth-century French socialist Louis Blanc, who regarded it not merely as an error but as a crime, was convinced that it was the work of Law's enemies. 'The decree of February 24 saved the system by ruining several great lords', he wrote; 'that of March 5 saved several great lords by destroying the system.' Dutot, who had worked in the bank as a cashier, expressed astonishment that his master had consented to such a disastrous step.

'He should have perceived the danger inherent in the government's purchase of shares', he wrote, 'and he should have realized that the excessive increase in note issue, which these purchases necessarily involved, was bound to impair confidence and spread alarm far and wide. He should not have overlooked the fact he was in a sense personally responsible for the notes, since he had made them national currency, whereas it was not the same with the shares, whose value was properly speaking fixed by public opinion.' Other contemporary economic writers, on the other hand, such as Forbonnais and du Hautchamp, considered the decree of March 5 to be a logical expression of Law's policy, and they have been followed in the nineteenth century by such leading economists as Thiers, Daire and Levasseur.

The question has now been resolved by the recent publication of the history of Law's financial administration by himself.[1] This leaves no doubt that Law put forward the decree of March 5 with his eyes open and in the full knowledge of the risks he ran. He states he had come to the conclusion that he could no longer 'maintain the value of the notes', i.e. preserve their purchasing power, since there were already too many in circulation; and, although he appreciated the arguments of Dutot and people like him, he also felt he had an obligation to the investors who had provided the capital which was now being employed to enable the government to liquidate the national debt. 'If he was carried at this moment to excess,' he wrote, 'it was because excess was necessary to cure the excessive complaints of the State . . . In spite of the remonstrances which were made to him he persisted in the purchases of shares which led to the multiplication of notes and his own downfall. He sacrificed the reputation which he had acquired by the establishment of his bank, whose collapse became imminent by reason of the extreme desire which he possessed to restore speedily the State's affairs through the extinction of all its debts. Thus this operation, which has commonly been considered an inexcusable folly, appears quite otherwise when its nature and objects are examined.'

However misguided he may have been in this instance, particularly when judged by subsequent events, it cannot be denied that the Controller-General at this time resorted to a number of other violent and unfortunate measures in an endeavour to sustain by force the 'system' which the public was declining to support voluntarily. 'I will compel confidence,' he said. A decree of January 20, 1720, had authorized the search of all houses, even those belonging to religious communities, for old coins which had been withheld from recoinage. This was followed by more sumptuary and tyrannical legislation. The wearing of diamonds and other precious stones on the person was forbidden under penalty of confiscation and a fine of 10,000 livres. Goldsmiths

---

[1] In 1934. See Professor Harsin's edition of Law's works, vol. III, pp. 367–373.

were prohibited from making any gold or silver articles except episcopal rings. Payments for all amounts in excess of 100 livres in future had to be made in notes and not in specie. Perhaps the height of tyranny was reached by the edict of February 27 which forbade any person of whatever rank or wealth from keeping gold or silver to the amount of more than 500 livres. The penalty was a fine of 10,000 livres and, of course, the confiscation of the specie. To this end informations were encouraged and the informer given a share of the treasure. It was laid down that the police might enter and search any house in execution of this decree.

The notorious decree of February 27 was rigorously enforced, and it naturally led to a mass of denunciations of individuals for hoarding specie. The inducements offered to informers appealed to the worst instincts and passions in the community at a time when manners and morals had grown particularly lax. Spiteful or jealous servants were especially prone to denounce their masters, and in one instance a son gave information against his own father. Not even religious establishments were exempt from these proceedings, and alms were confiscated on the ground that, if they were really what they purported to be, they should already have been given to charity. However, the law was not fairly administered as between rich and poor. Men like the Prince de Conti, who openly admitted having carted away several wagon loads of gold from the bank, submitted to the most perfunctory search of their houses and kept their treasure. Others less fortunate were relieved of their fortunes in quick order, including the brothers Paris, who unsuccessfully endeavoured to transport 7,000,000 lives to Lorraine.

It now only remained for Law to do away altogether with the circulation of gold and silver, even in small amounts. On March 11 it was announced that gold should cease to be employed for the payment of any debt as from May 1, and silver as from August 1. No individuals except goldsmiths were permitted to retain any specie in their possession, and goldsmiths were only to have so much as their business required. Thus was France to become the first country in the civilized world where a man could not pay a debt or conduct any normal commercial transaction with gold or silver coin. In defence of his unique innovation the Controller-General argued that gold and silver, like silk and wool, could now be put to some useful purpose, while the paper currency, having no intrinsic value, could not be diverted from its proper purpose which was to circulate as a medium of exchange.

All these legislative measures met with a mixed public reception. Two echoes, which reached Law, have been preserved.

'I think it hard', wrote the Regent's mother, 'that there is no more gold to be seen, because for forty-eight years now I have never been without some beautiful gold pieces in my pocket.'

Lord Stair's comment was more acid. 'There can be no doubt of Law's catholicity', said the British ambassador, 'since he has established the Inquisition after having first proved transubstantiation by changing paper into money.'

2

The Mississippi mania, which swept France and reached its height during the winter of 1719–1720, brought other evils in its train. As we have seen, there was a phenomenal rise in prices; and this inflation, accompanied by a great increase in gambling and a looseness of morals generally, was unhappily reflected by an alarming outburst of robberies and other crimes of violence. The popular resort of the gamblers in the capital was the so-called market of St. Germain near the Latin quarter on the left bank of the Seine. Notwithstanding an edict which prohibited gambling in public under heavy penalties, this neighbourhood abounded in gambling establishments of all kinds. According to Buvat, as much as 60,000 livres were commonly staked on a single throw of the dice or turn of a card, while the players seemingly treated the wads of notes, with which their pocket-books were stuffed, as nothing more than inconsequential pieces of paper.

Crimes against the person now assumed dreadful proportions. Eleven people were killed and robbed in Paris alone within the space of a few days. Quantities of arms, legs and trunks of corpses belonging to victims, who had been murdered for their money and then cut to pieces, were dragged out of the river. The crime wave spread to the provinces, where masked highwaymen infested the roads and held up travellers. A few unlucky speculators and gamblers committed suicide, but the majority turned to a life of crime in order to recoup themselves. The climax was reached in a sensational murder, which gained a wide notoriety, and firmly fixed public attention on the menace, not only from the revolting circumstances of its commission but also from the fact that the perpetrators were all men of aristocratic birth, of whom one was allied to several reigning houses and claimed kinship with the Regent himself.

Antoine Joseph Count de Horn was a young cavalry officer belonging to a well-known Dutch family. He had been drawn to Paris when the Mississippi boom was at its height, but a series of heavy losses in the Rue Quincampoix, accompanied by his natural extravagance, had left him, at the end of two months, without a sou. In a moment of weakness he entered into a conspiracy with two companions, the Marquis de Lestang and the Count de Mille, to rob a stockjobber named Lacroix, to whom they pretended they had a large quantity of stock to sell at a low price. A meeting was arranged in a tavern called *L'Epée de Bois* in the Rue Venise, near the Rue Quincampoix, where a private room was reserved for the ostensible transaction of the business. Lacroix had no sooner taken out his bulging pocket-book, which contained no less than 150,000 livres, when one of the conspirators, Lestang, left the room in order to keep watch on the staircase. Horn then got up and, passing behind the unfortunate jobber's chair, threw a napkin over his head. Whereupon de Mille fell upon Lacroix and stabbed him with his dagger. On the jobber's crying out Horn promptly snatched the dagger from his confederate and despatched his victim with repeated blows.

At this moment a water-carrier, who lived on the floor above, thought he heard some unusual noises and he hastened to inform the landlord. The latter made his way to the room and, seeing Lestang who had been keeping watch take to his heels, guessed there was something wrong and proceeded to lock the door from the outside, at the same time giving the alarm. Horn and de Mille made their escape by the window into the street below, but in the descent de Mille injured his leg. This latter circumstance attracted the attention of some passers-by, who had heard the alarm, and they promptly seized de Mille and carried him off to the nearest magistrate. De Mille, who had the dead jobber's wallet in his pocket, at first denied everything. He asked to be allowed to go to the lavatory where he succeeded in getting rid of the wallet undetected, having first abstracted several bank-notes which he unwisely concealed in his armpits and under his socks. On being searched, the notes, all bearing unmistakable bloodstains, were discovered, and de Mille thereupon made a complete confession. The wallet was also recovered and de Mille conducted to the scene of the crime. Meanwhile Horn had succeeded in making his way to another magistrate, to whom he pretended he had just himself been robbed. He was about to be released when the magistrate's clerk, whose suspicions had been aroused by Horn's anxious manner, whispered to his master that the Count was trying to save himself. The magistrate then demanded to be taken to the Rue Venise, and on their arrival they found the first magistrate with Count de Mille who, not knowing what had happened, clearly recognized his confederate as an accomplice. Both men were removed to prison where Horn eventually made a full confession under torture.

If justice in Regency France was not always sure, it was certainly expeditious. The day afterwards the two murderers were tried and condemned to death, and within the next forty-eight hours their appeal had been heard and dismissed by the Council. Frantic attempts were made to save young Horn's life, and several thousand letters on his behalf were addressed to the Regent. But Orleans, who was usually inclined to be merciful, on this occasion remained inexorable. There is no doubt that his attitude was strengthened by Law, who insisted that a conspicuous example must be made, since such a dastardly crime, committed in full daylight almost within a stone's throw of the exchange market, could not fail to cause widespread fear. Horn was moreover suspected by Law, not without good reason, of having been mixed up in other crimes of violence. At all events Orleans declined to yield to the solicitations of Horn's friends. 'I know that he is related to me through my mother,' he said, 'nevertheless he deserves death for his dreadful crime, and justice must take its course.' With these words the Regent shut himself up in his room and refused to emerge until he heard that justice had been done.

On March 22, four days after the murder, Horn and de Mille were executed in the Place Grève by being broken on the wheel. Horn, who refused to take poison which a friend had smuggled into his prison cell, met his end with courage, and is said to have survived for an hour and a quarter after all his limbs had been crushed by the executioner.[1]

The Controller-General, who had insisted on such a severe example as a deterrent to others, made use of the episode as an excuse for an action which he had had in mind for some time – the closing of the notorious Rue Quincampoix. When he was eager to foster speculation in the Mississippi Company's shares the activities which took place in this street had been of advantage, and on one occasion he had visited it himself, receiving a triumphal reception as he did so. But it was a far different story with a falling market which he was desperately anxious to sustain. In these altered circumstances, the street, which was the natural origin of every alarmist rumour, could only be an acute embarrassment. Law now declared that such a market for the Company's shares as the Rue Quincampoix was no longer required, since the price of shares had recently been fixed at 9,000 livres. On the same day as Horn and his confederate met their end in the Place Grève the celebrated street was declared shut to all dealings in securities. A few days later the prohibition was extended under heavy penalty to all other districts of Paris.

Clandestine dealings in stock continued to take place on a small scale, but generally speaking the era of unbridled speculation was over. But the day of reckoning was yet to come.

3

Now that affairs showed signs of going badly, Law began to lose favour with the Regent, and on several occasions hard words passed between them. Orleans complained petulantly that, since Law had become Controller-General, vanity and ambition had turned his head. 'You may depend upon it', wrote Lord Stair in a letter to Whitehall dated March 12, 1720, 'that Law is mightily shaken in his master's good opinion, who, within these few days past, has used him most cruelly to his face, calling him all the names that can be thought of, knave and

---

[1] The foregoing details are based on the account furnished many years after the event by Lestang, the third conspirator, who made good his escape and lived until 1764. The account will be found in the Appendix to vol. II of Buvat's *Journal de la Régence* (Paris, 1865).

madman, etc.' The British ambassador also heard from Le Blanc, the Secretary for War, who happened to be in the room, how Law called at the Palais Royal at a moment when the Regent was performing a certain act of nature. 'The Duke of Orleans was upon the close-stool when Law came in' and moreover he 'was in such a passion that he ran to Law with his breeches about his heels and made him the compliment above mentioned.' The Regent concluded his tirade of abuse by telling the Controller-General that 'he did not know what hindered him to send him to the Bastille and that there was never one sent thither that deserved it half so well'.

The effect of this extraordinary outburst, which was probably occasioned by a difference of opinion over the unpopular sumptuary edicts which Law had pressed upon the Council, soon passed and before long Law had succeeded in regaining a great measure of the Regent's confidence. At the same time Law was visibly worried, his own temper grew short and he became nervous and easily excited. He could not sleep at nights and was reported to pace and even run about his bedroom 'making a terrible noise, sometimes singing and dancing, at other times swearing, staring and stamping, quite out of himself'. One night Catherine, who was awoken by the disturbance he made, came into his room and was forced to ring and summon assistance. The officer of the guard was the first to arrive on the scene and, to his utter astonishment, discovered the Controller-General in his night-shirt with two chairs set in the middle of the room round which he was dancing wildly.

The fact that the government undertook to buy any shares that might be offered at 9,000 livres kept the printing presses working day and night turning out notes to pay for them. This proceeding provided an added stimulus to the general inflation. Prices of commodities, particularly food, soared to fantastic heights – a phenomenon which was scarcely surprising, since there were notes to the nominal value of nearly 3,000 million livres in circulation throughout France in the spring of 1720. It was with the design of checking the colossal rise in prices, which was inherent in the inflation, that Law consented to a step which was to bring disaster upon his system and ultimately upon himself.

On May 21, 1720, a royal edict was published decreeing the successive devaluation of both money and shares. A bank-note representing 100 livres on May 21 was to be worth 80 livres on July 1; it was to be lowered in value by degrees until the end of the year when it would be worth only 50 livres. In the same way the Mississippi Company's shares were to be reduced in value from 9,000 livres to 5,000 livres.

This famous edict produced a general public outcry, and in its effect it spelt the death knell of Law's 'System'. The man-in-the-street felt as one would today if he were suddenly told that his £1 note or $1 bill would be worth only half its face value in six months' time. In reality the edict was a mere juggling with figures, since the purchasing power of 50 livres in December would still be roughly equivalent to that of 100 livres in May – that is, the new 50-livre note would buy approximately as much in the way of food, cattle, houses, etc., as the old 100-livre note had done. But the public did not regard it in that light. They felt they were being robbed of half their riches, although in truth this wealth was no more than wealth on paper and really fictitious. Furthermore, the edict seemingly constituted a departure from the undertaking previously given by the government that whatever variations might take place in the coin of the realm, the standard of the bank-notes should remain fixed and invariable. The net result was to shatter confidence, so that holders of both notes and shares now rushed to convert them into more substantial assets.

As in the case of the edict of March 5, which initiated the process of ruin, opinions have been divided as to the extent to which Law must be held responsible for the edict of May 21. The talk of the day, on the tongues of such gossips as Buvat and Barbier, had it that Law was opposed to the edict and that it was in fact devised by D'Argenson and other enemies of the Controller-General with the object of ruining him. There is no doubt, however, that Law took part in framing it and was induced to give it his approval, even if it was not eventually promulgated in the exact form which he had originally suggested. There is no doubt too that, dazed and confused by ever rising prices on the one hand and the Regent's ever increasing extravagance on the other, he was in sympathy with the deflationary principle which it embodied. In later years Law admitted that the edict was the product of mature reflection and that its terms had been discussed with the Regent as long as two months before its promulgation by the Council.

As it stood, the ill-fated edict could not fail to produce universal consternation, since everyone persisted in thinking that he was
now only worth half as much as he had been. The public outcry
was prodigious. There was not a rich man, said Saint-Simon, who
did not see himself in straitened circumstances or a poor man as
reduced to beggary. Parliament, of course, promptly refused to
register so unpopular and detested a measure and sent a deputa-
tion of protest to the Palais Royal. The Regent hurriedly called the
Council together, and less than a week after its publication, the
edict was repealed.[1] But the damage had been done. Confidence,
that precious and intangible commodity indispensable to the successful operation of 'the system', had been irreparably damaged.
Nothing now could retard the painful process of liquidation.

The Parliament and public now clamoured for the sacrifice of
the obvious scapegoat in the person of the Controller-General.
To his credit the Regent was determined not to punish Law by
sending him to the Bastille or otherwise abandoning him to the
popular fury. Outwardly, however, Orleans pretended to placate
the general feeling. Within forty-eight hours of the repeal of the
edict the Regent sent Le Blanc, his Secretary of State, to Law,
with a message thanking the Controller-General for his services
and relieving him of his portfolio. In delivering this message Le
Blanc added, with a touch of understatement, that the ex-minister
should be given a bodyguard day and night, 'as many people in
Paris did not like him'. Law, who was not expecting to receive his
quietus in this manner, took the news quite coolly, his only
request being that he desired an audience of the Regent. He was
duly conducted to the Palais Royal, but apparently as part of a
pre-arranged act to impress the courtiers and public who habitu-
ally hung about the entrance to the palace the Regent refused to
receive him. But on the following day Law was secretly taken to
one of the private entrances and brought up the backstairs to the
Regent's apartments. Orleans concluded his little comedy by wel-
coming his visitor graciously and treating him as well as ever.
While reluctantly obliged in the public interest to relieve him of
his office of Controller-General the Regent hoped that Law would
continue to act as Director-General both of the bank and the
Mississippi Company. Nevertheless, although Orleans and the

[1] Law was present at this meeting and spoke against the repeal, but in the
temper of the times he was, of course, powerless to prevent it.

rest of the government and court had been too closely identified with Law's system in the heyday of its success to sacrifice its principal architect, it was clear that his continued presence in France was merely required to clear up the débris which the collapse of the edifice had produced.

Advantage was now taken of Law's temporary eclipse to repeal the edict which forbade the possession by any individual of more than 500 livres in specie. 'There is a decree', noted the lawyer Barbier ironically, 'which allows us to have as much money in our houses as we please. This permission comes when nobody has got any!' The evils of unbridled inflation were now to be brought home with a vengeance to all classes in France. The Dowager Duchess of Orleans summed up the general feeling at Court. 'The working people no longer want to work', wrote Madame, 'and they put a price on their goods three times higher than they are now worth because of the bank-notes. I have often wished that these bank-notes were consigned to hell fire. They are much more of a worry than a help to my son, and it is impossible to describe all the evil that has resulted from them . . . I should like to see Law go to the Devil with his system and I wish that he had never set foot in France.'

4

It has generally been assumed that Law's 'system' collapsed on the morrow of the ill-fated edict of May 21, and that the whole paper fabric which the financier had assiduously built up over the past few years immediately tumbled to the ground. According to the accepted authorities the value of the bank-notes virtually fell to zero at this moment. As Sir James Steuart put it in his famous *Principles of Political Economy*, published later in the eighteenth century, on the day following the edict anyone might have starved with 100 millions in his pocket. Families possessing fortunes of several hundred thousand livres, we read, were reduced to beggary or driven to suicide. But this was not so. Otherwise Law would in all probability have been obliged to leave the country immediately. The truth is that the legend of a catastrophic monetary depreciation is not reflected in the course of commodity prices at this time, and there is no evidence that in the day-to-day commercial transactions of the period the bank-notes only commanded a fraction of their face values. There was, of course, a widespread scramble on the part of the public to get rid of them as well as the shares in exchange for specie and other commodities of intrinsic value. Commodity prices, however, showed little rise in terms of notes. What happened was that during the months that followed, Law concerted various measures with the Regent which were designed to contract the circulation of the notes and maintain the price of the Mississippi Company's shares. It was a gallant effort to save the remnants of the System, but confidence continued to ebb away until by the end of the summer Law realized that the game was up. 'There is still a great deal of money in France', wrote the Regent's mother at this time, 'but everyone conceals it from selfishness and won't put it into circulation. They take no notice of the laws which Monsieur Law has made on the subject.'[1]

The rush on the bank caused by the edict of May 21 was so great that this institution was compelled to close its doors for ten days. When payments were resumed on June 1, only notes of denominations of 100 livres and less were honoured. Soon after 10-livre notes could be exchanged for specie, and then only at the rate of one note per customer. This restriction was dictated by the need of relieving the necessities of the working classes who had mostly notes of the lowest denomination in their possession, which many shopkeepers were disinclined to accept, and they were now faced with the difficulty of meeting their daily living expenses. The Rue Vivienne and other streets leading to the bank's spacious premises in the Palais Mazarin were again filled with excited crowds, but this time there were no eager speculators hopeful of gain. The majority whose feverish hands clutched 10-livre notes were simply actuated by fear of starvation. Crowds would begin to collect as early as two o'clock in the morning, though the bank did not open for business until nine. Since the bank closed at noon for the day many of those who waited were

---

[1] In his *Histoire des Finances pendant la Régence*, which he wrote several years later in exile, Law admitted that these laws were makeshift measures which were not based on the 'true principles' of the system. He dated the destruction of the 'system' from the repeal on May 27, 1720, of the edict of May 21. See John Law, *Œuvres complètes* (ed. Paul Harsin), III, 380. He repeated this opinion while conversing with Montesquieu in Venice in 1728.

unsatisfied. Accidents were frequent among jostlers in the crowd. Many suffered serious injuries and several people were trampled to death. On one occasion the troops on guard at the Palais Mazarin lost their heads and charged the crowd with fixed bayonets. One night in July fifteen thousand frantic individuals were tightly wedged in the Rue Vivienne and when dawn broke it was found that sixteen had died from suffocation.

This tragic incident so enraged the mob that some of them dashed off with three of the bodies to the Palais Royal, which they displayed before the gates, shouting for the Regent to come out as they did so. Others surrounded Law's house in the Place Vendôme, and threw stones at the windows, several of which they succeeded in breaking. The crowds were gradually dispersed by relays of soldiers and police. Law made his appearance about ten o'clock in the morning and drove to the Palais Royal in his coach. A woman, the widow of one of the victims, threw herself at the vehicle. Crazy with grief, she could think and speak of but one subject. Law offered her money. 'No,' she shouted, 'I want my husband.' The journey was accomplished in safety in spite of the fact that the financier had been recognized and his coach was pursued by a howling throng, '*Vous êtes des canaille!*' he shouted at them. He was seen to be white as a ghost when the Regent received him, and he not unnaturally judged it wise that he should remain inside the palace until the clamour had abated. In fact he stayed in the Palais Royal for the next ten days. Meanwhile the empty coach was again surrounded by the mob on its return to Law's house. The coachman got down from the box and, seeking to emulate his master's spirit of bravado, shook his fist at the people and declared: '*Vous êtes des canaille!*' He was immediately thrown to the ground, had a leg broken and was left for dead. The crowd then proceeded to smash the coach to pieces.

In the Palais Royal Law was also secure from the fury of Parliament, for the members of that body were still intent on hanging the financier if they could only lay hands on his person. Law's intense unpopularity likewise encouraged the Parliament to increased obstruction of the legislative measures now being formulated by him in defence of the 'system'. On the same day as the tragic deaths in the Rue Vivienne occurred, Parliament refused to register an edict granting the Mississippi Company a further extension of its privileges in return for an undertaking on the Company's part to withdraw from circulation every month bank-notes to the nominal value of 50 million livres. Parliament's blocking of this attempt to restore confidence in the notes determined the Regent on another *coup d'état*. A few days later the *Palais de Justice* was invaded by several companies of troops, the members were rounded up and told to transfer themselves and their deliberations to Pontoise, a village about forty miles from Paris. The gentlemen of the robe made no attempt to disobey this order and docilely went into exile. For them it was simply a matter of *force majeure*.

Backed by Orleans, Bourbon and other courtiers who had made money out of the Company, Law now struggled violently to save his beloved 'system'; but it was inevitably a losing battle that he fought during the hot summer days of 1720 in Paris. Notes to the value of 700 millions of livres were withdrawn from circulation, being exchanged for municipal bonds and other forms of security held by the bank. But in spite of all Law's efforts the notes steadily lost favour with the public. The price of Mississippi stock likewise steadily declined and, though there was a momentary rise in July by reason of the edict which led to the exile of Parliament, they continued to fall with increasing rapidity. An attempt by the government once more to fix their price failed, and before the summer was over they were at a discount of 80 per cent. Matters were not helped by the disappearance about this time of one of the bank's cashiers accompanied, it need hardly be added, by considerable funds. Also, one of Law's secretaries, an Italian named Angelini, thought it prudent to depart on the vain pretext that his father had died and that it was necessary for him to settle his affairs.

For a short time the government permitted the reopening of the stock market. Dealing took place in the grounds of the Prince de Carignan's spacious Hôtel de Soissons, but this became the scene of so many 'black' market operations in other commodities that the place eventually had to be closed down. While the shares continued to change hands in a very subdued market, the notes, on the other hand, were doomed. In announcing their complete withdrawal from circulation the Council formally marked the end of the 'system'. An edict of October 10 declared that in their present discredited state the notes constituted a hindrance to trade and that consequently, as from the beginning of November, the use of gold and silver would be resumed in all commercial transactions. Thus France's much-vaunted paper currency, which the Scots financier had promoted, was altogether extinguished after an experience of less than two years.

5

Law went about his business throughout these difficult months in constant fear of his life and, whenever he appeared in public, he ran the risk of personal insult and injury. 'I am like the fabulous hen which laid the golden eggs,' he remarked ruefully, 'but which, when it was killed, was found to be like any ordinary fowl.' According to Saint-Simon the financier suffered with singular patience all the annoyances which his operations had caused him until towards the end when he became quick and short tempered. We have already seen how his nerves had become affected. In August the Regent's mother wrote that he dared not stir out of his house, and that the women from the market had sent numbers of little boys to surround the house and carry the news to them should he venture forth into the street. He consequently again sought the sanctuary of the Palais Royal. 'Law is like a dead man and his face is as white as a sheet,' reported Madame. 'I expect there are times when he wishes he himself were on the Mississippi or in Louisiana.'

Nor was the financier's family immune from the animosity of the mob at this time. One afternoon, the lawyer Barbier happened to be walking near the Etoile when he saw a crowd gathered round a carriage and pelting it with stones. He heard shouts of: 'That's the livery of the filthy beggar who doesn't pay his 10 livre notes.' Law's young daughter Mary Catherine, who happened to be inside the vehicle, was struck and slightly injured by a stone, while the coachman barely managed to escape to safety by whipping up the horses. On another occasion Madame de Torcy, wife of the Foreign Under-Secretary, was mistaken for 'Madame' Law by some peasants and narrowly escaped being drowned in a duckpond before she succeeded in establishing her identity. The Duke of Bourbon, who had made enormous profits from speculating in Mississippi stock and had become momentarily attached to Law in consequence, extended the protective hospitality of his country place at St. Maur to Catherine and her daughter during this period.

The Mississippi Director and his 'system' now became the subject of numerous lampoons and much ribald verse. The knowing ones took this as a good sign for Law, and said that the French do not kill those they satirize. The story of the 'system' was jestingly recounted in pasquinades such as the following:

> My shares which on Monday I bought
> Were worth millions on Tuesday, I thought.
> So on Wednesday I chose my abode;
> In my carriage on Thursday I rode;
> To the ball-room on Friday I went;
> To the workhouse next day I was sent.

At all events Law was seen about again. On September 23 he began to sit for his portrait in crayons to Rosalba Carriera, the famous Venetian pioneer in the art of pastel painting, whose acquaintance he had made some years before. On November 1 the artist called at the bank, probably with the intention of getting paid for her work. (In fact she received 450 livres for it.) It was the date on which the notes ceased to be legal tender. 'A bad day,' she recorded laconically in her diary. 'I saw M. Law at the bank and talked to him.'[1]

Law's enemies at Court, led by the old Chancellor D'Aguesseau, did their best to persuade the Regent to consign him to the Bastille. To his credit Orleans once more declined to sacrifice a man who after all had done nothing criminal. At the same time it had become generally obvious with the collapse of the 'system' that the continued presence of its author in France was a danger to himself as well as an embarrasment to the government. One day, for instance, towards the end of November he happened to be in the bank when some late customers, who had come to dispose of their shares, insulted him to his face, calling him thief, rogue, and rascal. About the same time it was officially announced that the Parliament, which it had proved most inconvenient to keep in exile, would be recalled to the capital before the end of the year.

---

[1] This portrait was completed in less than two months on November 13, 1720. Its subsequent history to the time of its disappearance in 1842 is described below at p. 212. Portraits of Law during his residence in France were also executed by Alexis Simon Belle and Hyacinthe Rigaud.

It now seemed to Law that it would be best for everyone if he were to retire, certainly from Paris and possibly from France as well.

As soon as his mind was made up, Law acted quickly. During the first days of December he asked the Regent to relieve him of his remaining offices and let him withdraw to the country. He suggested Guermantes, an estate which he had acquired near Paris. He also asked for his passports. Orleans immediately granted his first request but said that he must refer the question of the passports to the King. A day or so later his retirement was publicly foreshadowed by the appointment of his subordinate in the finance ministry, Pelletier de la Houssaye, to the office of Controller-General which had remained unfilled since Law's enforced resignation in the previous June. Law himself proposed this appointment to Orleans as being that of the best man available, and the new Controller-General showed his gratitude by adding his voice to those which were daily petitioning the Regent for Law's arrest and imprisonment.

On December 12, 1720, Law made his last public appearance in Paris. Accompanied by his family he went to the opera where he was the object of some ill-willed curiosity on the part of the audience, but nothing worse. 'English impudence' was how the Parliamentary lawyer Marais described his behaviour on this occasion. Next day Law took leave of the Regent and twenty-four hours later he was on the road out of Paris to his country estate. One of the few to call at the large house in the Place Vendôme and wish the fallen financier good luck was the artist Rosalba, who had always been a close friend of the family. He explained that he was taking his son John with him, but that Mary Catherine would stay behind with her mother and help her to settle up his private affairs. There were his personal debts which would have to be paid and these, it may be added, were not inconsiderable. To the family butcher alone 10,000 livres were owing.

Although Orleans afterwards expressed himself as more than relieved when the financier had departed – 'I am delighted this man has betaken himself off' was what he said – nevertheless they had a touching farewell interview, and Law's parting words produced a deep impression on the Regent's mind. 'Sire,' said Law, 'I acknowledge that I have made great mistakes. I made them because I am only human, and all men are liable to err. But I declare that none of these acts proceeded from malice or dishonesty, and that nothing of that character will be discovered in the whole course of my conduct.'

As Law uttered these words – the last, had he but known it, that he was to speak to the Regent – it is said that his eyes were full of tears.

6

Law's public career was thus seemingly brought to an end before his fiftieth birthday. The collapse of his 'system' and the failure of his schemes were complete, and it was to take France more than one generation to recover fully from their effect. Many contemporaries were inclined to regard the financier as nothing more than a greedy adventurer who had lined his own pockets with riches at the expense of thousands whom his crazy schemes had ruined. At this distance of time from the period of Law's amazing operations it is easier to assess the character of the man and the real reasons for the misfortunes into which he plunged himself and his adopted country. In the economic field he realized, with remarkable foresight, how credit could be utilized so as to become the life-blood of industry. His great mistake was that he pushed forward his ideas too quickly for the country, while his encouragement of speculation, though it was inspired by perfectly honest motives, became a snowball whose movements he eventually found himself unable to control. Of his personal limitations, quite apart from the difficult political conditions by which he was bound, he afterwards showed that he was well aware.

Subsequent examination proved that, in his management of the Mississippi Company as indeed in all his commercial and financial enterprises, there was never any taint of dishonest or sharp dealing. The large fortune, which he brought with him to France, he put at the service of the bank and the Company, and he left it behind when he departed. All the landed property which he had bought in France was seized by the government, and he had not acquired any land or other assets outside that country. His administration of both bank and Company had been fair and honest, and he felt he could not properly be held responsible for their

John Law as Controller-General of Finance in France.
From an engraving of a portrait by Peter Schenk

(*Above*) Rue Quincampoix.

(*Below*) 'The wind buyers paid in wind, or those who are last will remain hanging on'.

From satirical prints in *Het groote Tafereel der Dwashied* (The Great Mirror of Folly), Amsterdam, 1721

debts. 'That Company owes its birth to me,' he was later to point out. 'For them I have sacrificed everything, even my property and my credit, being now bankrupt, not only in France but also in all other countries. For them I have sacrificed the interests of my children, whom I tenderly love and who are deserving of all my affection. These children, courted by the most considerable families in France, are now destitute of fortune and establishment. I had it in my power to have settled my daughter in marriage in the first houses of Italy, Germany and England; but I refused all offers of that nature, thinking it inconsistent with my duty to do so and my affection for the state in whose service I had the honour to be engaged. I do not assume to myself any merit for this conduct, and I never so much as spoke upon the subject to the Regent. But I cannot help observing that this mode of behaviour is diametrically opposed to the idea my enemies wish to impute to me.'

It was quite true that young John and Mary Catherine Law no longer received advantageous offers of marriage which they might have accepted but for the reasons given by their father. Meanwhile the daughter and her mother who remained behind in Paris were soon obliged to leave the magnificent house in the Place Vendôme, dismissing the staff of liveried servants and selling up all the furniture to pay off the more pressing creditors. To add to Catherine's troubles the truth of her relationship with Law, which had been suspected for some time, now became generally known. 'His wife is not really his wife,' noted the lawyer Marais in his journal at this time; 'she had a husband who only died a year and a half ago.'[1]

Receivers were now appointed to apportion the fallen financier's assets – he had none outside France since he had previously made over the Lauriston property to his brother – and he was treated in every respect as a bankrupt. Everything which he had was taken into account. Even the annuities on his own life and the lives of his family which he had bought, and which had been expressly exempted from sequestration at the time of purchase, were taken with the rest. The large sums of money which he had

---

[1] Mathieu Marais, *Journal et Mémoires*, II, 33 (Paris, 1863). Saint-Simon wrote similarly: 'His wife was not his wife . . . This was suspected towards the end. After his departure it became certain.' *Mémoires de Saint-Simon* (ed. Boislisle), XXXVIII, 74.

generously distributed to the needy at the height of his prosperity, were forgotten, among others by the very recipients of his bounty. The Regent's mother noted that he gave away enormous sums in charity, and when it was cast in his teeth that he had helped the Jacobites he could only reply that he had given succour regardless of political allegiance to many individuals who would otherwise have starved. Although Law bought estates to the value of nearly eight million livres in France, his profits in the stock market were modest compared with some of the fortunate Mississippians. But if he had sold out even a portion of his holdings when the boom was showing signs of collapsing, as he might well have done, it has been estimated that Law could easily have cleared the equivalent of £2 millions sterling. But he put no money away in a safe place and he made no investments in other countries. When he left Paris he had only a few thousand livres in his possession, and even this comparatively small sum, as will be seen, he was not allowed to take with him out of the country.

His impetuosity, of course, was not his only fault. His economic policy was not always consistent with the theories which he had enunciated, particularly in the matter of public confidence in bank-notes and securities. He thought unwisely that people could be compelled against their will to maintain their confidence in the instruments of his schemes. He believed that panic selling on the exchange could be checked by legislation, but once confidence had gone he did not realize until the end that the spate of decrees that he inspired the Council to issue were just so much waste paper. He placed too much faith in the arbitrary power of despotic authority and too little in the influence of public opinion in money matters, even under an absolute monarchy. Thus he anticipated state socialism in France by several generations. 'It is a fortunate country,' he once said, 'where action can be considered, decided upon and carried out within twenty-four hours instead of twenty-four years like England.' In these circumstances it was perhaps inevitable that the reforms which he had effected as a minister, particularly in the sphere of taxation, should be swept away in the ensuing catastrophe, and should afterwards find few advocates apart from his own somewhat pathetic voice in exile.

As one historian of the Regency put it: 'Two things were lacking in his make-up. Nature, which had endowed him with a spark of genius, denied him the quality of patience; and fortune, which provided him with a fine stage, did not always leave to him the choice of actors.'[1] But in spite of his shortcomings his patent achievements stand out forcefully. The bank created by the adventurous Scotsman became the prototype of the Bank of France and similar national banks. He introduced the bank-note into French commercial life, later recognized to be an indispensable instrument of credit. He familiarized the French people with methods of dealing in futures and on margin which are a prominent and useful feature of stock market transactions today. His whole aim and ambition were to increase the welfare of his adopted country. In this, as the famous French socialist Louis Blanc was later to show, he was a veritable pioneer of collectivist government. Because he identified himself so closely with this country's interests he emerged in the end a loser. 'For the rest,' as he wrote to the Regent in his last letter from French soil, 'time will show that I have been a good Frenchman. The institutions which I have founded are under attack, but they will survive, and posterity will do me justice.'

[1] P. E. Lemontey. *Histoire de la Régence et de la Minorité de Louis XV*, vol. I (Paris, 1832) at p. 344.

CHAPTER VII

THE EXILE

The estate of Guermantes, to which Law had chosen to retire, was pleasantly situated near the market town of Lagny in the rich agricultural district east of Paris known as the Brie. It was among the many properties which the financier had acquired when at the height of his prosperity and which he had never seen. This particular property had cost him some 160,000 livres (about £12,000); and, though it was situated less than forty miles from Paris, he does not appear to have visited it until the melancholy occasion of his fall and departure from the capital. His seventeen-year-old son, John, who was to accompany him on his journey to exile, was probably no stranger to Guermantes; while the elder John was engrossed in the fruitless business of saving the remnants of his 'system', during the preceding summer, the young man, after the manner of his French contemporaries, is said to have been in the habit of entertaining ladies of the *demi-monde* within the hospitable walls of the fine house which graced the estate.

According to his own account, Law expected to remain at Guermantes for some time, as he did not think that he would be allowed to leave France until all his affairs and those of the bank and the Mississippi Company had been liquidated. He was somewhat surprised, therefore, when two gentlemen of his acquaintance, the Marquis de Lassaye and M. de la Faye, appeared a day or two later with his passports and a considerable sum of money in gold, sent by his friend the Duke of Bourbon to defray his travelling expenses, with the Regent's concurrence. They wished him *bon voyage*. There were two sets of passports to cover the journey of himself and his son; one was made out in their real names and the other in a false name – that of Du Jardin – should they wish to travel incognito. With the imminent return of the Parliament to Paris it seems that the Regent wanted to get Law, in the interests of his personal safety, out of the country as soon as possible. Anyhow Law gladly accepted the protection which these documents afforded him. But he refused the money, as he judged he had a sufficient sum in his possession – 800 gold louis or about 36,000 livres which one of the bank clerks had obtained for him from the mint in exchange for paper which he held to that amount. Some conversation then took place between Law and his visitors as to the locality of his future residence; the two visitors said that the Regent had suggested Rome as eminently suitable. The financier replied that he would bear this suggestion in mind, although he thought that the social temptations of the 'eternal city' might prove too distracting for his son.

Next day, December 16, the travellers set out in a post-chaise kindly supplied by the Marquise de Prié, the Duke of Bourbon's mistress. The coachman and postilions wore dark coats over their liveries so as to avoid attention, since it was necessary for Law to slip into Paris unobserved so as to collect some papers from his house. They only stayed a few hours in the Place Vendôme; and, after the papers and some other possessions had been hastily packed up and a fond farewell taken of the women who were being left behind, Law and young John stepped into their coach and drove off in the direction of the Netherlands frontier. At Valenciennes they were stopped on the orders of the Marquis d'Argenson, *Intendant* of the district, who recognized them and demanded to see their passports. This d'Argenson was the son of the former finance minister whom Law had driven from office. The *Intendant* realized that here was a heaven-sent opportunity of avenging his father's dismissal, although, according to his own account, he was afraid to let such notorious travellers pass until he had received further confirmation from the authorities in Paris. He kept the two men waiting for forty-eight hours while he examined their passports, and it was only when a letter from the Regent in Paris, further authorizing the journey, arrived, that d'Argenson reluctantly allowed them to proceed.

In the course of a long conversation which he had with the *Intendant* Law was prompted to let fall some acid remarks on

French local government. 'Monsieur,' he said, 'I would never have believed what I have seen during the period I administered the finances. Do you know that this kingdom of France is really governed by thirty *Intendants*? You haven't got Parliaments nor committees nor estates nor governments, I would nearly add neither king nor ministers. These are the thirty masters of requests sent out to the provinces, on whom these provinces depend for their good or ill, plenty or want. Of what importance is it that these men should be good or bad and that pains should be taken to choose them well, to reward and punish them!'

D'Argenson's retort was to confiscate the 800 gold louis which a search of the financier's effects had revealed. To Law's protest the *Intendant* replied that it was illegal to export specie. 'If I remember rightly', he added with a sardonic smile, 'you were the author of the edict to this effect!'

Somewhat disgruntled the travellers resumed their journey to reach Brussels on the morning of December 22. Here they put up at the Hôtel du Grand Miroir in the name of Du Jardin. However, their incognito did not remain undetected for long, and before noon the Marquis de Prié, the provincial Governor, General Wrangel, the Commander-in-Chief, and other notabilities had called at the hotel to pay their respects. Among others whom Law saw was the French Minister, the Marquis de Rossi, to whom the financier gave the details of the unfortunate incident at Valenciennes; the minister promised to do his best to get the money returned. In the evening he went to the theatre with some friends; he was instantly recognized by the audience and received a tremendous ovation. During the next two days he was fêted by the civic authorities and leaders of Brussels society – 'like a Messiah', wrote one observer. During this period he managed to raise enough money to enable him to continue his journey.

He set off again with his son after two days, taking the road to Aix-la-Chapelle. This time father and son drove away in a hired post-chaise, since in the meantime Law had sent the other coach back to Madame de Prié. In the letter which he wrote thanking her for her kindness Law enclosed a valuable diamond ring, which in his altered circumstances he could really ill afford to give away.

Despite his magnificent reception in Brussels the fallen financier felt disillusioned and sick at heart. He would have liked to stay some time in Belgium, but he realized that it was too near France to be either comfortable or healthy for him, particularly when he heard the news just before he left that three of the principal officials in the bank had been arrested and sent to the Bastille. On Christmas Day he wrote to the Duke of Bourbon: 'I left Brussels yesterday evening and, although the roads are very bad, I propose to continue my journey to Italy. The Regent has expressed the desire that I should retire to Rome; that determines me. The enemies of the system have taken umbrage at seeing me within reach of France and have been seeking ways to cause me trouble, although I am outside the kingdom. It will cost me nothing to satisfy them. I have always hated work. A hope well-founded of doing good to a people and being of service to a prince who had given me his confidence – these were the ideas which inspired and sustained me throughout an unpleasant business. I have now returned to my natural self.'

Louvain, Liege, Aix-la-Chapelle, Cologne – the journey was made no easier for Law by the feeling that creditors both public and private would soon be on his track. In fact, a Jew named Rodriguez, to whom he is said to have owed 60,000 livres for some jewels, had already left Paris in pursuit of the financier. It is not known whether he ever caught up with his quarry. At Cologne (then an imperial free city governed by its Archbishop as Elector), the Elector, who had a considerable amount of notes of the bank in his possession, refused to have the travellers supplied with further relays of post-horses so as to continue their journey until his demands had been met. The following dialogue took place between Law and the Elector.

'Good morning, Monsieur Lass,' said the Elector, addressing the financier by the name by which he had commonly been known in France. 'I won't ask how you are, but how is France?'

Law, who did not relish this type of humour, replied civilly that there was an abundance of everything in France.

'And the notes? How much are they worth?'

'As much as they have always been.'

The Elector thereupon produced a large bundle of notes. 'I am very glad,' he went on. 'Here are 400,000 livres in notes. Please pay me cash for them.'

Law looked somewhat taken aback.

'You know very well, Sire, that I have scarcely any money with me.'

'Monsieur, you will not proceed until you have satisfied me. You have agents here. Give me bills of exchange on them.'

The result of this disagreeable encounter was that Law was obliged to draw bills for the amount requested by the Elector. Presumably they must have been accepted, as father and son were now allowed to proceed on their journey.

And so on through Bonn and up the Rhine. New Year, 1721, found the travellers on the road to Bavaria. It was rumoured that Law would go on to Vienna at the request of the Emperor Charles VI in order to set the Austrian finances in order, but there was no truth in the story. For at Munich they turned south to Innsbruck and then across the Brenner pass. They reached Venice on January 19, 1721.

He immediately wrote to Catherine, asking her to send on a memoir and some other papers he had left behind in the hurry of his departure from France, as he wished to put on record some justification of his official work. 'I am sensible that you suffer extremely by the resolution I have taken of going to Italy,' he told her. 'There was no choice in my situation. Holland was not proper. Your son and I are well, tho' much fatigued by the bad weather and bad roads . . . The memoir you will find with my papers may be sent with my baggage; put them in Lassaye's hands, with the papers that are in the little closet.' To his friend Lord Londonderry he wrote hopefully: 'What I have shall be employed to pay what I owe. If I have little, I can live on little; but as I am in great advances for the King's service abroad, the Regent has promised to lay aside a sum monthly for my payment.'

Carnival was in full swing and, in an endeavour to distract his mind from the worries of the past twelve months, Law threw himself enthusiastically into the gay life which he had known as a young man many years before. As he strolled across that part of the vast Piazza di San Marco known as the Broglio he happened to run into one of his former Venetian acquaintances, a senator named Contarini, who buttonholed him and wanted to know all about the 'system' and why it had failed. Law refused to be drawn.

'I have spoiled my life,' he said with a sigh. 'It is here that I should have stayed and developed my talents, dreaming of little pleasures and little scandals, living in song and fun, thinking only of how to win the ladies, and so heedlessly coming to die as one

suddenly comes up against the night on the threshold of a door-
way.'

2

The romantic capital of the Ven-
etian republic, where the fallen financier and his son were to spend
most of the next seven months, had always offered a convenient
haven for refugees of all types and all countries. Its government
by Doge, Council of Ten and Senate, was both autocratic and
aristocratic – Venice was in effect a police state – but natives and
visitors alike, provided they did not concern themselves with
politics, were left undisturbed to enjoy the manifold pleasures
which the city had to offer. The naturally gay disposition of the
Venetians, their love of the theatre and carnival, made the stranger
doubly welcome, while the exotic and almost mysterious character
of the place with its narrow alleys and canals and gondolas aided,
by the use of the mask, was ideal for amorous intrigues. The city's
famous carnival began on the day after Christmas and continued
until the beginning of Lent. During this period the mask was
universally worn by all classes, and its disguise afforded an excuse
for every kind of frolic and licentious adventure. Proceedings
were enlivened by dancing and masquerades. The most characteristic and picturesque festival, however, occurred on Ascension Day,
when the Doge in the state barge led a magnificent procession
across the lagoon, which culminated in the casting of a golden
ring into the water to symbolize the wedding of the state with the
sea.

To say the least, Venetian manners and morals in the eighteenth
century were easy going. The authorities made no attempt to
suppress prostitution and gambling, which flourished throughout
this period: in fact these occupations were regulated by law. There
is evidence that the government purposely tolerated if they did
not entirely encourage them, as a safeguard against the diversion
of men's thoughts towards politics and other interests which
might prove inimical to the state. The latest guest of the Republic
had long since had his fling with the ladies. He left the lively
courtesans to his son and betook himself to the Ridotto. This was
the great century-old gaming-house near the church of San Moisé

and but a few moments' walk from the Piazza di San Marco and the Grand Canal. In the large entrance hall, whose walls were hung with embossed leather, the gamblers met and talked, but only members of noble families might be unmasked in the Ridotto. Ten rooms were given up to gambling, the chief games played being bassett and faro, and there were two buffets generously stocked with refreshments of all kinds. At each table in the gaming rooms there sat a nobleman in patrician robe and wig with piles of sequins and ducats before him; he was prepared to hold the bank against all comers, including women who were admitted. As a rule play continued in absolute silence broken only by the declaration of the stakes, the rattle of dice and the clinking of coins.

After a few days in this congenial atmosphere Law decided to remain awhile in Venice and not to continue his journey to Rome until the Carnival was finished. He still passed under the name of Du Jardin, but his real identity soon became a matter of common knowledge and he found himself besieged by callers. The British Resident, Colonel Elizeus Burges, showed particular interest in his movements and hoped that he would not settle in Rome where the Young Stuart Pretender held his court and where Law might become involved in Jacobite plottings. The Council of Ten also kept the visitor under surveillance, deputing one of their secret agents to report upon his movements and conversation. However, Law characteristically made friends with the spy, a Sicilian ex-convict who was also a gambler, and even induced him to lend him some furniture when Law rented a house. The house was taken from the Austrian ambassador, Count Colloredo, and was conveniently situated in the same street as the Ridotto. It was here that he received his friends and, since he was determined to clear himself in the eyes of the world of any charges of duplicity and dishonest dealing, he planned to write a justification of his system. 'When my journey is over', he told his friend the Marquis de Lassaye, 'I will work at a memoir to justify the system, to explain the principles on which it was formed, the good which it has produced and which it should again produce, and the methods which are necessary to realize it. I will prove that it is to the advantage of all parties in the state to maintain my system.'

Besides the charges affecting his departmental record Law was worried by the rumours repeated to him in many quarters that he had succeeded in taking large amounts of money and jewels with him when he left France. Most assiduous in spreading this ill-founded story was the French minister to the Republic, M. Fremont, who stated that the ex-Controller-General of Finances had smuggled out of the country a box full of diamonds worth 10 million livres. 'He says all his effects are in France, and that he has secured nothing to himself out of it', wrote Burges to his colleague in Geneva at this time. 'How true that is I can't tell, but he has refused to pay me £5,000, which I have a commission from England to demand of him, upon no other pretence.' Nor had he the least desire for any further official employment. After he had been a month in Venice he wrote, on February 22, 1721, to Dubois's secretary, the Abbé Tencin: 'When I was in charge of affairs, I did what I conceived to be my duty as an honest man. If I have given any advice to the Regent which has not turned out well, I shall be the first to be deceived; and his ministers should not wish me ill, since I have now returned to private life and I wish to stay there. I have no further ambition nor desire for employment. I pity those who have, and I assure you that I would not wish to change my position or to get involved again in public business of any kind.'

A few days later the Carnival ended in a blaze of fireworks, streamers, confetti and orange peel, and Law began to pack up his belongings preparatory to leaving the territory of the Republic. Before he departed he sent the Regent a letter in which he asserted his good faith and asked for a fair liquidation of his property in France. It was the first of a fruitless series of letters which he addressed to the Palais Royal on this subject.

Venice, 1st March, 1721.

MONSEIGNEUR,

I have avoided hitherto availing myself of the permission, which Your Royal Highness has accorded me, of writing to you, in order not to give the least umbrage to those whom you officially employ. However, there are certain occasions when I am persuaded that it will be found advantageous if I take this liberty.

When I proposed to Your Royal Highness that I should retire, I proposed at the same time to assign to the Company of the Indies all my shares, lands and other assets of all kinds, only reserving to myself for the purpose of paying my debts a sum equivalent to that which I brought to France with me. Your Royal Highness was gracious enough to reply that I had children and that consequently it was not proper that I should assign all my assets to the Company.

Your example, Monseigneur, and that of the various noblemen and gentlemen who are members of the Council of Regency, justify my requesting Your Royal Highness anew to agree to the Company's entrusting one or two persons of my nomination with the task of paying what I owe, remitting to me a sum of 500,000 livres from what I estimate to be the total amount of my assets, and handing over the balance to the Company.

From the statement of accounts which has been sent to me, the item covering the amounts which I have advanced for use in foreign countries[1] will of itself be sufficient to pay my debts and to remit the sum which I desire. In case Your Royal Highness should find this too much, I shall be content with whatever you consider fit to determine. In my work I only aimed at being useful to a great people; I desired for myself neither riches nor offices except in so far as they could help me to succeed in my purpose. The Chancellor D'Aguesseau will bear me out in this; in talking to him on his return to office of those individuals who had suffered from the fall in their *rentes*, I offered him my own share holdings, at that time worth nearly 100 millions, so that he might distribute them amongst those who were in need.

I entreat Your Royal Highness to rest assured that I possess no property either abroad or within the kingdom which is not known, and I have no desire to be rich; but it is not right that I should fail to pay what I owe, while on the other hand it is necessary for me to subsist honourably.

I have the honour to be with the most sincere and respectful attachment, Monseigneur,

Your Royal Highness's most humble and obedient servant,

LAW.

The financier and his son set out for Rome on March 15 travelling overland. However, they did not get very far. Their route lay through Ferrara and Bologna, and at one of these towns it seems they received some news which caused them to change their plans

---

[1] Nearly 3½ million livres which Law had paid out of his own funds to various government agents abroad.

and retrace their steps. In order to protect himself from the un-welcome attentions of his creditors, real or supposed, Law had taken the precaution of having his name enrolled on the list of Roman citizens which rendered him immune from proceedings for the recovery of debts except at the suit of a fellow citizen. He now heard that some of his creditors had assigned their claims to a Roman citizen who was making preparations to have him arrested as soon as he set foot there. Accordingly after a week the travellers judged it advisable to return to the shelter of the Republic.

Back again in the Calle del Ridotto, Law received a significant communication from Count Guldenstein, the Danish minister. On the instructions of his master, King Frederick IV of Denmark, Count Guldenstein invited the financier to visit Copenhagen and set the finances of that kingdom in order. It was a tempting offer, since his services would be handsomely rewarded. But he had little hesitation in turning it down. In any case he doubted if he could stand a winter in northern latitudes. 'I will undertake no further engagements,' he told the Dane. 'I have done enough, and I now want to live quietly. This Republic pleases me. I am agree-ably prepossessed by it, and I think the longer I stay here the more I shall like it.'

3

On the morrow of Law's pre-cipitate departure from France a meeting of the Regency Council was called by King Louis XV in the Tuileries Palace to discuss the affairs of the Company and bank. Twenty-eight persons attended including the young monarch and all the principal dignitaries in the realm; and, thanks to Saint-Simon's pen, the proceedings at this remarkable session have been faithfully recorded. The main feature of the meeting was an ill-judged and unsuccessful attempt on the part of the Regent Orleans to disown any responsibility for the excessive issue of bank-notes which had been made.

De la Houssaye, the new Controller-General, opened the dis-cussion with a reference to the large outstanding note issue which still remained to be redeemed. The Regent interposed with the statement that Law had issued and circulated notes to the nominal value of 600 million livres in excess of what he should have done. These notes were issued without his (the Regent's) knowledge and without any authority from the Council. For this, Orleans went on, Law deserved to be hanged. However, when he discovered what had happened he consented to extricate Law from this predicament by ante-dating the decree which authorized the issue.

The Duke of Bourbon broke in at this point: 'How was it, Monsieur, knowing this that you allowed him to leave the country?' 'I have just furnished him with the means of doing so,' replied the Regent.

'I never asked you to allow him to leave.'

'But it was you yourself who sent him his passports,' insisted the Regent.

'That's true', rejoined Bourbon, 'but it was you who gave them to me to send to him. I never asked you for them or to let him leave the country. I know that the public has chalked up his departure to my account and I am glad to have this opportunity of explaining the true facts of the case. I was opposed to Monsieur Law being sent to the Bastille or to any other prison as was generally wished, because I did not think it was in your interests to permit this after the services which this man had rendered you. But I never asked you to let him leave the kingdom and I beg you, Monsieur, in the presence of the King and of all these gentlemen, to say if I ever did make any such request.'

The Regent saw that it was futile to attempt to prevaricate. 'It is true that you never asked me to,' he now admitted, 'I let him go because I thought his continued presence in France would injure public credit and hinder the process of liquidation.'

Bourbon got in a concluding thrust which incidentally revealed him in his true colours, as being anything but the friend of the financier that he pretended to be.

'So far was I from asking you to let him depart, if you had done me the honour of consulting my opinion, I should have advised you to take good care not to allow him to do so.'

De la Houssaye brought this unseemly altercation to an end only by continuing his financial statement. He pointed out that, as the Mississippi Company had been under the control of the government, it could not now be turned adrift as a private corporation. He estimated that no less than 80,000 French families had invested everything they had in the Company's shares, and that in order to save them from starvation, it would be necessary that this paper should possess some value. He proposed, therefore, that in order to facilitate the liquidation of the system on these lines special commissions should be appointed to scrutinize all notes and securities as well as title deeds to landed property, and confiscate all those which in their opinion had been acquired solely by process of speculation.[1] Securities not declared before August 1, 1721, were to be cancelled. In other words, there was to be another *visa*, similar to that which had been instituted in 1716 and which had caused so much consternation. The Council approved this proposal, and the commissioners were accordingly invested with plenary powers in the execution of their inquisitorial duties.

The task was entrusted to the Paris brothers, exponents of the 'anti-system', who conducted the inquisition with extreme harshness and injustice, besides hopelessly bungling the liquidation. When in the habit of defending his official conduct in later years Law used to point out that, while the fatal edict of May 21, 1720, had precisely the same deflationary object in view as the hated *visa*, it would within the space of twenty-four hours (if it had been allowed to operate) have fairly affected all classes of the community without arbitrary distinctions or penalizing one section more than another or putting the nation to expense. The *visa* on the other hand was carried out over a period of many months by a monstrous staff of 800 clerks, who toiled away in the Palais Mazarin, and was accompanied by such knavery and cruelty that many of them were subsequently arrested and convicted. Through the dishonesty of one of these clerks Law was wrongly debited by the Company with the sum of $4\frac{1}{2}$ million livres, whereas in fact he had already discharged this debt. All the financier's landed property in France, which had been seized, was administered most inequitably; his movables were simply sold up in the King's name. Catherine and her daughter were turned out of their house and forced to go into humble furnished lodgings. His brother William,

---

[1] The legality of such acquisitions had been pointed out by Law when he was still Controller-General. On April 27, 1720, he wrote from Paris. 'Those private persons, who have made vast fortunes by the paper commerce, have acquired their estate[s] by lawful ways. His Majesty could not forbid them the disposal of them. 'Twas in their own option to buy them at a dear rate. These men, being either guided by a wise foresight or a fortunate chance, have been justly rewarded for their confidence.' See *The Present State of the French Revenues and Trade* (London, 1720) at p. 28.

Teusday

can you not prevaile one the Duke.
so help me some thing more then the
half year or is there no body that
could have good nature enough to
lend me 1000ds. I bege that if nothing
of this can be done. that it may only
be betwixt us two. as I take you as
my real friend. & am very well assur
of it. by the honour, I had done me
yesterday at Court by the King. I had
another letter yesterday from
france with the same thing over
again. excuse this dear madame
& only put your self in my place.
& know at the same time. that you
are the only friend I have. yours sin Lee

Letter from John Law to the Hon. Henrietta Howard, 1721:
'You are the only friend I have'.
From the original in the British Museum

Regatta on the Grand Canal, Venice.
From the painting by F. Guardi

who had also been left behind and was living quietly at Versailles after having got rid of his coach and horses and dismissed all his servants, was suddenly arrested and thrown into prison.

Law hoped that Catherine would now leave Paris and meet him in Italy. 'You desire me to manage on the money you sent me,' he wrote to her on April 19, 1721. 'My table does not pass half a Spanish pistole a day, the servants eat in the house, and I am better satisfied than when in the greatest plenty. I want your company and to live as we used to before I engaged in public business. Don't sell any of my clothes; what you don't bring with you have packed up and sent me. Keep your tapestries and what furniture may be sent by sea. Tho' I determine you at present to come to Venice and tho' I like the place very well, I don't propose that we shall always stay here. I give you my word that if you don't like it, I'll determine you what other place you judge best.'

Naturally Law was anxious, as he put it at this time, 'to have the consolation of my family in my retreat'. He implored the Regent to grant him a moratorium of two or three months – 'during this time', he wrote, 'I will be able to concert with Madame Law means of satisfying my creditors' – and Catherine sent the Regent a pathetic letter in similar terms.[1] But it was no good. Catherine was refused passports when she applied for them, and the Regent washed his hands of the whole business. When 'Diamond' Pitt's son Thomas, now become Lord Londonderry, arrived at the Palais Royal and explained to the Regent that to oblige Law he had accepted bills of exchange to a considerable amount on the security of Company stock which was now virtually worthless, Orleans bluntly remarked: 'I don't interfere at all in Law's affairs. Take whatever steps you can.'

It was in vain for the exile to petition Orleans for the Regent took no notice of his letters. On June 21, 1721, Law wrote: 'This, then, is the condition to which I have been reduced by my design for serving Your Royal Highness and France. When I embarked

---

[1] The letter from Catherine Law to the Duke of Orleans, the only one of hers whose text is known to have survived, is signed 'K. Law'. It has been reproduced in Boislisle's edition of the *Mémoires de Saint-Simon*, Vol. XXXVIII at p. 407. 'Madame Law is again to be seen in Paris', wrote the banker Crozat to Rosalba at this time (June 7, 1721), 'and she cuts a striking figure there with her daughter, but she is surrounded by creditors.' See *Journal de Rosalba Carriera pendant son Séjour à Paris* (Paris, 1865), at p. 317.

on the King's service, I had as much cash as I wanted, I owed nothing to anyone, and I also had credit. I left the King's service without anything; those who have had faith in me have been forced into bankruptcy, and I have nothing with which to pay them. Yet I find that I am really in credit by reason of the very considerable sums which I have advanced at the King's order. The foreign affairs item alone would be sufficient to pay all my agents and remit me what I require for myself. I now entreat Your Royal Highness to consider that in according me the justice I demand you risk nothing. In refusing it on the pretext that I have removed certain assets with me, as time will prove to the contrary, you will only have to reproach yourself with the injustices which I have suffered.'

These disappointments now led Law to reopen with Colonel Burges, the British Resident in Venice, the question of his going to London where, since he would be much nearer the scene of his former triumphs, he thought he would have a better chance of settling his affairs. There were, of course, difficulties, as he explained to his fellow countryman. He no longer possessed the royal pardon which he had received for the offence of which he had been convicted many years before; he had sent this material document to the Regent in 1718 as proof of his intention at the time never to leave France. Likewise the discharge from the late 'Beau' Wilson's heirs which he had received had been left behind with his other papers in Paris. Burges, however, was reassuring. He thought that these difficulties could be overcome. He promised to write to Whitehall and he advised Law to move his friends at home in the matter. 'Alas,' remarked the financier sadly, 'a man in my position no longer has any friends.'

Money troubles are certainly apt to ruin the firmest friendships. Among them was that of the Venetian artist Rosalba, who returned to her native city at this time, and complained, not without good reason, it must be admitted, that her brother-in-law Pellegrini had never been paid for the paintings and other interior decoration which he had executed on Law's instructions in the bank's premises in the Palais Mazarin. But, if he lost one old friendship, he renewed others and made fresh acquaintances. Among them were two prominent political exiles like himself – the thirty-four-year-old Stuart Pretender and former Prince of Wales, James Francis Edward, Chevalier de St. George, and the fifty-eight-year-old Cardinal Giulio Alberoni, son of an Italian market gardener and lately Spain's all-powerful Prime Minister. The three men are said to have had a secret meeting in a Capuchin monastery. It would be interesting to know what they talked about, but no record of their conversation has been preserved.

There seemingly being little prospect of getting any money out of France, Law depended more and more upon the green baize tables in the Ridotto for supplies of ready cash. He had a great run of luck one day when he won 20,000 livres from a gentleman of Padua named Delphino who unwisely insisted on doubling his stakes. He also offered, as he used to do in his earlier gambling days, to stake the equivalent of £1,000 to a shilling that sixes would not be thrown six times running at dice. There were many takers, but as the odds against such a combination were something like 46,656 to 1 there were no winners, and Law soon found that he had increased his capital considerably. He was able to indulge in some of his accustomed luxuries, buying some pictures of which he had always been a connoisseur and having his own portrait painted again. He even attempted, but without success, so it is said, to purchase a title for his son in the ranks of the Venetian nobility.

An irritating wind which swept Venice during that summer depressed him somewhat and he developed a slight fever, but he cheered up when Burges told him that he had heard from Whitehall that there were no official objections to his going to England with his son. He had just packed up his bags once more and was all ready to leave when M. Baguerel de Presly, a Savoyard in Russian service, presented himself with a letter from Peter the Great begging Law to come to St. Petersburg and act as financial adviser to his government. The Tsar, who had not forgotten his visit to Law's bank in 1717, appears to have been anxious to introduce the 'system' into his empire; at all events his representative was authorized to offer its author a substantial capital sum if he would put it into operation on the spot. But to the financier this invitation was even less tempting than that of the Danish king Frederick, and, although he put off M. de Presly with the excuse that he must think it over, he never had any intention of accepting it. For one thing he was anxious not to jeopardize his chances of returning to England by becoming associated with a monarch whose growing power in the Baltic was causing real concern to the English government at this time. And then there was always the chance that, if any misfortune befell the experiment, as had happened in France, the outcome for himself would not be a graceful withdrawal from the scene but instead the road to Siberia or even the axe.

Towards the end of August, Law and his son left Venice and, travelling by easy stages through imperial Germany and the Kingdom of Hanover, reached Denmark early in October. They stayed a few days in Copenhagen, long enough to be presented to the imbecile Frederick who constantly shifted from one foot to the other and had not been known to finish a sentence for twenty years. A strong British naval squadron was then lying off Elsinore under the command of Admiral Sir John Norris; its purpose was to ensure that Sweden was not exterminated by Russia. Peace had just been concluded between the two countries and, as the Tsar had laid up his ships for the winter, Norris prepared to sail for home with his own fleet. The Admiral, who was known in the service as 'Foul-weather Jack' from his readiness to put to sea at all times, was glad to offer Law and young John a passage in his flagship.

On October 20, 1721, John Law, sometime Controller-General of Finance and Counsellor of State to His Catholic Majesty King Louis XV, disembarked at the Nore. It was the first time for twenty-seven years that he had set foot on English soil.

4

The Duke of Argyll and Lord Londonderry were waiting at Rochester to welcome the returning wanderer on his way to London. Londonderry, who was described by a member of his family – perhaps not without justice – as 'a man of no character and of parts which were calculated only for the knavery of business', was principally interested in ascertaining the chances for the repayment of the large sums which he had advanced Law. Argyll, on the other hand, was more sincerely attached to the fallen financier; their friendship dated from the days of the *Squadrone* in Edinburgh when the Duke had acted as viceroy in the early years of the late Queen Anne's reign. He too had invested profitably in the Mississippi enterprise, and he had expressed his readiness to help his fellow countryman within the limitations of his purse which, being a Scots one, were of course quite clearly defined. In addition both men had a piece of unpalatable news. Law's arrival was already known in London, and several ill-wishers were proposing to raise in Parliament the question of his being allowed to remain in the country as well as that of his journey to England in a British naval vessel.

To his friends Law made no secret of his delight at being back again in a democratic country where personal liberty enjoyed well-established safeguards. Outwardly the country and its people presented little change, although two sovereigns had passed away since the date of Law's sensational escape from the King's Bench prison, and a German prince now occupied the throne as King George I. 'I am at present among people who are governed by right', he wrote to Lassaye, 'I shall be safe and have justice. The Englishman does not allow himself to be taken in by any kind of accusation; he is not afraid to oppose the policy of the ministers, nor is unpopularity at Court considered a crime. Here cabals are sometimes formed against those in office, but no one plunges a dagger into the heart of the State.' The appearance of the country-side and the people he saw there as he drove along the London road likewise prepossessed him. 'I would rather have an income of £100 and live among a happy, well-fed and decently clad folk than live in a country where the people are continually hard up. You don't see great wealth here, but there is a considerable affluence. I was delighted to see the industry of the people. There are no *intendants* here and no arbitrary or solidary impositions of taxes. The prince, who is at the head of such a contented people, has himself good grounds for being content.'

The sixty-year-old prince, whom Law thus eulogized, though probably not the worst, was assuredly the least attractive monarch ever called upon to reign over the British people. He could not speak a word of English; his domestic companions were blowsy foreign mistresses, his divorced wife being incarcerated in a gloomy German fortress on the supposed ground of her adultery many years before with a Swedish adventurer named Count Konigsmark. But his great merit lay in his ignorance of the English tongue, since this apparent handicap limited intercourse with his ministers and thus immeasurably promoted the constitutional development of his kingdom by placing much of the powers exercised by his predecessors in the hands of Parliament and the Cabinet. This fundamental development constituted the greatest change to take place in England during Law's long absence from the country, and it was borne in upon the financier when he was received by King George I and rendered thanks (in French) for the royal pardon which it will be remembered had been transmitted to him three years previously. When Law left England in 1694 it was largely true to say that honours and office flowed from the sovereign; now, in 1721, they flowed from the King's ministers; in the present instance the leaders of the Whig party to whom Law saw that he must now address himself for any personal and political advantages he might hope to obtain. The outstanding Whig leader was Sir Robert Walpole, a shrewd and cynical Norfolk baronet and country gentleman whom events had raised to the position of virtual Prime Minister shortly before Law's arrival in London; the others were the two Secretaries of State Lords Townshend and Carteret, the former hard-working and uninspired, the latter youthful and brilliant.

As Argyll and Londonderry had foretold, it was not long before the fact of Law's presence in England was raised in Parliament. The matter was brought forward in the House of Lords by Earl Coningsby, a bigoted Protestant of bad manners and worse temper, who had recently been committed a prisoner to the Tower of London for a gross contempt of court. This noble lord stated that he, 'for his part could not but entertain great jealousy of a person who had done so much mischief in a neighbouring kingdom and who, being so immensely rich as he was reported to be, might do a great deal more hurt here . . . that his person was the more dangerous in that he had renounced not only his natural affection to his country and his allegiance to his lawful sovereign by being naturalized in France and openly countenancing the Pretender's friends; but, which was worst of all and weighed worst with him was that he had renounced his God by turning Roman Catholic.' His lordship concluded his speech by urging the House 'to inquire whether Sir John Norris had orders to bring him over'.

The financier was defended by the clever thirty-year-old Secretary of State Lord Carteret who declared that 'Mr. Law had many years ago the misfortune to kill a gentleman in a duel; but that, having received the benefit of the King's clemency and the appeal lodged by the relations of the deceased being taken off, he was come over to plead His Majesty's most gracious pardon; that there was no law to keep an Englishman out of his own country; and, as Mr. Law was a subject of Great Britain, it was not even in the King's power to hinder him from coming home if he thought fit.' After some desultory discussion the matter was allowed to drop. A week or two later John Law went down to Westminster Hall to plead his pardon formally before the Court of King's Bench. Quite a ceremony was made of the occasion, the suppliant being attended, according to contemporary accounts, by the Duke of Argyll, the Earl of Islay and several other friends.

Meanwhile Law had taken a house for himself and his son in Conduit Street where, so the *Historical Register* informs us, 'he was daily visited by persons of the first quality and distinction'. This series of visitations, which proved of short duration, was mainly induced by curiosity to see the figure of one who had lately made such a great stir across the Channel. In fact Law was generally regarded as an adventurer of doubtful honesty who had been lucky to escape from Paris with his head on his shoulders. The popular note was struck when Law with young John attended a performance of Ben Jonson's play *The Alchemist* at Drury Lane, and he heard declaimed from the stage an epilogue in which the members of the audience were exhorted not to model their conduct on that of the Scots financier:

> Though Law from France be landed on the coast;
> By sober arts aspire to guiltless Fame,
> And prove that Virtue's not an empty name!

5

England like France had lately passed through a disagreeable experience of economic crisis, and it was not long before Law began to feel its repercussions on his own person. This experience took the form of a series of financial projects which had originated in the South Sea Company. The latter concern, which was certainly inspired if not created by the Tory Daniel Defoe, author of *Robinson Crusoe*, had on its incorporation in 1711 been granted a monopoly of trade with South America and the islands of the Pacific, territories whose supposed

riches were generally regarded as being limitless. The Company
had thrived from the outset, and its trading prospects, which were
in reality extremely slender, were greatly enhanced by the acquisition from Spain in 1713, under the celebrated Asiento treaty, of
the monopoly of importing negro slaves into Spanish America.
In 1718 King George I had become governor of the Company.
Next year the directors put forward a gigantic national debt
conversion scheme. At this time the debt amounted to no more
than £51½ millions and consisted mostly of terminable annuities.
The board proposed to pay the government £3½ millions for the
privilege of absorbing the annuities, while at the same time giving
the annuitants South Sea stock in exchange for their gilt-edged
scrip. Since the Company's stock was at a premium in the market,
the directors hoped to extinguish a large proportion of the national
debt by the issue of a comparatively small amount of stock. This
is more or less what happened, except that the South Sea board
undertook to pay the government more than £7½ millions instead
of £3½ millions as at first proposed. Early in 1720 legislation
sanctioning this arrangement was passed by Parliament, and encouraged by the fortunes of the Mississippi Company in France,
which were now at their height, investors rushed to buy South
Sea stock which rapidly rose in price from 300 to 1,000. At this
latter figure the directors had sold about £5 millions of stock.

Unfortunately the South Sea venture produced a great number
of spurious imitators, which was to have an adverse effect on the
principal business. Vast numbers of companies of the 'bucket
shop' variety sprang up, several of which, through the enterprise
of their promoters, were accorded the patronage of royalty. A
credulous public was invited to subscribe to such objects as
'drying malt by hot air', 'a wheel for perpetual motion', and 'a
company for carrying on an undertaking of great advantage, but
nobody to know what it is' – the ingenious promoter of the latter
enterprise, it may be added, managed to collect £2,000 in the space
of a few hours, upon which he promptly set off for the continent
and was not heard of again. The government was now obliged to
intervene, and Parliament declared no less than eighty-six of these
so-called 'bubble companies' illegal. But it failed to check the fever
of speculation.

As with the Mississippi Company the crash came when those
on the 'inside' of the market sold out their holdings. In the course

of three months the price of South Sea stock fell from 1,000 to 135, and thousands of speculators who had exchanged their government annuities or bought at the height of the boom were ruined. As also with the Mississippi scheme in France, the public outcry was intense and widespread. A Parliamentary investigation was demanded, and, when it took place, this revealed the most flagrant corruption and fraud in the direction and management of the Company's affairs. The Company's books for instance, contained entries which were altogether fictitious, while many of the advantages obtained by the Company from the government had been purchased by the directors with gifts to the ministers of the day. Mr. John Aislabie, the Chancellor of the Exchequer, who had been in charge of the bill in the House of Commons authorizing the Company's debt conversion programme, was found to have acquired no less than £70,000 worth of South Sea stock in this disgraceful manner, and he was very properly expelled from the House and the government; he was also committed a prisoner to the Tower. Other members of the administration were involved in varying degrees of guilt; one of them, James Craggs, joint Postmaster-General, took poison rather than face the court of enquiry. All the directors' estates were confiscated and applied to the relief of the sufferers. The liquidation of the whole unsavoury business was entrusted to Sir Robert Walpole, whose labours in the process raised him to the offices of First Lord of the Treasury and Chancellor of the Exchequer: it meant that in 1721, when Law arrived in England, he had become in effect Prime Minister.

That the author of the Mississippi scheme should be linked in the public mind with the South Sea disaster was inevitable in the circumstances. An anonymous well-wisher, who addressed an 'open letter' to Law shortly after his appearance in London, warned him what he must expect. 'However distant it might be from your intentions', so ran this epistle, 'you may in one sense be termed the author of our misfortunes. You are not therefore to be surprised if the undistinguishing and unfortunate among us look upon you as the immediate cause of their calamities and ruin.' And so it happened that, after the novelty of Law's presence had worn off (which was soon enough), the unfortunate man became the object of considerable popular ill-will. 'Since my arrival in England', he wrote some time later, 'I have found the public very prejudiced against me, even some of the first in the land. The losses they have suffered in the South Sea Company have so distorted their judgment that they no longer listen to reason. I find myself condemned without being heard, while bad luck is represented as a crime. I am regarded as the author of their evils, on the ground that the system which I established in France led England to embark upon the South Sea venture. And, since the majority of people only pay attention to outward appearances and do not judge by realities, the general opinion is that my system had nothing substantial about it, and that, since it failed, it must have been unsound.'

Unfortunately for Law's memory the legend has persisted that the Mississippi scheme was a fraudulently promoted enterprise like the South Sea Company. We have seen, on the contrary, that the Louisiana undertaking was promoted throughout with clean hands and complete sincerity of purpose; and, however misguided by pressure from the Regent and Court Law may have become in the later stages of his career in France, he never at any time allowed himself to be corrupted like the South Sea directors and hand out presents of stock to the influential at the expense of the ordinary subscriber. Furthermore, the Mississippi enterprise was truly a scheme of some substance, enjoying as it did a trading monopoly of the entire French empire overseas. The South Sea venture, on the other hand, had no real prospects, since the Asiento treaty had turned out to be a much less lucrative proposition than was at first supposed, and in any event the outbreak of war with Spain in 1718 had put an end for the time being to trade with Spanish America. In the event the South Sea board was responsible for one of the greatest frauds ever perpetrated upon the English public, and there is no doubt that it caused incalculable harm to the Tory party in England, whose leaders had from the outset encouraged the concern. The popular association of Law with the South Sea disaster came as a crowning tragedy in the financier's life. The real truth was far otherwise, and it was summed up in a single sentence by Law himself at the time: 'The South Sea directors have worked *against* England; I have worked *for* France.'

6

Law's English creditors were now pressing him for settlement; and, while keeping them at bay, the financier found it increasingly difficult to get enough money to satisfy his daily wants and those of young John, who shared the rooms he had taken in Conduit Street. His largest creditor was George Middleton, a London merchant banker, who had been appointed agent for the *Banque Royale* after William Law had left for France. Middleton had assigned £15,000 of his debt to a Jew in the City named Mendes, who now became the most pressing creditor of all. In vain Law applied to his friends for further assistance. The Duke of Argyll had already put his hand in his pocket and he could do no more. To Mrs. Henrietta Howard, the kind-hearted but stupid mistress of the Prince of Wales (through whose good offices Law apparently owed his gracious reception at court), the unfortunate man wrote pathetically at this time: 'Can you not prevail on the Duke to help me something more than the half year? Or is there nobody that could have good nature enough to lend me one thousand pounds? I beg that, if nothing of this can be done, it may only be betwixt us two, as I take you as my great friend . . . I had another letter yesterday from France with the same thing over again. Excuse this, dear Madam, and only put yourself in my place, and know at the same time that you are the only friend I have.'

The news from France could scarcely have been more depressing. The liquidation of his affairs, whose mismanagement resembled barefaced robbery, was a standing reproach to the rulers of that country. On top of all this the power of attorney, which he had given Catherine on the eve of his departure from Paris, was now declared invalid on the ground that she was really not his wife, a fact which had recently been discovered by Law's enemies. At the same time Catherine and their daughter were still denied permission to leave the country. Such base ingratitude on the part of the country he had served provoked Law to the hardest words he ever addressed to the Regent. 'Monseigneur', he wrote, 'I am very sensible of the treatment I have had from France – the imprisonment of my brother and of those who have exhibited some attachment to me, and the retention there of Madame Law and of my daughter. But above all it is the indifference, which Your Royal Highness has seemingly shown in my affair, that touches me more than the condition to which I now see myself reduced.'

It is to Law's credit that, overwhelmed as he was at this time by fortune's reverses, he did not altogether lose heart and abandon himself to despair, 'The hope of being useful once more', he admitted, 'sustains me in my disgrace.' Meanwhile he set to work to write a history of his term of office as Controller-General. 'I am engaged on a work which will be interesting,' he told a friend. 'It is the history of my administration.[1] I hope to show that, if France suffers now, I am not the cause of it, and if I have done wrong, it has been unintentional, since I kept in view the people's welfare which I have always regarded as the true interest of the sovereign.' At the same time Law completed the essay in justification of his system which he had begun in Venice, including in it a comparison between the Mississippi and South Sea schemes, a subject which he never tired of explaining to anyone who cared to listen. Among those who heard him was Dr. William Stratford, Canon of Christ Church, Oxford, on whom Law called in college when showing his son the University one October day in 1722. 'Though I was no stranger to Law's character', noted the Canon afterwards, 'yet I did not grudge a bottle of wine for the sake of a little conversation with one who had made so much noise in the world. He spent the evening with me. I put him on talking of his own affairs, and he entered into them very readily. He seemed to take it as a great reflection on this that anyone should think our South Sea scheme to have been formed on the plan of his Mississippi . . . I perceive he takes our projectors to be great bunglers.'

The ensuing months found the wretched Law at the nadir of his fortunes. The winter of 1722–1723 was a particularly severe one, and at one period Law could not afford enough fuel with which to keep warm. On another occasion he could not pay for a hack-

---

[1] This work which Law entitled *Histoire des Finances pendant la Régence* was considered to be lost until Professor Paul Harsin of Liège University recently discovered it in the archives of the French Foreign Office in the Quai d'Orsay. It has now been published in the original text in Professor Harsin's edition of Law's collected works: see *Œuvres de John Law*, vol. III, pp. 282–430 (Paris, 1934).

ney coach to take him out to a dinner to which he had been invited. He sold the few pictures, including a fine Canaletto, which he had brought with him from Venice, but the money he got for them was soon spent. Eventually King George I, who had heard of the financier's plight, sent him a sum to relieve his immediate necessities. With the coming of spring there was better news. The Regent had decided to grant Law a pension, apparently with retrospective effect, and a substantial remittance reached him. Law's brother, William, was released from prison at this time. Apparently his arrest had been all a mistake. About the same time Law heard from Catherine that the Regent was greatly perturbed by the increasing distress in France and he was seriously considering his recall to advise him. However, Dubois, now a Cardinal Archbishop and Prime Minister of France, was said to be opposed to this move and, according to Catherine, it was imperative to convert him.

Law accordingly took up his pen and wrote a tactful letter to the minister offering his services. 'If you agree to my working under your orders, you can count on my attachment,' so he put it, 'and I will render service of the highest importance.' Hoping to soften Dubois he was able to arrange that the magnificent library which he had left behind in Paris should be acquired by the avaricious prelate for a nominal sum. At the same time he wrote to Orleans that he was ready to come over when summoned. 'I think the King and his ministers', he wrote, 'would not be sorry if I were to return to France in case Your Royal Highness should judge it good to recall me, being persuaded that I shall employ my influence in continuing and consolidating the friendship and good relations already existing between the two Crowns.' Meanwhile he offered to act as an intermediary between Orleans and Walpole in case the Regent had any matters which he preferred not to have dealt with through the usual official channels. According to Law, he had already offered his services in a similar capacity to the English government. 'Perhaps on this occasion it will be some secret commission to execute on behalf of the King in Hanover. I shall be able to undertake it without arousing suspicions on the grounds of making a journey for purposes of health and recreation.'

The truth was that for some time Law had been pestering Walpole for a job. At first the English Prime Minister was not encouraging, but on a hint from Lord Townshend, joint Secretary of State, Walpole began to show the financier 'all reasonable civilities', particularly when the serious possibility of Law's recall was reported from the Paris embassy. 'If the Duke of Orleans is disposed to recall him, as Mr. Law's friends here are very sanguine of hoping', wrote Walpole from Whitehall to Paris on April 10, 1723, 'it is not easy to judge what is most to be wished for in this case, unless we know the competition and upon whom the favour and confidence of the Duke of Orleans might probably fall.' Walpole was primarily concerned with the need for preserving the Anglo-French *entente* of which Dubois, in spite of his manifold personal failings, was a great protagonist. But the Cardinal Archbishop was reported to be a sick man and about to submit himself to an operation from which it was unlikely he would recover. 'If Mr. Law does not return', continued Walpole, 'there can be no doubt that the power might fall into worse hands; and if any who are neither Englishmen by birth or affection should prevail, we should have a less chance than by admitting one who has sundry ties to wish well to his native country.' Walpole finally uttered a word of caution to his minister in Paris, in case the question should be mentioned officially. 'Perhaps Mr. Law's being thought agreeable or acceptable in England would not at all forward his return to France; for nothing but his being thought not only an able but a good Frenchman can secure his being recalled.'

Law had recently made the acquaintance in London of the Earl of Peterborough, a friendly but eccentric nobleman who in the course of some sixty-five summers had had a somewhat chequered career as a soldier and a diplomatist. They were probably introduced by Mrs. Howard, for whom, unlike the Prince of Wales, Lord Peterborough professed a Platonic friendship which found expression among other ways in some remarkable verses. His Lordship was said to be secretly married to a well-known operatic singer named Anastasia Robinson (he was later publicly married to her, thus becoming the first member of the English peerage to ally himself thus with an actress); at all events he liked to travel about Europe with this lady, and as he was going over to Paris Law gave him the letter he had written to the Regent. What is more, when Peterborough called at the Palais Royal and presented it, Orleans gave a high opinion of Law's character. Peterborough expressed surprise that Law had acquired no assets outside France. 'No', replied the Regent, 'there was nothing base in Law's conduct.'

In his letter Law had suggested that, if anything should happen to Dubois, Orleans should henceforth act as his own 'first minister' in the interest of their two countries. '*Monseigneur, une liason étroite est nécessaire pour conserver les deux royaumes en l'Europe en paix.*' Events now began to take shape as Law had foreseen, and he went in high hopes of a summons from the Palais Royal. The Cardinal had his operation and died, and Orleans assumed control of affairs albeit with enfeebled vigour, since he was quite worn out by his excesses. The remaining opposition to Law's return was gradually overcome. In November the expected message arrived in London. It was from Law's friend the Marquis de Bully. 'Come back immediately', it read, 'without waiting for an express order from the Regent. I have reason to believe he will welcome you with pleasure.'

Then came the thunderbolt. On December 2, 1723, even as Law was packing up his bags, the Regent was sitting with his mistress, the Duchess of Falaise, in his apartments in the royal palace at Versailles. He asked her jestingly whether she really believed there was a God and a heaven and hell in the after-life. She replied that she did. 'If that is true', Orleans rejoined with his usual frankness, 'you are most unfortunate to lead the life you do.' They were almost the last words he uttered in this world. Suddenly he fell forward against his mistress, and, muttering that he felt unwell, died a few moments later in her arms.

'Here', wrote the chronicler Buvat, 'we can properly close the journal of the regency of this incomparable prince.' The courtier Duclos viewed the event more dispassionately. 'Thus', he wrote, 'perished at the age of forty-nine years and a few months one of the most amiable men in the world, full of wit, talents, military courage, goodness, humanity, and one of the worst princes – that is to say, one of the least able to govern.' Law heard the news from the French minister in London as he was on the point of setting out for the Channel. He unpacked his bags wearily and despondently. Paris seemed further away than ever now, for in spite of all his vices and failings the Duke of Orleans had been the only man in France who had really grasped the 'system'.

7

There is no doubt that, had Orleans lived a few months longer, Law would have returned to Paris where, taught by past experience, he might have reintroduced the 'system' in a modified form and perhaps have bestowed upon France the benefit of permanent credit institutions much sooner than in fact she came to enjoy them. 'A short time before his death this prince gave me several marks of his esteem', noted Law afterwards. 'He was convinced that my system would have succeeded if extraordinary events had not forced him to depart from its fundamental principles. He realized that he again had need of my knowledge; he asked my opinion on the present state of the kingdom, and he counted on my assistance to enable this great empire to achieve its true worth.' What had made the Regent hesitate so long – indeed until it was too late – was the fear of a popular outcry which the financier's reappearance in the country might provoke. Writing from Paris, shortly before the Regent's sudden end, the Venetian minister observed that Law's recall was regarded as very probable, but that the prospect was detested by the people even more than fresh taxes. The effect of the rumour on the Mississippi Company was otherwise. The price of shares advanced rapidly, but they fell again with equal rapidity when the rumour was contradicted after Orleans's death. Oddly enough the decision not to recall the financier was taken by Louis XV on the advice of Law's old friend, the Duke of Bourbon.

Having completed his thirteenth year early in 1723, the French king had now entered his legal majority and assumed power in person. Although no further regency was therefore necessary, the office of prime minister which Orleans had enjoyed since Dubois's death remained to be filled. The royal choice fell upon the thirty-one-year-old Louis Henri, Duke of Bourbon, head of the house of Condé and great-grandson of Louis XIV's celebrated general. The Duke, although he had made a huge fortune from speculating in the Mississippi stock, had no great aptitude for political affairs and was entirely under the influence of his mistress, the beautiful but faithless Marquise de Prié. (The Marquise, with whom he had been connected for the past five years, had received a good beating on this account from her husband, but the fact did not deter her from enjoying the Duke's embraces as well as those of a number of other lovers.) 'Madame', the Dowager Duchess of Orleans, could not understand how Bourbon could possibly inspire any woman with affection for him since he was so ugly: he had lost the sight of an eye in an accident, his lips were large, his cheeks hollow, his body bent, and his legs had practically no calves. Impatient and badly educated, he was content to leave the conduct of the government largely in the hands of his mistress. The result of this arrangement was unfortunate for Law, since the Paris brothers, who had been in charge of the profitable but scandalously bungled Mississippi liquidation, enjoyed her special protection. The Marquise, who had once lent Law her carriage and post-horses to enable him to leave France, said no. So the financier remained in London.

During the succeeding months, Law made a last attempt to have his own affairs in France settled, and to this end he addressed a number of lengthy letters and memorials to the Duke. What rankled with him most was the 4½ million livres which had been wrongly charged to his account with the Company. On the evening before he left Paris for his estate at Guermantes in the Brie, he had given one of the bank clerks named Pomier de St. Leger stock to the value of 14 million livres in order to discharge his obligations to the Company, but this payment had not been made in accordance with his instructions. 'Consider, Monseigneur', he wrote on August 25, 1724, 'if being in the country removed from my papers and books, it was in my power to put in order affairs that required not only leisure but also my presence in Paris to arrange properly; and if it is not a piece of great injustice for the Company of the Indies to wish to take advantage of the condition to which I was reduced, and of the dishonest conduct of clerks, in requiring from me payment of sums I do not in fact owe and which, even though I had been owing, were (as I have shown) expended for their service and payable in shares or notes, of which effects belonging to me they at that time had and still have on their books double or treble the sum they demand.'

It is unnecessary to examine the ground, which Law traversed in laborious detail, except to reiterate his own justification of his official conduct which this correspondence contains. How, he asked, could he possibly have sent huge sums of money out of the country for his own use? Were not the couriers always open to search at the frontiers? In any event would he have summoned his brother, who was his principal agent in London, to come over and establish himself in Paris, if he had wished to keep such a useful channel open? Because he wished to be regarded as a Frenchman he had declined honours and offers of property from foreign sources. When at the height of his power, for example, Dubois offered to persuade King George I to send him the patent of a dukedom and the Order of the Garter, he had refused both. He had also refused the offer of an Italian principality and an island off the North African coast which he might have accepted. With his supposed millions surely he would have great territorial influence in England, and could return numerous members to Parliament! Such was not the case. 'If I only had the half of what I brought into France', he added, 'Your Royal Highness would not be troubled today with my complaints.' Apart from a relatively small sum in ready cash, all he took with him out of France was a ring with a diamond of inferior water which he had been unable to sell before leaving: it was this ring that he had been wont to pledge when his luck of the green tables at the Ridotto went against him. As for Lauriston and his other Scottish property, he had assigned this to his brother William. It had been already burdened with charges in favour of his sisters and nieces: now William had mortgaged it heavily. Thus, far from being the millionaire he had once been, the erstwhile Controller-General was in fact penniless.

Law also reminded his one-time friend of the large sums he had disbursed by way of charity when he had been in power. For instance, he had cleared all the Paris prisons of debtors, setting aside no less than 60,000 livres from his private funds to discharge their debts. 'Every day', he went on, 'I gave Frenchmen I scarcely knew more than was required to maintain all my relations in comfort. But then I was French myself and I regarded my relations as foreigners, since they were not established in France.' And now he felt France owed him justice, or at least some recompense. To act otherwise would be inconsistent with her honour. What he wanted was a quick and just decision, now that more than three years had passed since he had left his house in the Place Vendôme. With that he would be satisfied to remain in London. 'If my affairs were decided,' he wrote, 'Madame Law, my daughter, my brother and his family would come to England; I would stay here, establishing myself in such a manner as to convince the public that I no longer think of returning to France.'

But it was not to be. While the financier was denied permission to enter France, neither Catherine, his daughter, nor William with his family, were allowed to leave it. Meanwhile the already long protracted liquidation of Law's affairs, public as well as private, dragged on. By means of the inquisitorial *'visa'* the existing amounts of bank-notes and company shares in the hands of the public were reduced by more than half. The enormous mass of paper which this process yielded was put in a huge incinerator, and days were occupied in the resulting combustion. Fire purifies everything, said the Paris wags, and thus the 'system' of Law passed away in smoke.

CHAPTER VIII

THE REFUGEE

Three years had passed since John Law had come back to England with his son; and, now that the Duke of Orleans was dead, his private affairs were seemingly in no better shape than the day he had stepped off Sir John Norris's flagship at the Nore in 1721. His pension had ceased to be remitted from France after the late Regent's death, and again he complained of being hard up. His health too had lately been giving him trouble. He had developed an unpleasant cough, he suffered from recurrent attacks of asthma, and an irritating nervous tic appeared at the right corner of his mouth. It is true that in 1724 he was only fifty-three, but the strain of the last years had told on his physique and he now began to look more than his age. It was absolutely necessary for him to obtain some employment, adequately remunerated but not unduly exacting, if he was to live. Hence he applied once more to Walpole.

The Prime Minister listened sympathetically to what Law had to say, for he was beginning to feel sorry for the Scotsman against whom fortune seemed to have turned permanently. Walpole scarcely had need to explain that any kind of official job at home was out of the question on account of Law's religion, since Parliament had enacted that no Roman Catholic could hold any office of profit under the Crown. However, he thought that some secret mission abroad might be possible, and he undertook to consult the King and Secretary of State Townshend about it. Some time later Walpole sent for Law and told him that it was proposed to despatch him on a secret mission to the Bavarian Elector in Munich. Bavaria, Walpole explained, was one of the satellite states of Austria which it was necessary in the interest of British policy to alienate from the imperial orbit. In 1718 Spain, under the ambitious Alberoni's guidance, had broken the treaty of Utrecht by seizing Sardinia for herself, and as a result the other principal European powers including Great Britain and Austria had gone to war with her. But now (May, 1725) the Emperor Charles VI, annoyed with England for various reasons, had suddenly made peace with Spain and thus broken away from the alliance which had been formed by Britain and France to restore the balance of power in Europe. It was necessary to isolate Austria before she could do any further damage. Would Law, therefore, undertake to secure Bavaria's adherence to the British side? When Law intimated that he was agreeable to execute this commission, Walpole told him that he must pretend to be an ordinary traveller making a tour for purposes of health, and that he should proceed first to Aix-la-Chapelle where he would receive further instructions. Whilst waiting there he would no doubt benefit his health by taking the waters.

On August 8, 1725, John Law left London for the last time, since, though he did not know it, he was destined never again to set foot in England. He had with him his son John, and a nephew 'Mr. Hamilton' (son of his elder sister Agnes, whose father-in-law, it will be remembered, had been Law's old schoolmaster in Renfrewshire), whom he proposed should act as his secretaries. Before setting out he had a final interview with Walpole whom he asked whether he might not be provided with official letters of credence accrediting him to some foreign court, preferably in Italy. The object of requesting this 'diplomatic protection', he explained, was a purely precautionary measure in case his person should be exposed to insults or injury at the hands of any ill-wishers in the countries through which he chanced to pass. He did not contemplate presenting the credentials except in case of dire urgency. Walpole advised Law to apply to Lord Townshend, the Secretary of State, adding that he would support his application. And the Prime Minister was as good as his word. 'Mr. Law has wrote to Your Lordship', he told Townshend next day, 'to desire that he may have some sort of commission from His Majesty to any prince or state, not to be made use of but to be kept as a protection in case of necessity. By what he says to me I really believe it may be of service to him, and I promised to use my interest with Your Lordship for the obtaining it.' The Secretary of State saw no objection and gave instructions for the necessary documents to be drawn up and sent after the traveller. The letters accredited Mr. John Law to the Republic of Venice.[1]

Although the successors of Charlemagne were no longer crowned Holy Roman Emperor within its gracious Minster, Aix-la-Chapelle, or Aachen (to give it its German name), was still regarded as the leading imperial free city in Germany. In addition, its famous hot sulphur springs had been known since Roman days for their curative properties, being particularly effective in the relief of rheumatism, gout and 'scrofulous disorders'. There was always a pleasant society to be met with there in the autumn and winter months, and so Law settled down to a round of assemblies, balls, concerts, and sulphur water. But by the end of October he began to feel bored and also worried at having received no communication from Lord Townshend apart from the letters of credence. He wondered what they were up to in Whitehall. Were they going to let him end his days in this miserable watering-place? The thought dawned on him that perhaps there was nothing in the alleged mission to the Elector. Could it have been a charitable ruse to get him out of the way, since though he heard nothing from Townshend his pay was regularly remitted to him at Walpole's orders through a local banker? He determined to write to the Secretary of State.

'No one has suspected that I am in the King's service,' he wrote to Townshend on October 24, 'or that I am here awaiting His Majesty's orders.' All he asked now was to be allowed to get to work. Perhaps the King had other employment in view for him. He reminded the Secretary of State that he had spent six years of his life in Italy before entering French service, and that he had become on intimate terms with the King of Sardinia as well as the principal families in Genoa and Venice. 'If the King has any commission to be executed in this country', he went on, 'I will willingly charge myself with it in the hope of being able to succeed in rendering good service to His Majesty.' Finally, he suggested that he might go to Vienna where by direct negotiation he could possibly win the Emperor back to the alliance.

---

[1] The letters, which were recovered after Law's death, are preserved in the Public Record Office in London (S.P. 104/210). They were never presented.

This letter evoked a curt response from Townshend instructing Law to proceed without further delay to Munich and there carry out his mission. Law obediently set off with his two secretaries. Towards the end of November they passed through Mannheim, and a week later found them in Augsburg, another of the imperial free cities. Here Law insisted on remaining for nearly a month in expectation of a letter from France about his affairs which he had been advised was on its way. While waiting for this communication he had several conversations with M. de Courtance, the Savoy-Sardinian minister to France, who happened to be passing through. Amongst the topics of the day on which they touched was the distribution of wealth in England, and Law shocked the minister by his opinion that the more the great landed estates in a country were divided up amongst small-holders, the more powerful that country would be. The minister replied that if Law should ever again come to Turin he should not repeat this to King Victor Amadeus who in so doing had already bade fair to ruin the nobility.

Law left Augsburg on New Year's Day, 1726, and arrived in Munich the following afternoon.

2

For the past forty-six out of his sixty-three years Duke Maximilian Emmanuel of the family of Wittelsbach had ruled Bavaria as its Elector. But he had not always done so from the capital's picturesque *Alte Residenz*. He had formerly spent many years in Brussels as Governor of the Austrian Netherlands; and, by foolishly siding with France during the Spanish Succession War and permitting French troops to occupy the Low Countries, he had temporarily lost his principality to Austria and had been fortunate to recover it, harried and exhausted, at the peace. Consequently, when Spain proceeded to upset the peace a few years later, the Elector gladly accepted French subsidies as a guarantee of his neutrality. Such an insurance policy was necessary, since Duke Maximilian Emmanuel was connected with Madrid through his first wife, who had been a granddaughter of the Spanish king Philip IV, and might otherwise have been tempted to enter the struggle on Spain's side.

When Law called at the *Residenz* to present his compliments, he learned that the Elector was in bed. Duke Maximilian Emmanuel had recently been taken ill with 'a kind of rheumatism in the neck which has tormented him greatly and keeps him from sleeping'. However, the Elector was able to receive Law in his bedroom on the next day, when they had a long and amicable interview. Maximilian Emmanuel had not forgotten the French subsidies which he had received and which had passed through Law's hands, and he hastened to explain that he was now paying the ruinous rate of from 10 to 12 per cent in interest on loans contracted from the Jewish bankers in Augsburg. Perhaps Law could help him, he suggested, since it was generally believed that the ex-Controller-General had got away from France with large sums of money. How this unfortunate legend of his wealth persisted, Law replied, as he pointed out that everything he owned he had left behind in his formerly adopted country. But he undertook to write to Sir Robert Walpole and raise the question of a loan from Britain. At this the Elector brightened up considerably and said that, when he recovered, Law must help him with the domestic finances of his principality. They could meet quietly, he went on, since there were secret passages connecting the palace with various churches in the city which he would show his visitor later on.

But Duke Maximilian Emmanuel did not recover, and Law never saw him again. He got gradually worse until, on February 26, 1726, barely six weeks after Law's arrival, he died. Duke Charles Albert, the new Elector, was only interested in Law as a possible means of obtaining a loan from Britain. When the possibility came to nothing, as appeared soon afterwards, the Duke took no further notice of the Scotsman. However, Law found an unexpected friend in the Dowager Electress, known as Cunegonde, who poured out her heart to him in her widow's weeds. Although well into middle age this prepossessing woman (she had been a Polish princess) still bore traces of her youthful beauty, and Law momentarily felt drawn to her. Now that her husband was dead she told Law that she had no intention of remaining in Bavaria, and it was suggested that perhaps they might contrive to meet in some congenial place away from the Court and outside the confines of the Electorate.

Law lingered on in Munich somewhat unhappily. In an almost

pathetic attempt to justify the salary which continued to reach him regularly from Whitehall, he sent detailed accounts of the strength and composition of the Bavarian army, as indeed befitted a secret 'agent'. He collected similar information about the resources of the neighbouring principality of Hesse-Cassel, whose ruler the Landgrave Charles was on a visit to Bavaria at this time. The Landgrave believed, like the rest, that Law had secretly removed millions from France, until the financier enlightened him when they were introduced. This prince was most anxious to discover the secret of Law's system which he conceived to be a method by which he might pay off his state debts at no cost to himself. To satisfy him Law said that, when he returned to England, he would travel by way of Cassel where he would explain how the system worked. The Landgrave repeated the invitation a little later, but it is doubtful whether Law had any intention of making such a journey. At all events Landgrave Charles never learned the details of the system, and to raise revenue he turned to the simpler expedient of hiring out his Hessian troops in foreign service. Indeed he is chiefly remembered as being the first European ruler to employ mercenaries in this manner. Having himself had more than enough of foreign service, Law also declined an invitation to go to Schwalbach, near Wiesbaden, and meet the Landgrave's kinsman King Frederick of Sweden.

Law's presence in Bavaria had been reported to the Austrian Emperor who promptly sent one of his ministers, Count Von Sinzendorff, to Munich to get what information he could. Law had met this emissary eleven years before in Holland, where the Count had been one of the Austrian representatives at the Peace of Utrecht, and in those days he had instinctively distrusted him. Now, noted Law, 'he wished to learn from my own lips the nature of my system, the means which I employed to create so much credit in France and the reasons why a system so well spoken of should have been abandoned'. To the Austrian's honeyed words the Scotsman replied that it would occupy too much time to enter into the details of the different operations which he conducted, but that he would give him a copy of the *mémoire justificatif* which he had written in 1721 and which proved that 'my system was well founded and that it would have lasted if extraordinary events had not upset it'. In handing over this document Law was careful to add that the late Regent of France had been convinced of the soundness of the propositions which it contained and that he would have summoned him to put them into practice had he lived. It did not, however, contain sufficient technical details to enable the Austrian Emperor to carry out the maladroit and compromising imitation of the system, which Law felt Charles VI might otherwise have done; and on any further particulars Law rightly refused to be drawn. Sinzendorff then proceeded to cross-examine Law on various budgetary questions, which revealed that on one controversial topic at least his opinions had changed with the years. When asked what he thought about state lotteries, the Scotsman replied that he did not approve of them, since they spread a 'spirit of debauchery' among the bourgoisie and the people. 'Wealth,' he said, 'should be acquired by industry, and not by luck or gaming.'

Long before the end of 1726 the futility of Law's mission had become apparent. His reports were filed away in Whitehall as useless pieces of information. There was no longer any question of detaching Bavaria from the Austrian orbit, since the new Elector Charles Albert heartily disliked the Emperor and indeed coveted the mantle of Charlemagne for his own shoulders. There was, therefore, no point in Law remaining any longer in Munich, so that, when he wrote to Whitehall and asked leave to retire to Venice, permission was readily granted. His departure was preceded by that of the Dowager Electress who arranged to meet him in the gay republic, but who first posted off in the opposite directtion to Bonn in order to avoid any suspicion of collusion.

It was Carnival once more when John Law and his small retinue stepped out of their gondola and walked across the Broglio to their lodgings. As old friends and acquaintances greeted him, the reason he gave for his visit was that the Venetian air suited his health. He was sorry he had ever left the lagoon. But now he was back again, and he intended to stay.

3

The exile soon settled down to his old life, as if he had only left Venice yesterday instead of nearly six years ago. He went regularly to the Ridotto and with his winnings was able to buy a number of pictures to replace those he had been obliged to sell in London. He finished writing the history of his official life in France which he had begun in 1722. He saw lots of old friends and acquaintances and made several new ones. Colonel Burges, the English Resident, was away, but there was a new French ambassador, Count de Gergy, and the French consul, M. de Blond, who treated him as an ex-minister with a kind of charitable consideration and gave him the latest news from Paris. In addition there was a constant stream of foreign visitors, some travelling for health or pleasure, some on business and others refugees like himself. The majority made a point of calling on the Scotsman and plying him with tiresome questions about the 'system' which they were convinced possessed a secret. To all and sundry he showed himself ready to discuss the subject at all times and with no lack of candour. 'The causes!' he declared to the young Duke of Richelieu who asked him what were the causes of the system's failure. 'My calculations were upset by happenings which human precautions could hardly foresee.' The Venetians liked him, though they were inclined to take what he said with the proverbial pinch of salt. 'This barbarian talks well,' they said, 'but he has nothing to show for it.'

In February, 1727, the Stuart Pretender spent a week in Venice; and although he was not seen in public with his compatriot, there is little doubt that he met Law privately. But, in spite of what his enemies said to the contrary, Law had little sympathy with either the Chevalier de St. George or the Jacobite cause. 'He is a thin ill-made man,' wrote the poet Gray of the person who now styled himself King James III of England, 'tall and awkward, of a most unpromising countenance, a good deal resembling King James the Second, and has extremely the air and look of an idiot, particularly when he laughs or prays. The first he does not often, the latter continually.' His Polish wife, who was a niece of the Dowager Electress of Bavaria, had recently left him to go into a convent, and her desertion had increased his habitual melancholy besides inclining him to discreditable bouts of dissipation. Incidentally, the Dowager Electress herself turned up in Venice about this time as indeed she had agreed to do when she left Munich. It is uncertain, nor is it of much consequence, to what extent she was able to comfort Law in the asylum he had found. She was seen one day with reddened eyes, as if she had been crying, and it is possible they may have quarrelled. She had a reputation for avarice, and it may be that the 'secret of the system' which she too endeavoured to ascertain was not what she expected.

For Law one day passed very much like another. Mass, coffee in Florian's, a little writing, the French mail, gossip, visits to the old picture dealers, masquerades, gondolas and the Ridotto. He even submitted some economic projects to the Council of Ten, so it is said, but the Republic's rulers were not impressed. Law was undismayed. Long before the next Carnival had come round it was clear that he had chosen Venice as his final refuge. Nor was he without companion adventurers in exile. One at least whom he knew had had a life as adventurous as his own and like himself had escaped death more than once by a hair's breadth. This was the French Count Alexandre de Bonneval, who, though but four years Law's junior, had already experienced an exciting career in the service of Austria as well as that of his native country, had been sentenced to death twice, and was now awaiting a summons from the Sultan to organize the Turkish army, become a pasha, and embrace the Mohammedan faith. But of the many visitors, both English and foreign, whom Law received in his rooms at this time, the most interesting as well as the most intelligent was unquestionably another Frenchman. His name, which Law heard announced by his servant on August 29, 1728, was Charles Louis de Secondat, Baron de la Brède et de Montesquieu.

President de Montesquieu – his office, which was in the Parliament at Bordeaux, he had inherited along with his title from an uncle – had just completed his fortieth year. Having recently satirized the inhabitants and institutions of his native country wittily but unmercifully in his *Persian Letters*, Montesquieu was now making a grand tour of Europe in order to observe men, things and constitutions. Although each was well known to the other, the two men had never met before this summer's day in Venice. Their meeting lasted several hours; and it was not unfriendly, in spite of the castigation which the author had inflicted on Law and the Mississippi rage in his now celebrated work. On his side Law was no stranger to the *Letters*, remembering in particular the allegoric description of himself in one of them.[1]

In an island situated not far from the Orkneys there was born a child whose father was Eole, god of the winds, and

---

[1] Letter CXLII. See also Letters CXXXVIII and CXLVI.

whose mother was a nymph of Caledonia. It is said that he taught himself without any help to count on his fingers, and that from the age of four years he was so perfectly well able to distinguish the various metals that once, when his mother wished to give him a brass ring instead of a gold one, he recognized the deception and threw it on the ground.

On this occasion Law spoke at great length of his experiences in France and, if he did not succeed in convincing his visitor of the merits of the 'system', he at least secured a patient audience. He recalled how it was the Duke of Noailles had had been the first to think of developing the Mississippi but with insufficient capital, and how the future Controller-General had outbid him. The destruction of public confidence in the system leading to its collapse he attributed to two factors: the repeal of the edict of May 21, which he was known to have sponsored a few days before, and the posting of a bodyguard to protect his house and person. How could people have any further confidence in the system after he had been disgraced in this manner? Indeed for some days he feared the worst and thought he might lose his head. He remembered what a perfectly appalling state of mind the Regent had been in when he next saw him at Court. Orleans had expected him to perform miracles at this crisis. It was too much. The climax was when he saw Orleans surrounded by all his enemies and heard him say: '*Qu'on me laisse seul avec Monsieur Law!*' That was the end.

Recollecting that he himself held office in a provincial Parliament, Montesquieu asked his host why he had not attempted to win over the members of the Paris body to his side by means of bribes as the English Prime Minister had done with the House of Commons. 'They may not be so smart in Paris,' replied Law, 'but they're much less corruptible.' From world prices and supplies of gold, on which the financier talked with his customary knowledge, the conversation drifted to general topics and personalities. One saying in particular of Law's Montesquieu remembered long afterwards. They were discussing the great stock of genius lost to the world in the countless throng of humanity such as the merchant classes. 'They are dead,' said Law, 'only they wont lie down'.

On the whole Montesquieu did not take to the Scotsman, and

he had no reason to revise the feelings which he had expressed in the *Persian Letters*. 'He is a captious man who must argue,' he wrote afterwards, 'and the whole force of whose arguments is to attempt to turn your reply against you, by finding some objection in it.' At the same time Montesquieu was bound to admit that Law was more enamoured of his ideas than of his money. If his financial resources were now depleted, his brain was as fertile as ever. 'He was still the same man, with small means but playing high and boldly, his mind occupied with projects, his head filled with calculations.'

Not long after President de Montesquieu's departure from Venice Law received two pieces of news from France which disturbed him greatly. First, all the contents and furnishings of the bank had been sold up; secondly, the grand ceiling, which had been decorated by Pellegrini but had never been paid for, suddenly collapsed in a cloud of dust. Law, who like many gamblers was inclined to be superstitious, regarded these incidents as extremely bad omens. In fact, they gave him the unmistakable impression that his own end was not far off. 'The material witnesses of my work have been destroyed,' he said to an acquaintance. 'I have a strong feeling that my own existence is about to disintegrate with them.'

4

The following winter in Venice was unusually damp and enervating, and Law's mood of depression increased as the Carnival approached its close. Colonel Burges had now returned to his old post of English Resident, and he tried in vain to cheer up the hypochondriac. They would often tour the canals and lagoons together by gondola. One evening after dinner during the last week of Carnival – the actual date was February 25, 1729 – the two men went out for half an hour on the Grand Canal. As their gondola passed under the Rialto Bridge, Law suddenly complained of feeling cold and his companion noticed that he was shivering. They returned immediately to Law's lodgings in the Piazza di San Marco, and the sick man was put to bed. His usual doctor, who appeared in due course, did not think there was any cause for alarm, and contented himself with bleeding the patient. He thought he had a slight fever. But the doctor was mistaken. Four days later an abscess appeared on one of the patient's lungs, and it was clear that he had pneumonia. The abscess was apparently syphilitic. Eminent physicians called in from the medical faculty in Padua declared there was no hope. 'They give me fifteen days to live,' Law told the French consul who called to see him, 'and I shall never find the time so long.'

The faithful Burges also appeared in the sick-room and sent an account of the patient's malady to Whitehall. 'He was first taken with a shivering cold fit which lasted him five or six hours,' Burges wrote on March 4, 'and that was succeeded by a violent hot one which has never intermitted but has continued upon him ever since. I saw him for the last time the day before yesterday. He was then very sensible of the danger he was in and, as he told me, very desirous to die, believing his death would be of greater service to his family at this juncture than any other, because the Cardinal [Fleury][1] has just now appointed three or four gentlemen to examine and state his accounts, and he thinks they will be more inclined to do him justice in France when they shall know how poor he dies and that he has nothing in any part of the world but in that country and in the King's hand. He has ordered his son, who is here with him, to go to France immediately after his death to throw himself at the King's feet and endeavour to move His Majesty's compassion and justice, for upon them must he rely for his future subsistence.'

Another caller was the French ambassador, Count Languet de Gergy. He began by telling the invalid that he should perform some act to show that he adhered to the Catholic faith, since the public thought that he had 'relapsed into the anglican creed which he had abjured in France'. Law appeared somewhat embarrassed at this remark and murmured something about having been accredited by King George I to the Venetian republic, that he had the letters of credence in his pocket but that he had never presented them.[2] The ambassador then promised to get the papal

[1] The septuagenarian Cardinal André Fleury who in 1726 had succeeded the Duke of Bourbon as Prime Minister of France. His administration was thrifty and statesmanlike.

[2] The presentation of the letters and his acceptance as an accredited diplomatic representative of Great Britain, had this taken place, must necessarily

nuncio to send a priest who might receive his confession. Count de Gergy then went on to advise Law to make his will, if he had not already done so. To this the sick man replied that there was no point in his executing such a document since everything he possessed was in France and had been seized by his creditors. The ambassador, in his own words, rejoined that 'a will executed in due form was always an authenticated proof of the faith in which one died, and it was only in that sense that I spoke to him'. Law thereupon agreed to send for a notary. 'The result of the varied conversation I had on this occasion with a man who saw death at the foot of his bed', wrote the ambassador to the Quai d'Orsay on March 5, 'has served to persuade me that M. Law has no other means than those which were seized by his creditors in France, that he had nothing else, not even in England, and that he was only able to subsist here by gaming on the considerable scale that he indulged in.'

The ambassador lost no time in getting hold of the Jesuit priest, Father Origo, whom the nuncio had recommended, and immediately conducted him to the sick-room. The Jesuit received Law's confession. The same day the nuncio also called to comfort him, while the local parish priest administered the sacrament and extreme unction. Since that time, noted the stoutly Protestant Burges, 'he has never been without three Jesuits with him who probably will not leave him till he dies'.

When the notary likewise arrived he took down the dying man's testament from his lips. Its contents are not known, since Law was dissatisfied with this form of disposition and shortly afterwards determined to change it. The will was accordingly recovered from the notary and in its place substituted a *donatio mortis causa*, a bequest known to both Roman and English law by which a gift of property is made in contemplation of death and intended to take complete effect only if the donor dies of the illness from which he is suffering at the time. This deed of gift, drawn up partly in Italian and partly in Latin, was dated March 19, 1729, 'from the residence of the most excellent John Law on St. Mark's Square in the parish of San Gemigniano'. In it the donor bequeathed all his possessions to Catherine who was

---

have involved Law in a further act of apostasy, since he could not legally have discharged his official functions while remaining a Catholic.

described not as Madame Law but as 'Milady Cattarina Knowel [*sic*], sister of the Earl of Banbury, the said lady residing at present in Paris in her house situated in the Place Louis-le-Grand'.[1] This circumstance appeared sufficiently curious for the notary to ask the French consul, who was also present, why his client, whom he understood to be married, should execute a deed in favour of a woman whom he did not describe as his wife. M. le Blond replied simply that 'the state of his affairs required it so'.

Next day the doctors attending him suggested that the inflammation of the lungs, against whose poisonous effects he had now been struggling for nearly a month, might be relieved through the application of leeches. The patient refused and asked for an emetic, as he had previously derived benefit from this remedy. He took the emetic during the night and suddenly became worse. Towards dawn of March 21 he lost consciousness, and a few hours later his breathing became shorter and gradually ceased altogether. Father Origo, M. le Blond and young John were with him at the end. 'He died with great calmness and constancy,' wrote Burges, 'and is spoke of here with much esteem.' A solemn requiem mass was said for the repose of his soul by the papal nuncio in the church of San Gemigniano, and his remains were then laid to rest within the same walls. Another month, and he would have completed his fifty-ninth year.

All the property the once rich and famous Controller-General left at his death was several thousand livres which he had won at the tables, a few pictures he had bought with his winnings, and the diamond ring of inferior water which he used to pledge when luck went against him in the Ridotto. Apart from these trifles, he told Father Origo in his last conscious moments, he possessed nothing outside France. He added, as Count de Gergy later informed King Louis XV, that 'for the rest he had nothing with which to reproach himself touching Your Majesty's finances throughout the whole period that he had their administration in his hands'.

Three months later Catherine and her two children in Paris heard the news for which the financier had waited so long and in vain. The French Council decreed that he owed nothing either to His Catholic Majesty or to the Company of the Indies.

[1] This shows that Law cannot have realized that Catherine and their daughter were no longer living in his former Paris house.

5

The day following Law's death Count de Gergy called to offer his condolences to young John, at the same time offering him the hospitality of his own roof on the pretext that he might wish 'to get away from the place where his father had departed his life'. But there was more in this offer than met the eye. The cunning ambassador was anxious to ascertain the contents of the last testament which rumour had it that the financier had executed. He was surprised that neither young John nor Le Blond, who had kept constant vigil at Law's bedside and were both in the house when he called, should have said anything about such a document. He accordingly took advantage of the son's being out of the way to get hold of the original, and have a copy made, which he promptly despatched to the Quai d'Orsay. The ambassador concluded that young John's reluctance to disclose the deed was due to his desire to conceal the fact that his parents were never married.[1] The same evening the ambassador spoke to Le Blond about the other papers he understood were in the dead man's possession and which must be of undoubted interest to the French authorities in Paris. But if he hoped to discover the secret of the system from this source, he was disappointed.

Next morning young John brought the ambassador a box containing, as he said, all his father's papers on his affairs in France. The ambassador eagerly seized upon the contents but found no memoirs or secrets. There were three quarto size letter books, containing copies of all Law's letters to the Regent and his other French correspondence between December, 1720, when he left

[1] De Gergy wrote to Chauvelin, the French Minister of Foreign Affairs, on March 26, 1729: 'Since I wished to be informed surreptitiously concerning the testament which everyone said the deceased had made, there fell into my hands a copy (which I take the liberty of sending you) of a deed of gift executed on the 19th of this month, of all M. Law possessed in favour of her who passes as his wife although, as you will see, he does not describe her as such in this deed.' See *Archives des affaires étrangères* (Venice, 183) quoted by Boislisle in the appendix to Vol. XXXVIII of his edition of the *Mémoires de Saint-Simon*, at p. 410; also Armand Baschet, *Histoire du Depôt des Archives Etrangères*, pp. 204–209, Paris, 1875.

France, and September, 1726, when he was in Munich and about to set off for his last sojourn in Venice. There was also a number of bundles of miscellaneous letters to various French friends like Lassaye, the whole making thirteen packets which the ambassador proceeded to seal up and despatch to the Quai d'Orsay. Unfortunately M. Chauvelin, the Foreign Minister, insisted on regarding the collection as his private property when he vacated his office some years later, since he removed all the items with him. As a result almost the entire collection must now be regarded as lost with the exception of one of the quarto letter books which somehow found its way into the public library in Aix-en-Provence.[1]

The papers of interest to the English Government were handed over to Colonel Burges. They were not many – a handful of letters which was all that Walpole and Townshend had deigned to send him, and the credentials never presented to the Doge. The remaining scant possessions young John gathered together and took off with him to Paris. They included for the most part the few pictures which Law had collected in the last years of his life, among them a Correggio entitled 'Jupiter and Io' and a study of a naval battle between the English and Dutch fleets in 1665 by W. Van der Velde, said to have been commissioned by Samuel Pepys, formerly belonging to Robert Harley, Earl of Oxford, from whom Law had acquired it.[2] Another picture which young John inherited was the portrait of his father done in happier days by Rosalba. This work subsequently passed into the hands of Horace Walpole, who for many years displayed it prominently in his famous picture gallery at Strawberry Hill but always refused to let it be moved for copying, 'being in crayons by Rosalba under glass and any shaking being very prejudicial to crayons'. At the Walpole sale in 1842 it was knocked down to '— Brown,

---

[1] This portion of the collection consists of 164 letters written by Law to Orleans, Lassaye, Bourbon and other correspondents in France between December, 1720, and May, 1722. It is preserved in the Bibliothèque Méjanes (MS. 335), Aix-en-Provence, and has been used by the present author.

[2] At an auction of some of Law's possessions, which took place in Christie's sale-rooms in London in 1782, the Correggio fetched 39 guineas and the Van der Velde 73 guineas. According to Baschet (*Histoire du Depôt des Archives Etrangères* at p. 207) the whole of the small picture collection had previously been sent to Holland in 1735 where it was dispersed among private buyers.

Esq., Pall Mall' for 15 guineas, after which it unfortunately disappeared from view and knowledge.

Arrived in Paris young John saw his mother and sister for the first time for more than eight years, and showed them the deed of gift. But when he approached the authorities with the document, he could obtain no satisfaction. Grounds were advanced to impugn the deed's validity and it was declared inadmissible. Neither young John nor Mary Catherine could now legally inherit under their father's intestacy, since they had both been born out of wedlock. Nor for that matter could William Law since he was not naturalized. Eventually, after protracted negotiations, William's two infant sons were, in 1735, by virtue of their birth as French citizens, jointly declared the legal heirs to their uncle's estate in France. Meanwhile young John, who had left Paris in disgust, had succeeded in obtaining a commission in an Austrian regiment of dragoons serving in the Netherlands. While on garrison duty at Maastricht early in 1734 he suddenly caught small-pox and died. He was unmarried and about thirty-one years old at the time of his death.

Numerous private creditors still remained to be satisfied but, since the financier's estate was relieved of any further liability to the government, Catherine and her daughter were at last allowed to leave the country. They settled in Belgium so as to be near young John, first in Brussels and later at Utrecht. Voltaire, who visited her there, liked to recall how he had once seen Law's 'widow' in Brussels 'so humbled as she had once been proud and exultant in Paris'. That she was in straitened circumstances there seems no doubt, as about this time she sold the late financier's small picture collection which she presumably acquired after her son's death. She then moved to Liege where she seems to have been cared for by a community of Benedictine nuns. Mary Catherine had now left her to marry her cousin Lord Wallingford and live in London. However, her mother was not entirely alone, for she had the companionship of the widowed Lady Peterborough, the one-time actress who had come to find consolation in the Convent of the Holy Sepulchre after her husband had died on board his yacht 'of a Flux by eating Grapes'. In 1747 Catherine herself died and was buried in a cemetery in Liege. On this last occasion it was agreed that she should be called 'Madame Law'. Three years later her nephew and son-in-law Wallingford unexpectedly followed her to the grave (a strange attack of cramp finished him off), but the widowed Mary Catherine lived on for half a century longer, a gracious if ageing figure in the London of Horace Walpole and Doctor Johnson. (Mrs. Delaney found her 'civil and good natured'.) As she had no children, her death in her elegant house in Park Street in 1790 removed the last direct descendant of the financier.

There were still William's children. It took fifteen years from the time they were declared their uncle's heirs until a final compromise was reached with all the private creditors. By this time William Law was dying – in 1752 he was laid beside the body of his father in the chapel of the Scots College in Paris – and his two boys were getting on in the service of the French East India Company which they had entered through the patronage of the Duchess of Bourbon. Jean, the elder, became a general and governor of Pondicherry, while his son, Jacques Alexandre Bernard, rose to be both a marshal and a peer of France during the revolutionary and Napoleonic era. To the latter it fell as military governor of Venice and Count de Lauriston to re-inter the remains of his celebrated great-uncle when the Church of San Gemigniano was pulled down in 1808. He arranged for Law's bones to be moved to the nearby Church of San Moisé where they now rest just inside the entrance to the west door. The inscription which Count de Lauriston had cut in the stone floor recorded in brief but appropriate Latin terminology the achievements of his ancestor and the reasons for the transfer of his remains.[1] It is perhaps worthy of note that these remains should finally have been laid to rest within a few paces of the adjacent building, the once famous Ridotto, so familiar to the 'projector' but long since closed down with the prohibition of public gaming in the latter part of the preceding century.

A few years later the last link connecting the French side of the family with Britain was broken. The only member capable of inheriting the Scotch property by reason of his not being a Catholic was Count de Lauriston's younger brother, Francis John

---

[1] Honori et memoriae Johannis Law Edinburgensis, regii Galliarum aesarii praefecti clarissimi, a MDCCXIX aet. LVIII defuncti gentilis. Sui cineres ex aede D. Geminiani diruta huc transferri curavit Alexander Law Lauriston, Napoleoni maximo adjutor in castris, praefectus legionis, gubernator Venetiarum a MDCCCVIII.

William Law. This individual, who was served heir of Lauriston in the same year as his ancestor's remains were transferred to San Moisé, succeeded in breaking the entail, and in 1825 he sold the whole of the property to an Edinburgh banker named Thomas Allan. Thus Lauriston acquired a new laird, after having been in the possession of the Law family for upwards of a century and a half.[1] Long before this, however, the place had fallen into decay, due partly to the absenteeism of successive lairds and partly to an expensive and protracted Chancery suit for possession instituted by another branch of the family which exhausted the rents for many years.[2] The Scottish judge Lord Cockburn remembered the bleak aspect of the castle when he was a boy towards the end of the eighteenth century. 'Lauriston, since I knew it,' he wrote, 'was a bare solitary keep, fenced from the farmer's cattle by a crumbling Galloway dyke, with scarcely a single comrade tree, and staring on the Firth as if it had been looking out for the reappearance of the South Sea schemer who was once its master.'

6

For the realization of the hope, which he expressed on leaving France in 1720, that posterity would do him justice, John Law has had to wait a long time.

[1] The estate frequently changed hands in the nineteenth century. Its last private owner, Mr. W. R. Reid, who died in 1919, bequeathed the castle and grounds to the City of Edinburgh. The castle is now a museum. A full and scholarly account of Lauriston has been written by its present curator, Mr. John A. Fairley, *Lauriston Castle: The Estate and Its Owners* (Edinburgh and London, 1925) to which, as to its author personally, I am greatly indebted.

[2] The financier John had a younger brother Andrew (b. 1673) who should have been next in succession, thus coming before William (b. 1675). But for some reason Andrew had incurred his mother's displeasure with the consequence that he was excluded from the entail which she executed in 1703 (see above p. 52). Andrew's daughter married a Scottish lawyer named Brebner. They had in turn three daughters Lilias, Law and Berthia Brebner, who claimed to be William Law's heirs on his death in 1752 as against his elder son Jean, governor of Pondicherry, who was not 'of the reformed religion'. The suit of *Brebners v. Laws* dragged on for eight years in the Edinburgh Court of Session, with the apparent result that Jean continued to hold the estate, although he never entered into possession. The estate was managed by a series of factors until Jean's sixth son, Francis John William Law, established his ownership in 1808.

With the exception of the relatively unknown Dutot and Melon, both of whom had worked in the bank as cashiers, all Law's contemporaries in France, whether economists, politicians or journalists, united in their writings to condemn the 'system' and its author. Politicians like Voltaire and Montesquieu, journalists like Saint-Simon, Duclos, Marais and Barbier, and economists like du Hautchamp, Forbonnais and Paris-Duverney, all succeeded in sounding the same hostile note in their publications. Across the Channel he was only spoken of as a disreputable 'schemer' and 'projector' who had brought untold ruin and misery upon countless French men and women. Apart from the spurious attribution of an economic work to his pen in 1751, his name was not seen on any title page in his native islands until nearly a century after his death. The general feeling was summed up by Horace Walpole. 'Law was a very extraordinary man,' wrote this great observer in 1783, 'but not at all an estimable one.'

In France the outbreak of the Revolution, of which in a sense he had been a precursor, and the issue of paper money based on landed security (*assignats*), led to a revival of public interest in the Scotsman and his works. In 1790 a Frenchman named de Senovert brought out what purported to be a collected edition of Law's writings. A year later this publication encouraged the Scottish antiquarian John Philip Wood to produce a biographical sketch which he expanded into a more lengthy work in 1824. But the learned editor of Douglas's *Peerage of Scotland*, although he included a number of interesting genealogical and personal details in his book, made no attempt to examine the 'system' objectively or even to analyse his subject's character in the light of his career.[1] Apart from two or three scattered essays[2] and a well-meant but largely imaginative effort of fiction on the part of the novelist Harrison Ainsworth,[3] only one serious work exclusively devoted to Law has been published during the past 120 years by a native author in the country of Law's origin, and that is so little known that the British Museum does not possess a copy.[4] It has been left almost entirely to foreign historians and economists to justify

[1] P. Wood, *Memoirs of the Life of John Law of Lauriston*, Edinburgh, 1824.
[2] Notably by Charles Mackay, J. S. Nicholson and R. H. Mottram. For particulars see Bibliography below.
[3] W. Harrison Ainsworth. *John Law, the Projector*. London, 1864.
[4] A. W. Wiston-Glynn. *John Law of Lauriston*. Edinburgh, 1908.

the achievements of the remarkable Scotsman. First and foremost there is the socialist Louis Blanc who was the first writer to give a sympathetic and at the same time graphic interpretation of the man and his work. And it is not altogether surprising that the initial volume of his history of the French Revolution, in which Louis Blanc set out to do this in 1847, should never have found an English translator.[1]

Other international authorities have added in different ways to our knowledge of John Law – in particular, Emile Levasseur (1854), Andrew McFarland Davis (1887), Fritz Karl Mann (1910–1913), and Paul Harsin (1933) – but none of these has attempted to alter the judgment of the great socialist writer formed a century ago. Blanc rightly regarded Law as a collectivist pioneer and his system as a powerful instrument of social change. 'What especially struck Law', he wrote, 'and what his generous soul revolted against was the tyranny exercised by certain owners of dead riches over the people, who constitute the living riches of the nation. The deliverance of the people was his aim and credit his means.' Law steadfastly believed that the more widely these 'dead riches' whether in the form of land, houses, goods or money were divided up and distributed throughout the population, in reality the more powerful and truly prosperous the State would be. He tried hard and he was absolutely honest, but he was constantly handicapped by two factors which gradually undermined and eventually ruined his 'system'. First, he was always having to work against time; secondly, the greedy and reactionary elements of a dissolute court combined against him.

Neither by tradition nor by education nor by legislation were the French people properly prepared for the gigantic credit experiment which Law launched upon the country. He moved too quickly for popular understanding and with characteristic impatience neglected to explain all the steps in his programme as he should have done. That he subsequently realized this fault there is no doubt. 'If I had the work to do over again,' he wrote from exile in 1723, 'I would proceed more slowly but more surely and I would not expose the country to the dangers which must necessarily accompany the sudden disturbance of generally accepted financial practice.'

[1] Louis Blanc, *Histoire de la Révolution Française*. Vol. I. Paris; 1847, see particularly pp. 271–328.

His plans for the overseas development of trade and industry were ambitious and patriotic. Unfortunately the speculation, which he quite wisely promoted in the early stages of the Mississippi scheme in order to attract public attention, developed into a fever for which he cannot fairly be held responsible. No more justly can he be saddled with the exclusive blame for the colossal inflation which marked the final months of his residence in France. The final blow to the 'system' was struck, not by the decree of May 21 devaluing both notes and shares (as has often been supposed), but by its revocation less than a week later at the instigation of the reactionary elements at Court. These elements of disaster may be found in the policy of Archbishop Dubois, the greed of the nobility and the extravagance of the Regent and his mistresses.

'Do not forget,' Law once said towards the end of his life, 'that the introduction of credit has brought about more changes among the powers of Europe than the discovery of the Indies, that it is the duty of the State to provide the people with this commodity, and that the people's need of it is so complete that they must always return to it in spite of themselves and any distrust for it they may have.' Distorted and perverted as the 'system' became by events which its founder could not control, John Law unfortunately did not live to witness the ultimate results for which his peculiar genius had hoped and striven. Nevertheless by his achievements and ideas he did contribute in a vital and distinctive manner to the history of the French people. By his marvellous device of credit he opened the road to commercial and industrial expansion; by his ameliorative legislation in the sphere of taxation he attacked vested interest and alleviated the heaviest popular burden; and by his impetus to speculation he promoted a redistribution of wealth which in its long-term effects, whatever personal hardships may have been caused at the time, could not be otherwise than beneficial to France. In short Law and his 'system' helped not a little to fan the breeze, barely perceptible when he came to France but beginning to blow when he left it – a breeze which increased in force with the years until, as a powerful revolutionary gale towards the century's close, it swept away priests and kings and nobles into the unwanted limbo of an ancient and outworn order of things.

BIBLIOGRAPHY

A. MANUSCRIPT SOURCES

Thanks largely to the recent researches of MM. Mann, Prato, Harsin, de Boislisle and Daridan, there is little MS. material of any importance on the Continent relating to John Law and his 'system' as yet unpublished. Such material as exists has been described by Professor Harsin in his introduction to his edition of Law's writings. It is distributed mainly among the following repositories: Paris – *Bibliothèque Nationale*, *Archives Nationales*, *Archives du Ministère des Affaires Etrangères*, *Bibliothèque d l'Arsenal*; Aix-en-Provence – *Bibliothèque Méjanes*; Nantes – *Bibliothèque Municipale*; Brussels – *Bibliothèque Royale*; Turin – State Archives. The lengthy correspondence concerning the liquidation of Law's affairs after his departure from France is preserved in the *Archives Nationales* in Paris.

The disappearance of the greater part of Law's papers, which were despatched to Paris from Venice at the time of his death, has been described in the text (see above p. 212). Further details are given by A. Baschet, *Histoire du Depôt des Archives Etrangères*, pp. 204–209. Besides the portion of this collection now preserved in the *Bibliothèque Méjanes*, Aix-en-Provence, some other letters have reappeared in private collections, e.g. the important letter from Law to the Duke of Orleans dated March 1, 1721, quoted above p. 172, originally used with other lost material by P. E. Lemontey in writing his *Histoire de la Régence* (1832) and now in the possession of Major J. G. Morrison. See, on this and other letters, *Historical Manuscript Commission, 9th Report*, Appendix, at p. 475, and *Catalogue of Collection of Autograph Letters and Historical Documents formed by Alfred Morrison*, Vol. III, pp. 106–109. (Privately printed, 1888.)

The principal English source is the Public Record Office in London. Law's letters to Lord Townshend while on special mission to the Elector of Bavaria in 1725 and 1726 are in S.P. 81/91. Correspondence of Colonel Elizeus Burges, English Resident in Venice, relating to Law is in S.P. 99/63. Such letters of Lord Stair, British Ambassador in Paris, as have not been published either in the *Hardwicke State Papers* (1778) or in J. Murray Graham's *Annals and Correspondence of the Viscount and the first and second Earls of Stair* (1875) are in S.P. 78/160–167. A few other letters are in the British Museum Add. MSS. 22, 521 and 22, 628, and Stowe MSS. 251.

A copy of J. P. Wood's *Memoirs of the Life of John Law of Lauriston* (Edinburgh, 1824) with interesting MS. annotations and additions in the author's handwriting is in the possession of the author's great-granddaughter, Dr. Marguerite Wood, in Edinburgh.

B. PUBLISHED SOURCES

A most comprehensive list of printed materials (to 1933), which it is unnecessary to recapitulate here, has been given by Professor Paul Harsin at the end of his monograph, 'Le Banque et le Système de Law', in J. G. Van Dillen's *History of the Principal Public Banks*, The Hague, 1934. The reader is also referred to the bibliography in *The Cambridge Modern History*, Vol. VI, Cambridge, 1909.

The most important biography recently published (since 1933) is by Jean Daridan, *John Law, Père de l'Inflation*, Paris, 1938. This work, which covers the financier's life after 1720, is based on unpublished material in French and British archives. The most recent biography is by Salvatore Magri, *La Strana Vita del Banchieve Law*, Verona, 1956. The best recent study of Law's 'system' and economic ideas is to be found in Charles Rist, *Histoire des Doctrines Relatives au Credit et à la Monnaie*, Paris, 1938. (English translation: *History of Monetary and Credit Theory from John Law to the Present Day*, London, 1940.) See also an article by Earl J. Hamilton, 'Prices and Wages at Paris under John Law's system' in *The Quarterly Journal of Economics*, Vol. LI, Boston, Mass., 1937.

The principal authority on Law's life and work is the financier's own writings. Few of these were published during his lifetime – only his celebrated *Money and Trade Considered*, Edinburgh, 1705, and several letters which he wrote to the *Mercure de France* in 1720 in support of his policy as Controller-General of Finances (subsequently republished in English under the title *The Present State of the French Revenues and Trade and of the Controversy betwixt the Parliament of Paris and Mr. Law*, London, 1720). The work of disinterring Law's literary remains was begun by General E. de Senovert with his first edition of the *Œuvres de Jean Law*, Paris, 1790; continued by Eugene Daire in his *Economistes Financières du XVIIIe Siècle*, Paris, 1843, by F. K. Mann in a series of articles contributed to the *Revue d'Histoire des Doctrines Economiques*, Paris, 1910, *Revue d'Histoire Economique et Sociale*, Paris, 1913, and *Jahrbuch für Gesetszgebung Verwaltung und Volkswirtschaft*, Leipzig, 1913, and by G. Prato in *Memorie della Reale Academia della Scienze di Torino*, Vol. LXIV, Series II, Turin, 1914; and completed by Paul Harsin in his monumental *John Law, Œuvres Complètes*, 3 vols., Paris, 1934. Besides a number of new letters, Professor Harsin has discovered thirty-nine of Law's compositions, of which unquestionably the most important is the financier's so-called memoirs, in reality the account which he wrote from exile of his administration in France, *Histoire des Finances pendant la Régence*, completed in 1726 and long considered lost.

Law's official activities have been described, often with scant impartiality, by various contemporary French economists in their writings. These are Marmont du Hautchamp, *Histoire du Système des Finances sous la Minorité de Louis XV, pendant les Années 1719 et 1720*, 6 vols., The Hague, 1739; Dutot, *Reflexions Politiques sur les Finances et le Commerce*, The Hague, 1738; S. F. Melon, *Essai Politique sur le Commerce*, 1734; V. D. de Forbonnais, *Recherches et Considérations sur les Finances de la France*, 6 vols., Basle, 1758; and Paris-Duverney, *Examen*, 2 vols., The Hague, 1740. The financial decrees of the Regency Council, many of which were drafted by Law, are contained in Vols. V and VI of du Hautchamp's work.

The chief secondary authority on the 'system' is the scholarly work by E. Levasseur, *Recherches Historiques sur le Système de Law*, Paris, 1854. Besides recounting the 'system's' history in detail, Levasseur summarizes and assesses the economic writings of Law's contemporaries. An informative and recent account of

Law's economic ideas and their application is by Reinhard Rohr-bach, *Die Geld- und Kredittheoretischen Anschauungen John Laws*, Berlin, 1927. The best work on the 'system' in English is by an American economist, A. McFarlane Davis, *An Historical Study of Law's System*, Boston, Mass., 1887 (reprinted from *The Quarterly Journal of Economics*, Vol. I, 1887). Other short but useful studies have been made by Charles Mackay in his *Memoirs of Extra-ordinary Popular Delusions*, Vol. I, London, 1852; by S. Alexi in his *John Law und sein System*, Berlin, 1885; by J. S. Nicholson in his *Money and Monetary Problems*, London, 1897; by R. H. Mottram in his *History of Financial Speculation*, London, 1929; and by Peter Wilding in his *Adventurers in the Eighteenth Century*, London, 1937. See also René Trintzius, *John Law et la Naissance du Dirigisme*, Paris, 1950.

Short biographies have been written in French by P. A. Cochut (1853), A. Thiers (1858) and Georges Oudard (1927), and these are all available in English translations. Law's only English biographers proper are J. P. Wood (1824) and A. W. Wiston-Glynn (1908), but biographies in the form of fiction have been written by Harrison Ainsworth, *John Law, the Projector*, London, 1864, and by Michael Harrison, *Gambler's Glory*, London, 1940. None of these is satisfactory, although Wood's book has considerable genealogical interest and Cochut has collected most of the contemporary anecdotes. The two short anonymous sketches which appeared during Law's lifetime, *The Memoirs of the Life and Character of the Great Mr. Law*, London, 1721, and *Het Leven en Caracter van den Heer Jan Law*, Amsterdam, 1722, must be regarded with caution. An exhaustive account of the history of Law's family and Lauriston, based largely on original Scottish sources, has been given by John A. Fairley in his *Lauriston Castle: The Estate and its Owners*, Edinburgh and London, 1925.

The period is rich in memoirs and journals of contemporary Frenchmen, who had an opportunity of observing Law and the operation of the Mississippi scheme at close quarters. The principal works in this category are by Barbier, Buvat, D'Argenson, Dangeau, Duclos, Marais, Narbonne, Noailles, Villars, and Saint-Simon. Of these the most valuable is the *Mémoires de Saint-Simon* in the erudite edition by A. M. de Boislisle, Vols. XXX to XXXVIII, Paris, 1919–1926. Most informative of the private correspondents of the period is Charlotte Elizabeth, Duchess of

Orleans ('Madame'), whose letters have appeared in numerous editions both in French and English.

French historians of the Regency have naturally included accounts of Law and the 'system' in their works. The chief are Voltaire, Millot, Massillon, Lemontey, Louis Blanc, Martin, Michelet, and Leclercq. Best of these is Dom H. Leclercq, *Histoire de la Régence*, 3 vols., Paris, 1921. P. E. Lemontey's *Histoire de la Régence et de la Minorité de Louis XV*, 2 vols., Paris, 1832, is important in that it is based in part on materials which are now lost. Louis Blanc's account in his *Histoire de la Révolution Française*, Vol. I, Paris, 1847, is extremely interesting, but the author may have been led by his own peculiar political and economic views to overstress Law's popular sympathies. The best history in English is by J. B. Perkins, *France under the Regency*, London, 1892.

Interesting iconographies of the Mississippi scheme and its promoter will be found in the anonymous *Het groote Tafereel der Dwashied*, Amsterdam, 1720, and in Benjamin Betts's *Descriptive List of the Medals relating to John Law and the Mississippi Scheme*, Boston, Mass., 1907.

INDEX